Vengeful Citizens, Violent States

From crusading in the Middle Ages to genocide in the twentieth century, from ancient blood feuds to modern urban riots, from tribal warfare to suicide terrorism, revenge has long been recognized as a root cause of violence in human societies. Developing a novel theory linking individual vengefulness to state behavior, Rachel M. Stein brings the study of revenge into the field of International Relations. Stein argues that by employing strategically crafted rhetoric, leaders with highly vengeful populations can activate their citizens' desire for revenge and channel it into support for war, thereby loosening the constraint of democratic accountability and increasing their freedom to use military force as a tool of foreign policy. This book will change the way scholars think about how citizens form their opinions regarding the use of military force and about the role those opinions play in shaping when and how democracies go to war.

RACHEL M. STEIN is an Assistant Professor of Political Science at George Washington University.

Vengeful Citizens, Violent States

A Theory of War and Revenge

RACHEL M. STEIN

George Washington University

CAMBRIDGE
UNIVERSITY PRESS

CAMBRIDGE
UNIVERSITY PRESS

University Printing House, Cambridge CB2 8BS, United Kingdom

One Liberty Plaza, 20th Floor, New York, NY 10006, USA

477 Williamstown Road, Port Melbourne, VIC 3207, Australia

314–321, 3rd Floor, Plot 3, Splendor Forum, Jasola District Centre,
New Delhi – 110025, India

79 Anson Road, #06–04/06, Singapore 079906

Cambridge University Press is part of the University of Cambridge.

It furthers the University's mission by disseminating knowledge in the pursuit of
education, learning, and research at the highest international levels of excellence.

www.cambridge.org
Information on this title: www.cambridge.org/9781108492751
DOI: 10.1017/9781108686266

© Rachel M. Stein 2019

First published 2019

Printed and bound in Great Britain by Clays Ltd, Elcograf S.p.A.

A catalogue record for this publication is available from the British Library.

Library of Congress Cataloging-in-Publication Data
NAMES: Stein, Rachel Michelle, 1983- author.
TITLE: Vengeful citizens, violent states : a theory of war and revenge / Rachel Stein,
George Washington University.
DESCRIPTION: 1 [edition]. | New York : Cambridge University Press, 2018. |
Includes bibliographical references and index.
IDENTIFIERS: LCCN 2018045075 | ISBN 9781108492751 (hardback : alk. paper) |
ISBN 9781108734493 (pbk. : alk. paper)
SUBJECTS: LCSH: Revenge. | War.
CLASSIFICATION: LCC BF637.R48 .S74 2018 | DDC 303.6–dc23
LC record available at https://lccn.loc.gov/2018045075

ISBN 978-1-108-49275-1 Hardback
ISBN 978-1-108-73449-3 Paperback

To Hugo and Dalia
You are my whole heart times two.
I hope this book makes you proud.

Contents

Figures

Tables

Acknowledgments

"Nothing great was ever achieved without enthusiasm." It is highly unlikely that Ralph Waldo Emerson was thinking of a newly minted assistant professor trying to write her first book when he wrote those words, but that does not make them any less apt. Without enthusiasm, this book would never have been written. It was the spark of enthusiasm that kept me going through the long years of research, writing, and rewriting. But it was also the enthusiasm of friends, family, colleagues, reviewers, and editors – for the project itself, and for helping, supporting, critiquing, and comforting its author – that made this achievement possible. I cannot hope to thank all of them sufficiently here, but it is my pleasure and my privilege to try.

My first thanks are for a place and not a person. Thank you, Stanford University, for being my dream for so long, and for changing everything forever in 2006, when I started graduate school and found both my life's passion and my life's partner. I am forever grateful for my amazing dissertation committee: Mike Tomz, Ken Schultz, and Gary Segura. They always welcomed my somewhat unorthodox ideas and helped me make them clear and strong. They were and are true role models, and the examples that they set of both scholarship and mentorship continue to light my way. I also owe a special thanks to David Laitin, whose course in comparative politics offered me my first real insight into what we actually do in this profession. I will use the tools he taught me throughout my career. My fellow graduate students at Stanford were truly inspiring, and I am proud to call many of them friends and colleagues today. I especially want to thank Aila Matanock, who was the best officemate, friend, and fellow chocolate addict that I ever could have asked for.

In writing this book, I have also enjoyed the support of two other great institutions: George Washington University and Princeton University. At the former, I have been blessed to begin my academic career in a place that values intellectual diversity, open-mindedness, and camaraderie. I don't know if I could have written this particular book in any other place, and I thank my wonderful colleagues for making me a part of such a special community. I am particularly grateful to Alex Downes, who has been my mentor and unflagging supporter, and Elizabeth Saunders, who (among many other things) opened my eyes to the fact that I actually was writing a book, even if it didn't feel like it at the time. At Princeton, I owe a great debt to the Center for the Study of Democratic Politics (CSDP) and the Niehaus Center for the fellowship year during which I wrote the first draft of the words that appear in these pages. I could not have done it without that precious time to breathe and to think. At Princeton I also gained two invaluable friends: Melissa Lee, whose feedback on an early draft of the theory chapter gave me the confidence to keep going, and Keren Yarhi-Milo, who helped me navigate the early stages of the publication process.

The shape and scope of this book owe a great deal to the generous colleagues and friends who participated in my book workshop: Charlie Glaser, Steve Biddle, Caitlin Talmadge, Alex Downes, Elizabeth Sauders, Yon Lupu, Danny Hayes, Sarah Croco, Olivier Henripin, Michelle Allendorfer, and Michael Joseph. Thank you all for reading the whole, horrible first draft and for spending a day of your lives helping me work out the kinks. Thanks to you, I realized that I didn't have to choose between writing a book about public opinion or a book about war; I could (and did) write a book about both. I am especially grateful to Charlie Glaser, who hosted the workshop at the Institute for Security and Conflict Studies (ISCS) in addition to offering his always astute comments.

Much of the research in this book was accomplished with financial support from the Columbian College Facilitating Fund (George Washington University), the Graduate Research Opportunity Grant (Stanford University), and CSDP (Princeton University). I am also grateful to Mike Tomz for funding some of my earliest exploratory efforts, and to the undergraduate and graduate research assistants who worked with me over the years: Ryan Krog, Zixiang Zhou, Connie Chau, Daniel Edgren, and Gabriella Jiminez-Garcia. I am also thankful to Robert Dreesen at Cambridge University Press for seeing the value in my project from the beginning and making this process a positive experience from start to finish.

And last, but never least, I will try to thank my family for so many things that are hard to put into words. I owe my parents, Gretchen and

Sam Stein, for so many things, but especially for being my earliest models of a life spent in love of learning and passion for work.If there is anything commendable in the writing of this book, it is due to my mom, who taught me how to write and who is still the best proofreader around. My sister, Sarah Stein, was always there no matter how many times I screened my phone calls, and helped me keep my love of reading alive when if felt like I might never want to look at a book again. Finally, to my husband, Ali Valenzuela, thank you for ... everything. Love, adventure, a home, children, dreams, plans, purpose. Because of you, I can walk this path without knowing where it will lead in the end. The destination does not matter; we are together.

1

Introduction

Does revenge play a role in fomenting international conflict? Scholars have long recognized revenge as one of the root causes of violence in human societies. From crusading in the Middle Ages to genocide in the twentieth century, from ancient blood feuds to modern urban riots, from tribal warfare to suicide terrorism, the fingerprints of vengeance can be found on acts of violence both commonplace and cataclysmic.[1] Historical accounts have also cited revenge as a contributing factor in a number of interstate wars, including World War II, the Indo-Pakistani conflict, the 1973 Yom Kippur War, the 1980 Iran-Iraq War, the 1988 Eritrean-Ethiopian War, and the 2003 Iraq War (Lowenheim and Heimann 2008: 689). Yet scholars of International Relations (IR) have paid surprisingly little attention to the topic of revenge. The purpose of this book is to develop a general theory of war and revenge. In particular, I examine the link between the vengefulness of a country's population and its propensity to use force against other states. This leads to a powerful and provocative insight: among democracies, where domestic political institutions make leaders accountable to the mass public, the most violent states are those with the most vengeful citizens.

My theory takes ordinary people rather than leaders or states as its starting point. In doing so, I advance a conceptualization of revenge that

---

[1] On the role of revenge in the Crusades, see Throop (2011). On genocide, see Hinton (1998). On blood feuds, see Bohem (1984); Daly and Wilson (1988); Ericksen and Horton (1992); Fletcher (2004). On urban riots, see Horowitz (2001) and Gullace (2005). On tribal warfare, see Blick (1988); Chagnon (1988); Beckerman et al. (2009). On suicide terrorism, see Moghadam (2003) and Speckhard and Ahkmedova (2006).

pushes back against the pejorative outlook that has long dominated discussions of revenge in Western philosophy and law. Over the centuries, this so-called anti-revenge discourse has variously painted revenge as an immoral, irrational, pathological, and atavistic impulse that has no place in a civilized society (Miller 1998). I make no such normative judgments in this book. Rather, I take an evidence-based approach, drawing on a growing multidisciplinary body of research to argue that revenge is best understood as a core value – rooted in the belief that those who hurt others deserve to be hurt in return – that shapes individuals' behavior and opinions across a wide variety of contexts, both personal and political. Revenge, in other words, is not just something people do, it is something they believe in, and those beliefs have consequences that reach far beyond each individual's sphere of personal concern.

The link between individual vengefulness and state violence lies in the dynamic interaction between elected leaders and their citizens. As with many complex political issues, ordinary people rely heavily on their values to inform their opinions toward the use of military force (Hurwitz and Peffley 1987), and studies have shown that vengefulness can be an important predictor of support for the use of military force, even if there has not been a direct attack on the nation's homeland or its citizens (Liberman 2006, 2013, 2014; Gollwitzer et al. 2014; Washburn and Skitka 2015; Liberman and Skitka 2017). Building on this research, I argue that citizens' desire for revenge against an adversary is a potent force that national leaders can mobilize into support for war by using strategically crafted rhetoric that frames the use of force as a punishment the adversary deserves to suffer.

For democratic leaders, whose political fortunes are inextricably linked to public opinion, the ability to generate popular support for war in this way is highly consequential. When the public is generally averse to war, democratic accountability acts as a constraint on leaders' freedom to use military force as a tool of foreign policy. Embarking on an unpopular war can undermine leaders' popularity, sap their political capital, and ultimately place their position in office in jeopardy (Mueller 1973; Edwards 1976; Ostrom and Simon 1985; Rivers and Rose 1985; Hurwitz and Peffley 1987; Aldrich, Sullivan, and Borgida 1989; Krosnick and Kinder 1990; Bueno de Mesquita and Siverson 1995; Goemans 2000; Karol and Miguel 2007; Kernell 2007; Croco 2015). These risks create a strong incentive not to use the hammer of military force on every single nail but only on those rare occasions when the stars align for a swift, victorious, and popular war. However, if a leader can generate a significant boost in popular support for war by framing the conflict in a way that resonates with citizens' beliefs about revenge, then the political risk will be lessened and the constraints of accountability will be loosened.

In a world where there are significant cross-national differences in vengefulness, this logic implies that leaders with more vengeful populations are less constrained because they have a larger reservoir of latent support for war that they can galvanize by framing the use of force as a punishment. Consequently, they are more likely (on average) to initiate the use of force in their disputes with other states. Thus, the vengefulness of a country's population is best understood as an underlying risk factor rather than a proximate cause of war. In order for two states to traverse the path from peace to war, a conflict of interest must first arise between them, and they must then fail to find a peaceful bargain that both sides prefer to war. My claim is not that the vengefulness of a country's population creates conflicts of interest or causes bargaining to fail. Rather, I argue that once a conflict of interest has emerged and bargaining is under way, a highly vengeful population can exacerbate the proximate causes of bargaining failure by lowering the expected costs of military action for leaders, thereby shrinking the set of peaceful outcomes that both sides would prefer to a fight. The smaller this "bargaining range," the more likely it is that bargaining will fail and that war will be the result (Fearon 1995).

The theory that I develop in this book stands apart from prior attempts to theorize about the role of revenge in interstate conflict both in its focus on ordinary individuals as the locus of the desire for revenge and in its attention to tracing out the domestic political mechanism whereby that desire is externalized as state behavior. By locating the theory's microfoundations at the individual level, this approach overcomes the primary problem that has plagued the existing literature on war and revenge: the state as the unit of analysis. In this respect, this book is part of what Hafner-Burton et al. (2017: S2) refer to as "the behavioral revolution" in International Relations. The defining feature of this revolution is "the use of empirical research on preferences, beliefs, and decision making to modify choice- and game-theoretic models." While much of the work in this vein has concentrated on leaders, studies of public opinion have also flourished.[2]

---

[2] For recent examples of work on leaders, see Hafner Burton et al. (2014); Yarhi-Milo (2014); Renshon (2015); Rathbun et al. (2017); Saunders (2017). For recent examples of work on public opinion, see Kertzer and McGraw (2012); Tomz and Weeks (2013); Bayram (2015); Rho and Tomz (2017).

One of the fundamental challenges faced by the public opinion arm of the behavioral revolution is aggregation, i.e., "how individual-level findings can be aggregated to understand collective as well as individual decision making" (Hafner-Burton et al. 2017: S17). Studies of public opinion in IR often posit that their findings regarding individual preferences are "intrinsically interesting because they act as constraints on national decision makers in democratic settings," but they do not often address aggregation directly (Hafner-Burton et al. 2017: S19). In contrast, this book attempts to provide a more fleshed-out account of how individual heterogeneity in values translates into differences in state behavior by relaxing the assumption – common to many theories of democracy and war – that democratic leaders cannot manufacture popular support for war, and by recognizing that the core values that inform individuals' preferences about the use of military force vary both across individuals and across cultures. These two theoretical moves turn the constraining effect of accountability to the public into a variable rather than a constant and defining feature of democracy.

In this respect, the theory that I develop in this book stands apart from much of the previous research on domestic politics and war, which has largely focused on differences between democracies and autocracies rather than variation among democracies themselves.[3] This has been a productive line of research, but it has also obscured important variation within the group of democracies. The existing literature paints a fairly rosy picture of the conflict behavior of democracies. Compared with autocracies, democracies tend to fight shorter, lower-cost, and more victorious wars (Siverson 1995; Bennett and Stam 1996; Bueno de Mesquita et al. 1999; Reiter and Stam 2002; Filson and Werner 2004; Slantchev 2004; Valentino et al. 2010). Yet it is also true that some democracies behave much more belligerently than others in their international relations. How can we explain why similar institutions can nonetheless produce these different patterns of conflict behavior? In this book, I contend that cross-cultural differences in core values, and particularly in endorsement of revenge, are an important part of the answer to this question.

Democracy is no longer a rare and radical form of government but one that has taken root in a large and culturally diverse set of nations, and the differences among democracies are just as consequential as their

---

[3] For other recent work that focuses on democratic heterogeneity, see Caverley (2014) and Baum and Potter (2015).

similarities. Although my theory deals specifically with conflict initiation, it has broad implications for other aspects of interstate war, including the democratic peace. Indeed, it suggests that the increasing diversity of democracies may have the potential to weaken the separate peace that has prevailed among democratic nations for more than two centuries.

PRIOR APPROACHES AND THEIR LIMITATIONS

The central challenge of integrating revenge into IR theory is the state as the unit of analysis. Revenge, which involves perceptions, beliefs, and emotions that we typically think of as fundamentally human attributes, does not map neatly or easily onto an abstract, corporate entity like the state. Prior work has dealt with this challenge in two main ways. The first approach makes national leaders the locus of the desire for revenge. The most prominent recent example of this kind of argument is the 2003 Iraq War. It has long been suggested that part of President George W. Bush's motivation for going to war with Iraq was his long-standing desire to get revenge on Saddam Hussein for orchestrating an assassination attempt that targeted his father, former President George H. W. Bush, during a visit to Kuwait in 1993 (Lebow 2010). This narrative was fueled in part by President Bush's own words. For instance, he once referred to Saddam Hussein as "a guy that tried to kill my dad at one time."[4]

However, this case also illustrates the limitations of leader-centric accounts. As a general matter, it is difficult to look inside leaders' hearts and minds for the personal motivations that might be driving their policy decisions, and there is little concrete evidence that President Bush acted out of a desire for revenge. Furthermore, such accounts tend to deal with single, idiosyncratic cases – e.g., a current president seeking to avenge an attack on a former president who also happens to be his father – making it difficult for them to give us any generalizable insights into when and how revenge helps to fan the flames of conflict. Finally, this type of argument equates the whims of individual leaders with national policy while ignoring the fact that in most modern polities, decision makers are embedded in a set of domestic political institutions that serve to constrain, to varying degrees, their freedom of action, and that create channels through which other domestic actors can influence the policy-making process.

---

[4] The White House, Office of the Press Secretary, 2017, *Remarks by The President at John Cornyn for Senate Reception*, https://georgewbush-whitehouse.archives.gov/news/releases/2002/09/20020926-17.html.

The second approach makes the state itself rather than individual leaders the locus of the desire for revenge, as exemplified by the works of Harkavy (2000) and Lowenheim and Heimann (2008). According to Harkavy, national humiliation, such as military defeat or long-term domination, leads to "collective narcissistic rage," which motivates states to go to war in order to exact revenge. Lowenheim and Heimann add some additional nuance, arguing that vengeful behavior by states is driven by three factors: the degree of moral outrage that a state experiences following a harm done against it, the intensity of the state's humiliation following that harm, and the extent to which negative reciprocity is institutionalized in international politics. Both these arguments ultimately rest on the attribution of emotions, such as anger and humiliation, to states themselves. In other words, they posit that states have an emotional capacity that is not reducible to "the mere aggregation of individuals' (decision makers, members of the public) emotions" (Lowenheim and Heimann 2008: 689).[5]

The concept of state emotions has both empirical and theoretical limitations. First, it cuts against the mainstream perspective on emotion, which views emotion as something that can be experienced only by living beings with brains and bodies.[6] Lowenheim and Heimann attempt to deal with this problem by positing that individuals within the state – its rulers, officials, and citizens – experience the state's emotions on its behalf. The essence of this argument is that these individuals assume particular "role identities," as a result of which they experience emotions that are specific to those roles and that are distinct from their personal emotions. However, there is little empirical evidence to support the idea that such role-based emotions exist and can be distinguished from an individual's personal emotions.[7] Moreover, even if individuals' role-based emotions

---

[5] For more on emotions in international relations, see Crawford (2000); Bleiker and Hutchison (2008); Sasley (2011).

[6] See Niedenthal (2007) on the "embodiment" of emotion.

[7] In their case study of the Second Lebanon War (2006) between Israel and Hezbollah, Lowehheim and Heimann use the statements of key decision makers as evidence that the desire for revenge drove Israel's behavior during the conflict. Even setting aside the obvious issues with inferring emotions from leaders' publicly available statements, the authors do not indicate how they separate the emotions that these individuals feel because of their particular role identities from their personal emotions. Nor do they indicate how such an analysis could be replicated outside of those few (and mostly recent) cases of conflict for which we have access to a similarly detailed documentary record. Thus, in practice their approach does little to improve on the lack of generalizability that characterizes leader-centric accounts.

could be reliably identified, individuals in different roles might have very different emotional reactions to the same event, raising the thorny question of whose role-based emotions should be assigned to the state.

More broadly, as with the leader-centric arguments discussed previously, the state emotions account fails to recognize the political nature of the decision to go to war. The story it offers is a simple one: the state experiences some kind of harm or humiliation, feels a desire for revenge, and acts on it by going to war. Yet we know that state action does not spring directly from emotional drives as the actions of individuals often do. Rather, it is the result of a policy-making process that is shaped by a state's political institutions and by the set of domestic political actors who are enfranchised by those institutions. Thus, even if they exist, state emotions cannot translate directly into policy, because policy-making is a political process.

Given these limitations, it is not surprising that neither the leader-centric approach nor the state emotions approach has established revenge as important topic of study in International Relations. What is needed is a new approach that identifies both when and how revenge enters into the political processes that lie behind the decision to go to war. The theory that I develop here rises to meet that challenge by grounding itself firmly in the existing research on revenge, public opinion formation, and democratic accountability.

A NEW APPROACH: FROM VENGEFUL CITIZENS TO VIOLENT STATES

Ordinary people do not have a direct say in when and how their country uses military force, but this does not mean they are necessarily lacking in influence. They have the power to give voice to their opinions, and those opinions can enter into the decision-making process when leaders have an incentive to take the preferences of their citizens into consideration. Thus, in order to link individual vengefulness to state violence, we need to answer three key questions. First, how do ordinary people think about revenge and what role does it play in their everyday lives? Second, when and how does revenge influence individuals' attitudes toward war? Third, when and how do those attitudes shape the choices of state leaders?

My answer to the first question is that at the individual level, revenge is best understood as a core value. An individual's core values are his or her deeply held and enduring beliefs about "desirable modes of conduct or desirable end states of existence" (Rokeach 1973: 7). These beliefs play an essential role in human behavior by providing the evaluative criteria that people use "to select and justify action and to evaluate people (including the self) and events" (Schwartz 1992: 1). Due to the strong anti-revenge bias in Western thought (Miller 1998), revenge has not traditionally been recognized as a core value. However, thanks to the growing body of empirical research on revenge, we now know a great deal about how ordinary people, as opposed to philosophers and legal scholars, think about revenge. Building on this research, I argue that the essence of revenge is the belief that wrongs deserve to be repaid and that like other core values, this belief serves as an important standard of judgment in matters both personal and political.

In particular, the belief that wrongs deserve to be repaid has a profound effect on individuals' attitudes toward violence. For those who hold revenge as a core value, the use of violence in response to a perceived harm or injury is seen as an act of moral virtue. This is not a view that accepts the old adage that "two wrongs don't make a right." Rather, the return of harm for harm and suffering for suffering is necessary to balance the scales of justice. In other words, when the target of an act of violence is viewed as deserving of punishment, that act of violence is imbued with an aura of righteousness, transforming it from something vicious into something virtuous. Consequently, individuals who hold revenge as a core value are more likely to express support for the use of punitive violence in a variety of forms, including, as I show in Chapter 3, corporal punishment, vigilante killing, police repression, the death penalty, and torture.

War is also a form of violence, which leads to our second key question: when and how does revenge influence individuals' attitudes toward war? My answer here draws on the extensive literature on the role of core values in the formation of public opinion. Scholars have long recognized that core values serve as heuristics or decision-making shortcuts that allow individuals to develop a coherent set of opinions across a wide range of political issues without paying the (often prohibitive) costs of gathering extensive information about each new issue (Hurwitz and Peffley 1987; Wildavsky 1987; Sniderman et al. 1993). Instead, a person can figure out where he or she stands on an issue simply by asking whether or not it accords with his or her core values (Feldman 1988).

However, values do not always translate automatically into specific issue positions (Zaller 1992; Alvarez and Brehm 2002). Indeed, most political debates are complex and multifaceted, touching on a variety of competing considerations that may point in opposite directions. Ordinary people therefore rely on the cues and information carried in elite political discourse to help them connect their values to the political debates of the day (Zaller 1992). When elite discourse frames an issue in a way that highlights a particular value, citizens are more likely to see the issue in terms of that value and to base their opinions on it (Iyengar 1991; Zaller 1992; Kinder and Sanders 1996; Nelson et al. 1997; Chong and Druckman 2007). For this reason, the ability to influence how an issue is framed is a source of political power. By using strategically crafted rhetoric that resonates with their citizens' core values, political elites can sway public opinion in favor of their preferred policies.

This, I argue, is the process by which revenge becomes salient to citizens' opinions about the use of military force, including the use of force in cases that do not involve an attack on the nation's homeland or citizens. By framing the use of force as a punishment that the adversary deserves to suffer in return for some prior transgression (real or invented), political elites, and particularly national leaders, can transform a complex international crisis into a simple and familiar narrative – a bad guy getting his just deserts – that will resonate strongly with their more vengeful citizens. In turn, these individuals will be more likely to support aggressive action against the adversary because, to them, going to war against an evildoer is more than a matter of security; it is a matter of justice. Thus, leaders can use the power of their rhetoric to boost popular support for war by appealing to their citizens' basic beliefs about revenge.

Having identified revenge as a potentially powerful source of popular support for war brings us to our third key question: when and how does this relationship influence the choices of state leaders? The answer to this question has two components. First, the relationship between revenge and support for war will have bearing on the choices of state leaders in places where those leaders can be held accountable by the public. In democracies, public opinion must be part of leaders' calculus about matters of war and peace. An unpopular war carries many political costs, and democratically elected leaders therefore have a strong incentive to use all the resources of their office, including the bully pulpit, to frame the use of force in a way that garners maximum popular support (Rosenblatt 1998). The more successful they are at doing so, the more freedom they will have to use military force as a tool of foreign policy. In autocracies, by contrast, leaders are constrained less by public opinion than by other regime insiders (Weeks 2008), whose support can be garnered through more direct methods like payoffs and threats, (Bueno de Mesquita et al. 2005).

Second, the degree to which democratic leaders can loosen the constraint of accountability to the public by appealing to their citizens' desire for revenge against evildoers depends on the prevalence of revenge in their populations. Due to diverse cultural legacies, cross-national differences in endorsement of revenge as a core value persist even in today's highly globalized world, and these differences impact leaders' ability to generate popular support for war by using a punishment frame. Put another way, all elected leaders have a set of tools that they can use to manage public opinion about war. Framing the use of force as punishment is one of those tools, and leaders with more vengeful populations will, on average, find it to be more reliable and more effective than leaders with less vengeful populations. With such a powerful tool at hand, leaders with more vengeful populations can behave more hawkishly in their foreign policies knowing that they have the capacity to bring the public along with them. Consequently, there are systematic differences in the conflict behavior of democracies with highly vengeful populations compared with democracies with less vengeful populations. In other words, vengeful citizens help to create violent states.

BROADER CONTRIBUTIONS AND IMPLICATIONS

Theories of Democracy and War

My theory joins a large and growing body of IR scholarship that gives individual preferences an important role in shaping states' foreign policies. In the area of international trade, for instance, scholars have long argued that models of trade policy-making must incorporate individuals' preferences over trade policy (Scheve and Slaughter 2001). Nor have theories of war been neglectful of the political relevance of the mass public. Indeed, the role of public opinion – and the constraint it places on the behavior of democratically elected leaders – is often held to be one of the fundamental reasons why the conflict behavior of democracies differs from that of autocracies along many different dimensions (Reiter and Tillman 2002).

According to the existing literature, democracies display a number of desirable tendencies when it comes to the use of military force. They are more likely to win the wars they initiate and to win them quickly, more likely to seek a negotiated settlement if a quick victory is not forthcoming, and less likely to incur high costs in terms of both civilian and military casualties (Siverson 1995; Bennett and Stam 1996; Bueno de Mesquita et al. 1999; Reiter and Stam 2002; Filson and Werner 2004; Slantchev 2004; Valentino et al. 2010).

Theories that attribute this democratic exceptionalism to elected leaders' need to take popular preferences into account typically rest on two key assumptions about public opinion toward the use of military force. The first assumption, rooted in the work of the philosopher Immanuel Kant, is that ordinary citizens are generally averse to war. It is they who are called on to sacrifice both their blood and their treasure in times of war, and they will therefore have a strong underlying preference for peace (Chernoff 2004). The second assumption is that elected leaders cannot easily manufacture support for war. If they could, then they would have very little incentive to attend to their citizens' preferences in matters of war and peace (Reiter and Stam 2002).

Together these assumptions undergird the view that public opinion is a powerful source of constraint on elected leaders' freedom to use military force as a tool of foreign policy. Because their political fortunes are tied to the opinions of a public that is generally war-averse and difficult to manipulate, their choices are circumscribed by the imperative of avoiding any serious or sustained dissatisfaction on the part of their constituents. When they do use force, they will strive to produce only short, low-cost, and victorious wars, selecting only those conflicts they believe they are likely to win, spending less on defense in peacetime but more in wartime, minimizing the costs of fighting, and using negotiated settlements to end wars that are getting too expensive (Caverley 2014).

The theory that I develop in this book challenges both the assumption that democratic publics are generally war-averse and the assumption that there is very little that leaders can do to rouse popular support for war. Mass attitudes toward war are not set in stone, and leaders do not behave as if they are (Rosenblatt 1998; Western 2005). Rather, the public's willingness to support the use of force depends on how a particular conflict is framed, and national leaders can sway public opinion in their favor by employing a frame that resonates strongly with their citizens' core values. At the same time, leaders cannot expect to play the role of puppet master, effortlessly steering their citizens in any direction they choose. Leaders' capacity to generate popular support for war is limited by the values that their citizens hold and by their ability to construct a narrative that aligns with those values. Thus, *among* democracies, there will be important differences in the degree of constraint that leaders face depending on the prevalence of values, such as revenge, that can be used to mobilize popular enthusiasm for war.

Indeed, as democracy spreads around the globe to encompass an ever more diverse group of nations, it is becoming increasingly important to move beyond the simple division of the world into democracies and autocracies and to ask why some democracies appear to be less constrained than others in terms of both when and how they use military force. By and large, existing studies that have addressed this variation in constraint have argued that it is the product of institutional differences among democracies, such as the type of electoral system, the timing of elections, political competitiveness, media freedom, the degree of transparency in national security, the extent of political participation, and the strength of legislative constraints on the executive (Morgan and Campbell 1991; Auerswald 1999; Gaubatz 1999; Reiter and Tillman 2002; Leblang and Chan 2003; Clark and Nordstrom 2005; Boehmer 2008; Colaresi 2012; Baum and Potter 2015).

However, these institutional differences cannot fully account for the diversity of democratic conflict behavior because they do not allow for variation in the preferences of the people who are enfranchised by those institutions. Institutions that enhance leaders' accountability to the public will be a force for peace only when public opinion is averse to going to war. If public opinion favors the use of military force, the constraining effect of accountability evaporates. Thus, similar democratic institutions can produce very different patterns of conflict behavior depending on prevailing public attitudes toward war. Although a few studies have noted that the pacifism of democratic publics is by no means guaranteed (e.g., Morgan and Campbell 1991; Gaubatz 1999; Mansfield and Snyder 2005), mainstream scholarship has yet to recognize that mass attitudes toward war can vary systematically across countries. An important exception is Caverley's (2014) theory of democratic militarism. He argues that differences in economic inequality across democracies affect how heavily the costs of war fall on the median voter. Where these costs are relatively low, the public is more likely to favor aggressive foreign policy strategies. In contrast, this book highlights the importance of cross-national differences in core values as a source of variation in mass attitudes toward war, and in Chapter 5, I demonstrate that taking these differences into account can shed new light on the question of why some democracies behave more belligerently than others.

More broadly, recognizing that attitudes toward war are shaped by persistent cultural differences across nations has important implications for work on the democratic peace. For decades, scholars have argued over how best to explain the fact that mature democracies rarely, if ever, fight major wars against one another (Maoz and Russett 1993; Farber and Gowa 1995; Siverson 1995; Gartzke 2007; Dafoe et al. 2013). A groundbreaking study by Tomz and Weeks (2013) suggests that public opinion may play an important role. Using survey experiments conducted in the United States and the United Kingdom, they find that people are much less likely to support using military force against a democratic adversary and that this is due in large part to the belief that going to war against a fellow democracy is morally wrong.

This study suggests that democratic leaders may be constrained in their relations with one another by their citizens' reluctance to use force when the adversary is a democracy. This is a significant advance in our understanding of the causes of the democratic peace, but in light of my theory, it also raises additional questions. Specifically, the United States and the United Kingdom are both long-established democracies that share many cultural similarities. Would citizens of Brazil or India be equally reluctant to go to war with another democracy? Would we expect the same attitudes to hold in a democratic Iran or China? Given that values vary substantially across cultures (Schwartz 1999; Henrich et al. 2010), it is by no means a foregone conclusion that moral opposition to fighting a fellow democracy will be equally strong in all nations.[8] Indeed, the club of democracies has long been populated primarily by states that share the same Western cultural heritage, and the values that are part of that heritage may have helped to promote and sustain the democratic peace. If this is the case, then we must consider the possibility that the democratic peace could weaken as democracies become more culturally diverse.

Finally, these insights about the role of core values in determining the degree of constraint that democratic leaders face carry an important message for both scholars and policy makers who have advocated for democracy promotion as a way to enhance international peace and security. The message is one of caution: there is no guarantee that democratization will produce a sizable peace dividend. Some democracies are highly pacific in their relations with other states, but others regularly behave belligerently. The democracies of the past have refrained from fighting one another, but the democracies of the future may not adhere so rigorously to this pattern. Whether newly democratic states will join the ranks of the pacifists depends, at least in part, on the

---

[8] I develop this idea in greater detail in the Conclusion.

vengefulness of their citizens. Given the wealth of evidence that revenge continues to flourish in many societies around the world, the "perpetual peace" that Immanuel Kant believed would prevail in a world populated by representative governments is likely to remain, for now, a dream rather than a reality.

The Sources of Public Support for War

The theory that I develop in this book also speaks to the growing literature on the sources of public support for war. In large part, this literature has been dominated by a debate between two competing theoretical perspectives: the cost–benefit model and the elite cues model. The cost–benefit model views support for war as the product of a rational assessment of the costs and benefits of fighting, including the objectives of the conflict (Jentleson 1992; Jentleson and Britton 1998; Eichenberg 2005), expectations of success (Kull and Ramsay 2001; Gelpi, Feaver, and Reifler 2006, 2009), and US military casualties (Mueller 1973; Burk 1999; Gartner and Segura 2000; Gartner 2008).

In contrast, the elite cues model contends that most people lack the information and experience necessary to make complex cost–benefit calculations, especially about something as remote from their everyday lives as international warfare. Instead, they rely on elite cues, i.e., signals of support or opposition, which serve as heuristics that obviate the need for extensive information-gathering and complex calculations by outsourcing those tasks to trusted political elites. Influential cue-givers include elected officials (Zaller 1992, 1994; Berinsky 2007, 2009; Baum and Groeling 2009), military elites (Golby et al. 2013), and foreign voices such as allied leaders and international organizations (Chapman and Reiter 2004; Grieco et al. 2011; Chapman 2012; Hayes and Guardino 2013).[9] The part of my theory that connects revenge and support for war aligns most closely with the elite cues model, drawing on some of the same

---

[9] Outside this central debate, there is an important strand of research that has focused on how media coverage, including the type of news sources that people consume and the framing of news stories that they encounter, can influence support for the use of military force (Iyengar and Simon 1993; Berinsky and Kinder 2006; Baum and Groeling 2009, 2010). There are also a number of studies that focus on individual attributes or predispositions, including gender (Conover and Sapiro 1993; Eichenberg 2005; Brooks and Valentino 2011), race/ethnicity (Nincic and Nincic 2002; Berinsky 2009), ethnocentrism (Hurwitz and Peffley 1987; Kam and Kinder 2007), authoritarianism (Doty et al. 1997; McFarland 2005), and trust (Brewer et al. 2004).

foundational ideas about the essential role that elite communication plays in the formation of citizens' political attitudes (e.g., Zaller 1992). However, I introduce additional nuance to this perspective by considering how leaders frame their arguments for war rather than classifying all discourse into signals of either support or opposition.

More generally, this book stands apart from both the cost–benefit model and the elite cues model in its focus on the moral dimension of war. Statesmen and scholars of international politics alike have long recognized that public support for war has moral roots (Carr 1939; Kennan 1951). Even the staunchest proponents of a *realpolitik* approach to international affairs acknowledge that moral arguments are critical when leaders communicate with their people. According to Hans Morgenthau, "The statesman must think in terms of the national interest, conceived as power among other powers. The popular mind, unaware of the fine distinctions of the statesman's thinking, reasons more often than not in the simple moral and legalistic terms of absolute good and absolute evil" (Morgenthau and Thompson 1985: 165). In reflecting on American foreign policy, Henry Kissinger observed that "Americans cannot sustain major international obligations that are not justified by their moral faith" (1994: 50). John Mearsheimer takes a similar view in his treatise on great power politics: "It is difficult to imagine a modern political leader openly asking the public to fight and die to improve the balance of power. No European or American leader did so during either world war or the Cold War. Most people prefer to think of fights between their own state and rival states as clashes between good and evil, where they are on the side of the angels and their opponents are aligned with the devil" (2003: 22). Yet the both the cost-benefit model and the elite cues model treat the decision to support the use of military force – one in which lives hang in the balance – as an entirely amoral one.

A few important studies do consider the moral basis of support for war, but each has significant limitations. Hurwitz and Peffley's (1987) groundbreaking work on the structure of foreign policy attitudes identifies the morality of warfare as one of the core values that shapes individuals' attitudes toward a host of specific foreign policy issues, including defense spending, nuclear arms buildup, and military intervention. Unsurprisingly, they find that individuals who say that it is morally acceptable to kill during war take more militaristic stances on those issues. However, this study leaves unanswered the question of why some people accept the morality of warfare while others do not. Where do those views come from? Are they rooted in other, more basic values? Several more recent studies have found that individuals who say that the use of force in a particular situation is "morally justified" or has a "moral basis" are more likely to express support for going to war than those who do not (Gelpi et al. 2009; Tomz and Weeks 2013; Reifler et al. 2014), but here again we are left to wonder about the source of those beliefs.

To understand the moral roots of public support for war, we need to know not just whether individuals believe that going to war is morally justified, but *how* they arrived at their convictions in the first place. In this respect, the work of Peter Liberman stands out from the crowd, and the argument that I make in this book owes much to his pioneering research. Liberman was the first to call attention to the importance of moral views about punishment as a source of public support for war, and the first to show empirically that endorsement of revenge is an important predictor of support for the use of force in both hypothetical scenarios (Liberman 2013, 2014) and real cases of conflict (Liberman 2006; Liberman and Skitka 2017). The theory I develop in this book builds on Liberman's work but also departs from it in several key respects.

The most important point of commonality between my theory and Liberman's is the conceptualization of revenge as a core value. From this starting point, Liberman goes on to argue that the same values that structure attitudes toward punishment in the domestic context are likely to do so in the international realm as well. Thus, given the importance of revenge in shaping individuals' attitudes toward both interpersonal and criminal punishment, revenge should also influence popular support for punishing foreign actors. The main problem with this argument is that it does not push the idea of revenge as a core value far enough. It incorporates one key idea from the literature on core values – that values are "trans-situational" and can therefore shape a person's thinking across different domains of social and political life – but it misses a second and equally important insight: that in the political arena, a person's values may not translate directly and automatically into positions on specific issues.

Why is this so? The literature on core values and opinion formation provides a two-part answer. First, most political issues are sufficiently complex that they touch on multiple (potentially competing) considerations. Rather than trying to weigh and combine all these different considerations, the average citizen tends to base his or her position on whatever consideration is foremost in his or her mind at a particular moment (Zaller and Feldman 1992). Thus, values will exert their influence only when they are "at the top of the head." Second, values are by definition abstract and general, and their implications for specific policies are not always straightforward and obvious. For example, the value of equality has been invoked by both supporters and opponents of affirmative action (Brewer and Gross 2005). Thus, people often require additional contextual information in order to translate their values into a concrete policy stance. In sum, we cannot assume that simply because a person holds a particular value, that value will automatically shape his or her opinions about politics. In order to influence opinion, values must be made salient and individuals must have sufficient contextual information to determine which policy or course of action is consistent with those values.

Liberman's work takes the crucial first step of recognizing that revenge is best understood as a core value and that it therefore has the potential to profoundly influence how people think about the use of military force against foreign enemies. However, his theory does not clearly and systematically specify the circumstances under which we should expect this potential to be realized, and consequently, his empirical results amount to a 'proof of concept' – a demonstration that revenge *can* influence people's attitudes toward the use of military force – rather than a fully fleshed-out picture of *when* and *how* they do so.[10]

The theory and evidence that I present in the following chapters help to fill in these important gaps in our knowledge. I engage much more extensively with the existing literature on core values and issue framing to identify the key actors and processes involved in making revenge salient to ordinary citizens' opinions on matters of war and peace. This allows me to develop and test a novel set of theoretical expectations about the conditions under which individual vengefulness will (and will not) lead to heightened support for war. In particular, my theory highlights the key role that leaders – and the frames they construct and disseminate in their political communication – play in activating their citizens' desire for revenge.[11] This in turn is a crucial step in establishing the connection between individual vengefulness and state behavior. It is the strategic

---

[10] At various points, Liberman suggests that the effect of revenge may be heightened or attenuated by certain situational and dispositional factors, such as nationalism, interest in foreign affairs, the strategic stakes of the conflict, and the availability of vivid information about the adversary's transgression. However, these factors are all proposed as potential moderators, which is separate from the more fundamental question of what makes revenge salient in the first place.

[11] Liberman does note that leaders' wartime rhetoric often appears designed to appeal to the vengeful among us, e.g., by making "frequent references to foreign enemies' crimes and evil natures" (2013, 286), but leaders do not have a central place in his theory.

behavior of leaders, conditioned by their degree of accountability to the mass public, that leads states with more vengeful populations to act more belligerently in their international relations.

Ultimately, it is by theorizing and testing the international implications of the relationship between individual vengefulness and support for war that this book most clearly distinguishes itself from Liberman's prior research on revenge, and indeed from much of the existing literature on public opinion and war. These studies often motivate the importance of their endeavor by citing the role of public opinion in a number of important theories about the domestic politics of international conflict (e.g., Gartner and Segura 1998; Chapman and Reiter 2004; Gartner 2008; Horowitz and Levendusky 2011). However, they rarely draw out the theoretical implications of their findings, much less test them empirically.[12] Consequently, it remains to be seen whether what we have learned about the sources of popular support for war will have a broader impact on IR theory. This is, in essence, the problem of aggregation that Powell (2017) identifies as one of the fundamental challenges facing the behavioral revolution in International Relations. The theory that I develop in this book tackles this challenge directly, building a much-needed bridge between the literature on public support for war and the literature on the domestic politics of international conflict, and providing a model for how to approach the issue of aggregation in future work.

EMPIRICAL APPROACH

Because the logic of my theory rests on a series of arguments about when and how revenge influences the attitudes of ordinary individuals, the empirical approach that I employ in this book places equal weight on testing both the theory's individual-level micro-foundations and its international implications.

At the individual level, I test two main hypotheses derived from my theory. The first, which I label the *core value hypothesis*, predicts that vengeful individuals (i.e., those who endorse revenge as a general principle) will be more supportive of punitive violence than non-vengeful individuals across a wide variety of contexts, regardless of their personal involvement. The second, which I label the *framing hypothesis*, predicts

---

[12] For a notable exception, see Caverley (2014).

that vengeful individuals will be more supportive of the use of force than non-vengeful individuals when (and only when) that use of force is framed as a punishment. Establishing that revenge is a core value that transcends the realm of the personal, and that by framing the use of force as a punishment, leaders can activate their citizens' desire for revenge and channel it into support for war in many different scenarios, are both essential steps in demonstrating the validity of the mechanism that I have proposed to link individual-level vengefulness with state-level violence.

To test these hypotheses, I rely on public opinion data from the United States. Some of these data are publicly available and some are from my own original surveys. When it comes to publicly available survey data, I am restricted to the United States for purely practical reasons. The record of public opinion is broader, richer, and extends further back in time in the United States than in any other country, and even so, I was able to find only a single survey that included both a measure of endorsement of revenge and questions about attitudes toward violence. Outside the United States, I was able to identify one multi-country survey that included a measure of revenge, but this survey did not ask any questions about the use of violence or military force. Thus, while this survey can tell us about the range of cross-national variation in endorsement of revenge, it does not allow for a direct test of my theory. Instead, to address the question of whether my theory has cross-cultural validity, I exploit regional cultural differences within the United States itself.

In collecting my own original data, I chose to focus on the United States for a different reason. Given its current position as the sole superpower and its immense military power projection capabilities, the United States has the capacity to use military force almost anywhere in the world. This allows me to ask questions about individuals' attitudes toward the use of force in a wide variety of contexts, both real and hypothetical, without straying into the realm of the fantastical. Americans can readily give their opinions about humanitarian intervention, the use of nuclear weapons, killing terrorists, intervening in a territorial dispute, and using force to secure oil supplies because these are things their country either has done in the past or could realistically do in the future. In any other country, at least some (if not most) of these scenarios would strain credulity because the military capabilities to carry out these kinds of missions are simply lacking. Being able to ask such a wide variety of questions about the use of military force allows me to conduct a much more rigorous test of my theory than would otherwise be possible.

At the international level, the main hypothesis that I derive from my theory is the *conflict initiation hypothesis*, which predicts that democracies with more vengeful populations will be more likely to initiate the use of military force than democracies with less vengeful populations. The main empirical challenge in testing this hypothesis is finding a measure of cross-national variation in vengefulness that is available both across countries and over time. Cross-national survey data on endorsement of revenge is too sparse to be used for this purpose. Instead, I use the legal status of the death penalty as a proxy measure.

Existing research on individual attitudes toward the death penalty shows that support is driven primarily by the desire for revenge rather than instrumental considerations (Ellsworth and Ross 1983; Bohm 1992; Cotton 2000; Carlsmith et al. 2002; McKee and Feather 2008), and my own analysis shows that democracies with more vengeful populations, as measured by the existing survey data, are more likely to retain the death penalty in the present day. Together, this evidence indicates that retentionist democracies are more likely to have highly vengeful populations than democracies that have abolished the death penalty. Moreover, information on the legal status of the death penalty is readily available for all countries in the international system. Using this measure as a proxy for the vengefulness of a country's population thus allows me to test the *conflict initiation hypothesis* using data on all militarized disputes initiated by democracies between 1945 and 2001 while simultaneously controlling for a number of other factors that are known to affect the likelihood of initiation.

By taking a multimethod and multilevel approach to theory testing, this book furnishes a rich set of insights into the mechanism that connects individual vengefulness with state violence.

PLAN OF THE BOOK

In the next chapter, I develop my theoretical argument in detail and lay out the three hypotheses that I will test in the book's subsequent empirical chapters. Chapter 3 tests the *core value hypothesis* by examining the relationship between endorsement of revenge and attitudes toward various kinds of punitive violence, including corporal punishment, vigilante killing, police repression, the death penalty, and torture. Chapter 4 tests the *framing hypothesis* by exploiting differences in question wording on public opinion surveys, leveraging the power of survey-based experiments to establish causal effects, and comparing two real-world cases of conflict involving the United States (Kosovo in 1999 and Iraq in 2003) to demonstrate external validity. Chapter 5 tests the *conflict initiation hypothesis* with a large-N statistical analysis of all militarized dispute initiations by democracies from 1945 to 2001. Finally, the book's Conclusion summarizes the argument and main findings, elaborates on their implications for our understanding of the conflict behavior of democracies in general and US foreign policy in particular, and makes the case that revenge ought to be recognized as an important ingredient in the production of political violence both between and within states.

2

Linking Individual Vengefulness to State Violence

Although revenge has long been recognized as a root cause of violence in human societies, the question of whether it plays a role in international conflict has received scant attention in the field of International Relations, and prior approaches that have focused on either individual leaders or states themselves as the locus of the desire for revenge have proved both theoretically and empirically unsatisfying. In this chapter, I present a theory that explains both when and how the desire for revenge, as experienced by ordinary individuals, influences the conflict behavior of states.

I develop my theory in three parts. In part 1, I consider the role that revenge plays in the lives of ordinary individuals. Drawing on the growing body of empirical social science research on revenge, I argue that at the individual level, revenge is best understood as a core value, rooted in the belief that those who hurt others deserve to be hurt in return. For individuals who hold revenge as a core value, this belief serves as a guiding principle that shapes both their personal conduct and their political opinions across a wide variety of contexts.

In part 2, I connect revenge to popular support for war, highlighting the crucial role played by elite discourse and particularly the rhetoric of national leaders. By using rhetoric that frames the use of force as a punishment the adversary deserves to suffer, leaders can activate and channel their citizens' desire for revenge into support for taking military action in many different circumstances, including situations that do not involve a direct attack on the nation or its citizens. Consequently, framing the use of force as a punishment is a powerful tool that helps leaders sway public opinion in favor of war when it is in their interest to do so.

In part 3, I argue that for democratically elected leaders, the ability to influence popular support for war in this way is highly consequential because it allows them to loosen the constraint that accountability to the public places on their freedom to use military force as a tool of foreign policy. The more effectively a leader can stimulate his or her citizens' desire for revenge against foreign adversaries, the less constrained he or she will be in taking the nation to war. This dynamic helps to explain why some democracies behave more belligerently than others. Here, the crucial ingredient is cross-cultural variation in attitudes toward revenge. As a result of these different cultural legacies, some democratic leaders face constituencies in which revenge is broadly endorsed, while others do not. This gives leaders with highly vengeful populations a systematic advantage in generating popular support for war, and consequently, these democracies tend to behave (on average) more belligerently than democracies with less vengeful populations.

I conclude the chapter by deriving three testable hypotheses from this theoretical discussion and by highlighting its broader implications for how we understand the role that public opinion plays in shaping the conflict behavior of democracies.

PART 1: CONCEPTUALIZING REVENGE AS A CORE VALUE

I begin by discussing how I conceptualize revenge for the purposes of this study. In brief, I define revenge as a core value, rooted in the belief that wrongs deserve to be repaid. This is an explicitly non-consequentialist belief about punishment, meaning that it does not judge the rightness or wrongness of a punishment based on its consequences. From a consequentialist perspective, punishment is justified only when the good it does outweighs the harm it causes. In contrast, revenge refers to the belief that when a wrong has been committed, giving the perpetrator his or her "just deserts" is a righteous act in and of itself, regardless of what happens after. In other words, justice requires that those who hurt others be made to suffer in return, even if doing so causes more harm than good.

Defining Core Values

Research on core values has a long history both in social psychology, where the concept originated (Rokeach 1973), and in political science. In social psychology, there is a general consensus that core values are defined by five key properties that distinguish them from related concepts like needs and attitudes. As summarized by Schwartz (1994): "A value is a (1) belief (2) pertaining to desirable end states or modes of conduct, that (3) transcends specific situations, (4) guides selection or evaluation of behavior, people, and events, and (5) is ordered by importance relative to other values to form a system of value priorities" (20). Core values serve an essential psychological function by providing standards by which both the self and others can be judged and actions can be selected and justified. For this reason, they are widely viewed as one of the basic building blocks of human behavior (Kuklinski 2001; Feldman 2003).

In political science, a large body of work has demonstrated that core values also play an important role in the formation of public opinion toward a range of political issues, both domestic and international (Hurwitz and Peffley 1987; Feldman 1988; Pollock et al. 1993; Wilcox and Wolpert 2000; Goren 2001; Alvarez and Brehm 2002; Jacoby 2006; Pantoja 2006). Politics is a complex and constantly mutating landscape, and many people have only a minimal level of political knowledge (Delli Carpini and Keeter 1997). Values serve as heuristics or mental shortcuts (Hurwitz and Peffley 1987; Sniderman et al. 1993), which allow people who "possess only inches of fact to generate miles of preferences" (Wildavsky 1987: 8). Political actors, events, and policies can all be judged as either good or bad, desirable or undesirable, depending on whether they are consistent with a person's values (Feldman 1988), thus enabling him or her to express coherent views across a range of issues with relatively little cost in terms of information gathering or cognitive effort (Alvarez and Brehm 2002).

In general, political scientists have adopted Schwartz's (1994) definition of core values with the exception of the fifth and final element, the idea that values must be ordered in importance relative to one another. According to Jacoby's (2006) review of the literature, the prevailing view in social psychology is that "it makes little sense to examine the impact of a single particular value on public opinion. Instead, it is necessary to observe how choices among different values impinge on individual political orientations. This, in turn, requires taking the hierarchical structure of value preferences into account" (707). In contrast, political scientists tend to regard the existence of value systems or hierarchies as an empirical question rather than a necessary part of the definition of core values. Moreover, in their view, values do not necessarily need to be fully ordered in order to exert their influence. In many cases, contextual information can alter the relevance of particular values, causing them to increase or decrease in importance relative to other values. Thus, for any individual, the hierarchy of values may vary over time or across issues without producing any overt conflict in the mind of the individual and without diminishing the importance of values in the opinion formation process. Furthermore, even when values do come into direct conflict with one another, those conflicts do not necessarily get resolved in a way that produces a clear value hierarchy. For instance, Alvarez and Brehm (2002) identify the phenomenon of value ambivalence, which occurs when people are unable to make choices between conflicting values, and which has its own set of unique effects on opinion formation.

For these reasons, I follow the rest of the political science literature in defining core values according to the first four elements of Schwartz's (1994) definition. To summarize:

1. Core values are beliefs.
2. Core values pertain to desirable end states or modes of conduct.
3. Core values transcend specific situations.
4. Core values guide the selection or evaluation of behavior, people, and events.

Thus, to say that revenge is a core value is to say that it has these four essential properties. I base this assessment in part on the growing empirical literature on revenge, which I discuss in greater detail later, and in part on the additional evidence that I present in Chapter 3.

This understanding of revenge stands in sharp contrast to how revenge has traditionally been treated in Western thought. Beginning with the Stoic philosophers, revenge has variously been decried as immoral, irrational, and pathological (Horney 1948; Jacoby 1983; Elster 1990; Miller 1998; Murphy 2000). Most recently, it has become fashionable to liken revenge to a disease, with forgiveness as the cure (McCullough et al. 2013). The overall message of this "anti-vengeance discourse" is that revenge has no place in a civilized society, which must be governed by the rule of law rather than the law of the jungle. Indeed, many proponents of this view have argued that the demise of revenge is an essential element of social progress, either because vengeance will disappear naturally as societies evolve toward the rule of law or because it will be deliberately extirpated by wise social planning (Miller 1998). However, the growing body of empirical social science research on revenge has produced three key insights that suggest a new perspective on revenge is needed, and that conceptualizing revenge as a core value offers the most promising way forward.

New Insights from the Empirical Research on Revenge

Revenge Is Not Obsolete

The first insight that emerges from the empirical research on revenge is that far from being an anachronistic remnant of a less civilized era, revenge remains an integral part of the fabric of everyday life, even in the most developed and democratic societies. Taking revenge is something that many people readily admit to contemplating or fantasizing about when they or someone close to them has been victimized (Cardozo et al. 2000; Crombag et al. 2003; Orth et al. 2006; Schadt and DeLisi 2007; Tripp and Bies 2009). For example, Crombag et al. (2003) report that in a sample of American college students, 64% could recall at least one incident within the past year that made them feel the desire to get revenge. Another study of US undergraduates by Schadt and DeLisi (2007) found that almost 80% said they would be tempted to hurt a person who had harmed a member of their family, and 34% said they would be tempted to go as far as killing that person. Outside the United States, Cardozo et al. (2000), interviewed a sample of Kosovar Albanians one year after the 1999 war in Kosovo and found that nearly 40% of those surveyed said they experienced "feelings and fantasies of taking revenge" for what had happened to them and their families during the war. Similarly, a 2011 study of victims of the Khmer Rouge in Cambodia reported that approximately one-third said they would seek revenge if they could.[1] Of course, it is likely that only a small proportion of people who experience these vengeful feelings choose to act on them.[2] Nevertheless, acts of revenge are a commonplace occurrence in many different domains of social life.

According to McCullough et al. (2013), the desire for vengeance is a causal factor in 10%–20% of homicides worldwide, and blood feuds, with their cycles of revenge-driven violence, occur with considerable frequency in countries such as Albania, China, India, Iraq, Turkey, and Yemen (Schumann and Ross 2010). Revenge is also cited as a

---

[1] Astrid Zweynert, "Cambodia Seeks Way out of Post 'Killing Fields' Mental Health Crisis," *Reuters*, October 5, 2015, www.reuters.com/article/us-health-mental-cambodia-idUSKCN0RZ2LC20151005.

[2] In the Crombag et al. (2003) study, 29% of those who said they felt the urge to seek revenge reported acting on it. In Schadt and de Lisi's (2007) study, 36% of the students said they would actually hurt the person responsible for harming their family member and 10% said they would follow through on killing the person. In Cardozo et al. (2000), 18% of those surveyed said that they thought they would act on their vengeful feelings.

primary motive for many other kinds of interpersonal aggression and violence, including arson (Pettiway 1987; Barnoux and Gannon 2014), rape (Scully and Marolla 1985), kidnapping (Concannon 2013), domestic violence (Kernsmith 2005), and school shootings (Vossekuil 2002). More broadly, revenge shapes how people behave in their romantic relationships (Mongeau et al. 1994; Yoshimura 2007a, 2007b; Boon et al. 2009) and in their workplaces (Fox and Levin 1994; Bradfield and Aquino 1999; Aquino et al. 2001; Bies and Tripp 2001; Sommers et al. 2002; Moreno-Jimenez et al. 2009; Tripp and Bies 2009, 2010). It influences how they drive (Wiesenthal et al. 2000; Hennessy and Wiesenthal 2001, 2005), the brands and products they purchase (Nasr Bechwati and Morrin 2003; Gregoire et al. 2009, 2010; Zourrig et al. 2009), and for whom they cast their vote (Nasr Bechwati and Morrin 2007). Revenge is also a perennial theme in advertising, music, books, and movies of all genres, where it is often depicted in a positive light (Barecca 1995; Miller 1998; French 2001; Schumann and Ross 2010; Maynard et al. 2010). Clearly, far from fading into obsolescence, revenge continues to be one of the primary forces that structure human relations.

Revenge Is a Kind of Self-Help Justice

The second insight is that acts of personal vengeance are a kind of self-help justice (Stuckless and Goranson 1994; Nasr et al. 2003; Tripp and Bies 2009, 2010; Schuman and Ross 2010). According to Stuckless and Goranson's (1994) seminal review of the literature, revenge is a "righteous response to perceived harm or injustice." Avengers view themselves as 'doing the right thing' and 'getting justice,' even if doing so comes at a high personal cost or involves illegal acts (Tripp and Bies 2010). This sense of righteousness is rooted in the conviction that the transgressor deserves to be punished and that payback is therefore "appropriate and morally justified" (Tripp and Bies 2009: 11). For this reason, revenge is often said to be 'backward-looking.' Its fundamental motivation and justification lie in the original act of wrongdoing. To get revenge is "to impose suffering on those who have made one suffer, *because* they have made one suffer," as Elster (1990) puts it, rather than because the infliction of punishment will serve some instrumental purpose, such as improving the transgressor's behavior or deterring future injury. These may be incidental benefits of revenge, but they are not the source of its "moral character" (Rieder 1984: 131).

The idea of revenge as self-help justice will be familiar to anthropologists, historians, and others who study societies without strong, centralized institutions (Hallpike 1977; Posner 1981; Boehm 1984; Chagnon 1988; Daly and Wilson 1988; Fletcher 2004), but in the modern world, this kind of "wild justice" is supposed to have been supplanted by the rational and impartial justice provided by civil authorities.[3] However, this narrative is belied by the fact that even in the most developed countries, the state does not have a de facto monopoly on violence, and individuals routinely take the law into their own hands in large and small ways (Black 1983). Indeed, criminologists and sociologists have long argued that much of what the state defines as crime should be understood not as predatory behavior but as the private pursuit of justice by those who cannot access official remedies for their grievances or who simply resent the intrusion of law into their personal business (Black 1983; Zimring and Hawkins 1997; Kubrin and Weitzer 2003). "They seem determined to have justice done," writes Black (1983), "even if this means that they will be defined as criminals ... They do what they think is right, and willingly suffer the consequences" (34).

Revenge Is More Than Personal

The third key insight from the empirical literature is that revenge transcends the realm of the personal. People want to see wrongdoers get the punishment they deserve as a matter of general principle. In other words, revenge informs how individuals respond to acts of wrongdoing, even when they themselves have no personal stake in the situation. Research in behavioral economics has established that many people are willing to punish harm-doers for transgressions against third parties, even when it is costly for them to do so (Fehr and Fischbacher 2004; Henrich et al. 2006; Buckholtz et al. 2008). These "third-party punishers" appear to be acting against their own self-interest in order to achieve justice for a victim with whom they have no prior relationship or personal connection.

The phenomenon of third-party punishment poses a deep puzzle for classical economic theory, and as such it has stimulated a great deal of scholarly interest. The burgeoning literature on third-party punishment suggests that observers often have strong emotional reactions to injustice even when they themselves have not been made to suffer and that these

---

[3] The epithet "wild justice" is attributed to Sir Francis Bacon, who wrote, "Revenge is a kind of wild justice; which the more man's nature runs to, the more ought law to weed it out."

emotions play a key role in motivating third-party punishment (Skarlicki and Kulik 2004; Nelissen and Zeelenberg 2009; Lotz et al. 2011). Moreover, work by Buckholtz et al. (2008) suggests that within the brain itself, the same cognitive processes that are at work when a person retaliates against a transgressor who has harmed him or her personally (i.e., "second-party punishment") also underlie third-party punishment. This innovative study scanned the brains of participants while they assigned punishments in a wide variety of real-world crime scenarios and found that many of the regions of the brain that are active during second-party punishment were also active during this task, leading the authors to conclude that third-party decision-making in the context of the legal system and second-party punishment in interpersonal interactions may have a common neural mechanism. Although it does not deal with revenge specifically, this research is important because it indicates that many people think about punishment in much the same way regardless of whether they are in the role of the victim or a third-party observer.

Other research has investigated the role of revenge in this kind of third-party punishment decision more directly by examining the roots of individuals' attitudes toward criminal justice, i.e., how the government should punish those who flout society's rules. Overwhelmingly, this literature finds that in spite of the dominant place that utilitarian justifications for punishment, such as deterrence or rehabilitation, hold in official discourse about crime and punishment, many ordinary people want punishments to be assigned based on what they feel the offender *deserves* rather than on what would produce the greatest benefit to society (Darley et al. 2000; Carlsmith et al. 2002; Alter et al. 2007; Carlsmith et al. 2007; Carlsmith 2008; Carlsmith and Darley 2008; Aharoni and Fridlund 2012).

Indeed, support for particularly harsh penalties, such as capital punishment and torture, appears to be driven primarily by this desire for revenge, rather than by instrumental motives (Ellsworth and Ross 1983; Bohm 1992; Cotton 2000; Carlsmith et al. 2002; McKee and Feather 2008). These studies typically use the term "retribution" rather than revenge to refer to desert-based punishment, a distinction that has its roots in Western legal and philosophical thought, where scholars have long argued that there is a categorical difference between retribution as exacted by civil authorities (legitimate) and private revenge (illegitimate). I do not adopt this distinction. My aim is not to cast judgment on the morality or legitimacy of revenge but to understand what it means in the minds of the ordinary people who are its proponents and, in many cases,

its practitioners. In that respect, it seems clear that many people understand revenge as a form of justice based on the principle of desert and that
they do not make a sharp distinction between the individual versus the
state as the agent of punishment.

For instance, consider the results of an experiment conducted by Skitka
and Houston (2001), in which participants read a fictional story about a
man who murdered a young couple. Half the participants were told that
the man received a fair trial and was sentenced to death. The other half
were told that the man was shot and killed by a vigilante before his trial
commenced. The authors find that participants who said they believed
strongly in a moral duty to punish the guilty evaluated the man's death as
equally fair regardless of whether it was achieved by trial and execution
or by vigilantism. In contrast, participants who did not recognize punishment as a moral duty rated death by vigilantism as significantly less fair
than death by court-mandated execution. A study by Schadt and DeLisi
(2007) also finds that among college students, those who expressed a
greater willingness to seek revenge against someone who hurt a member
of their family were also substantially more likely to express support for
the death penalty. For these people, the means appear to matter little,
provided that the wrongdoer ultimately gets the punishment that he or
she deserves.

Evaluating the Evidence for Revenge as a Core Value

To summarize, the empirical literature on revenge shows that acts of
revenge are a common phenomenon, even in the most developed and
democratic societies; that individuals view these acts as way to achieve
justice by giving wrongdoers their "just deserts"; and that they treat this
principle as a general standard by which to judge the righteousness of
punishment, including those punishments meted out by civil authorities
through the criminal justice system. Taken all together, this body of
evidence strongly suggests that revenge belongs in the pantheon of human
core values. Consider in turn each of the four key elements of our
definition of core values.

Core Values Are Beliefs
Does the evidence support thinking about revenge as a belief rather
than a behavior? Standard definitions of revenge often conflate the two.
For instance, Stuckless and Goranson's (1994) widely cited literature
review defines revenge as "the infliction of harm in righteous response
to perceived harm or injustice" (803). This definition includes both a

behavior – the infliction of harm – and the belief that doing so is morally right and justifiable in light of what the victim has suffered. However, there are good reasons to treat belief and behavior as analytically separate and to define revenge in terms of the former rather than the latter.

As Schumann and Ross (2010) point out, "there is no objective standard for declaring an act to be motivated by revenge or not. Revenge is a label that is ascribed based on perceivers' attributions for the act. It is an inference, regardless of whether the individuals making the inference are the harm-doers themselves, the injured parties, or outsiders" (1195). In other words, the crucial ingredient that makes us call something an act of revenge, as distinct from the broader category of hostile or aggressive behavior, is found not in the nature of the act itself but in the avenger's beliefs about the righteousness of his or her action.

The evidence that I surveyed in the previous section makes it clear that there is a vast spectrum of behavior, ranging from office gossip to road rage to mass murder, that can fall under the umbrella of revenge. What ties these behaviors together and enables us to recognize them as part of a common phenomenon is the observation – which I encountered repeatedly in the diverse literatures I reviewed – that avengers, victims, and observers alike view them as motivated by the desire for justice and the conviction that justice requires wrongs to be repaid. Put another way, virtually anything can be an act of revenge if it is understood as arising out of the belief that those who hurt others deserve to be hurt in return. It is this belief, therefore, which is the essence of revenge.[4]

Core Values Pertain to Desirable End States or Modes of Conduct

Core values can be divided into two broad categories: terminal and instrumental. Terminal values pertain to desirable end states of existence (e.g., freedom, national security, a comfortable life), while instrumental values pertain to desirable modes of conduct (e.g., ambitious, obedient, forgiving) (Alvarez and Brehm 2002). Both logically and empirically, revenge appears to fit best in the category of terminal values. The essence of revenge is the belief that justice requires repayment. This is about the state of the world – in a just world, all wrongdoers get the punishment

---

[4] Defining revenge as a belief rather than a behavior does not mean that vengeful behavior cannot or should not be studied. Rather, it means that the link between vengeful beliefs and vengeful behavior should be treated as an empirical question instead of being baked into the definition of revenge. Indeed, there are many factors that can affect whether belief in revenge translates into action when the opportunity arises (Diamond 1977; Schumann and Ross 2010).

that they deserve – rather than any specific way of behaving. In other words, the fact that the punishment happens is more important than the means by which it comes about. This is evident in the literature on attitudes toward criminal justice that I reviewed in the previous section. It is clear from this body of work that individuals who believe in revenge do not limit the application of those beliefs to their personal conduct. They want to live in a world where all wrongdoers get their just deserts, and they therefore want their government to mete out criminal penalties accordingly (Darley et al. 2000; Carlsmith et al. 2002; Alter et al. 2007; Carlsmith et al. 2007; Carlsmith 2008; Carlsmith and Darley 2008; Aharoni and Fridlund 2012).

Core Values Transcend Specific Situations

Core values "transcend specific situations" in the sense that they are beliefs that are abstract and general and that can therefore apply in a wide variety of contexts. The diverse body of work that I reviewed in the previous section indicates that revenge is at play in many disparate areas of social life, both private and public. Even so, a skeptic might argue that this element of the definition is not fully established because the literature on revenge is drawn from many different fields, each of which employs its own methods, measures, and standards of research, and which rarely communicate with one another. Thus, while they may use the common term "revenge," these separate streams of research may actually be studying different phenomena.

I do not believe this is the case, particularly because the three key insights that I gleaned from this literature were ones that showed up again and again across a wide variety of studies. However, given that conceptualizing revenge as a core value runs contrary to a long tradition of thinking and writing about revenge as an uncivilized anachronism (Miller 1998), I also present additional empirical evidence to support this element of the definition. I take up this task in Chapter 3, where I analyze both contemporary and historical public opinion data from the United States to show that the same measure of endorsement of revenge predicts attitudes toward punitive violence under a diverse set of circumstances, which is precisely what we would expect if revenge is a belief that transcends specific situations.

Core Values Guide the Selection or Evaluation of Behavior, People, and Events

Finally, the existing literature provides substantial evidence that core values perform this essential psychological function. The research

I reviewed furnishes numerous examples of individuals who account for their own attitudes and behaviors by citing their beliefs about revenge (Scully and Marolla 1985; Barecca 1995; Speckhard and Ahkmedova 2006; Tripp and Bies 2009;). To take just one example, in the United States, where a majority of people approve of the death penalty for the crime of murder, revenge has long been the most cited reason on surveys that ask respondents to explain their reasons for supporting capital punishment (see Figure A6.1 in the Appendix for details). Moreover, a number of studies show that individuals who believe in revenge display distinctive attitudes toward the use of force or violence across different contexts, including vigilante justice, torture, and the use of military force (Skitka and Houston 2001; Liberman 2013, 2014), indicating that their beliefs about revenge serve as an important guide for forming their attitudes toward these issues. The evidence that I present in Chapter 3 also bolsters the case for this element of the definition by showing that the views of vengeful and non-vengeful individuals diverge across an even broader spectrum of personal and political issues.

In sum, although revenge has not previously been studied as a core value by either social psychologists or political scientists,[5] the broader empirical literature on revenge clearly points in that direction. Combined with the new evidence I present in Chapter 3, this literature makes a compelling case for rejecting the old "anti-vengeance discourse" and recognizing revenge as part of the human value system (Miller 1998). In the next section, I show how conceptualizing revenge as a core value illuminates the role that revenge plays in shaping attitudes toward the use of military force and calls attention to the crucial role that political elites play in this process.

PART 2: RHETORIC, REVENGE, AND PUBLIC SUPPORT FOR WAR

Revenge as a Source of Popular Support for War

Both the historical record and contemporary scholarship suggest that revenge can have a powerful influence on support for the use of military force abroad. In the case of the United States, observers have cited the desire for revenge as a source of popular enthusiasm for war at several

---

[5] Peter Liberman's work (2006, 2013, 2014) is an important exception to this generalization. I discuss the relationship between my theory and Liberman's work in more detail in the Introduction.

critical junctures in American history, including the Revolutionary War (Engels and Goodale 2009), the Spanish-American War (Perez 1989) and World War II (Steele 1974; Mueller 1996). More recently, studies have identified individual differences in vengefulness as an important predictor of support for the Gulf War, the War on Terror, the Iraq War, the killing of Osama bin Laden, and a potential US intervention in Syria (Liberman 2006; Gollwitzer 2014; Washburn and Skitka 2015).

Most importantly, this research shows that revenge has an impact on attitudes toward the use of military force under a wide variety of circumstances, including situations in which the nation has not experienced a direct attack on either its homeland or its citizens. Of the recent uses of US military force that scholars have examined, only the war in Afghanistan and the killing of Osama bin Laden can plausibly be considered responses to a direct attack. The Gulf War, the Iraq War, and any future US intervention in Syria are all, to a certain extent, "wars of choice." Further evidence comes from Liberman (2014), who presented participants in his study with three hypothetical scenarios, a North Korean attack on a US Navy warship, a Pakistani-sponsored terrorist attack in India, and a Chinese invasion of Taiwan. Only the first involves a direct attack on the United States, yet across all three scenarios, vengeful individuals were more likely to support using military force to respond to the situation.

This body of evidence is consistent with my conceptualization of revenge as a core value that informs individuals' attitudes toward punishing wrongdoers, regardless of the identity of the victim. However, in order to connect individual vengefulness with state violence, we need to know not just whether revenge *can* influence individuals' attitudes toward war but *when* and *how* it does so. The existing literature clearly establishes the former, but does not sufficiently address the latter, either empirically or theoretically. Even Liberman's (2006, 2013, 2014) pioneering work, which also recognizes that revenge should be understood as a core value, does not provide a well-developed account of the process that leads individuals to connect their abstract beliefs about revenge to concrete questions about the use of military force abroad.

In a nutshell, Liberman argues that because values are "trans-situational" and are known to constrain attitudes across different domains, the fact that revenge is such an important determinant of individuals' attitudes toward both interpersonal and criminal punishment suggests that it will also shape their reactions to the use of military force to punish foreign actors. As discussed in the previous section, the trans-situational nature of core values is one of their essential properties and a key reason why they are considered one of the building blocks of human behavior and a fundamental ingredient in the formation of public opinion. However, just because core values have the *potential* to influence people's attitudes across disparate social and political contexts does not mean that they will always do so.

Ultimately, Liberman's work falls short of providing a fully fleshed-out theory of the relationship between revenge and support for war because it does not recognize or grapple with the fact that for ordinary people, values rarely translate directly and automatically into concrete positions on specific political issues or events (Zaller 1992; Alvarez and Breham 2002). In the remainder of this section, I first explain why this is so and then make the case that political elites, and particularly national leaders, play a crucial role in mobilizing and channeling their citizens' latent vengefulness into support for the use of military force against foreign adversaries.

The Role of National Leaders

To understand why it is not enough simply to know that a person espouses a particular value, we must first recognize that most people are fundamentally ambivalent toward most political issues, meaning that they feel differently toward different aspects of the issue (Nelson and Kinder 1996). Some of those aspects may touch on their values, but others will touch on their material self-interest, for example, or their social group attachments and antipathies. These considerations may point in different directions, and an individual's expressed opinion will depend on which consideration is foremost in his or her mind at the moment of decision (Zaller and Feldman 1992). In other words, values must be made salient in order to exert their influence on opinions, and given the multitude of potential considerations on any given issue, we cannot simply assume that values are always "at the top of the head." Furthermore, because values are abstract and general, connecting them to specific issues often requires additional information about the context that the average citizen, who is relatively uninvolved and uninformed about politics, does not typically possess (Almond 1950; Converse 1964; Delli Carpini and Keeter 1997). Instead, people rely on information gleaned from the political environment to signal to them how their values should map onto particular policies (Zaller 1992).

For most people, the values that ultimately become salient to a given issue and the way in which those values translate into opinion will depend on how the issue is framed in elite discourse. In keeping with the main-stream view in political science, I use the term "framing" to refer to the way in which an issue or event is described in communication (Chong and Druckman 2007). In this view, a frame is "a central organizing idea or story line that provides meaning to an unfolding strip of events" (Gamson and Modigliani 1994: 376). Frames create this central organizing idea or story line by emphasizing certain aspects of an issue and minimizing or obscuring others. As Entman (1993) explains, framing involves both selection and salience. In constructing a frame, a communicator selects certain pieces of information to highlight while choosing to diminish or omit others, thereby increasing the salience of the former and decreasing the salience of the latter. The same political issue can be framed in a variety of different ways because such issues are – by their very nature – multifaceted, encompassing a web of potentially relevant (and potentially contradictory) facts, symbols, images, metaphors, etc. A frame takes this "kaleidoscope of potential realities" (Edelman 1993: 232) and distills it down into a simpler, more coherent, and more familiar package that fits within citizens' established worldviews. Thus, as Nelson and Kinder (1996) put it, "Frames are more than simply positions or arguments about an issue. Frames are *constructions* of an issue: they spell out the essence of the problem, [and] suggest how it should be thought about" (1058).

The extensive literature on framing effects shows that framing the same issue in different ways can have a marked impact on public opinion by making certain considerations more accessible (i.e., more easily retrieved from long-term memory) and by increasing the weight that individuals place on them when forming their opinions (Iyengar 1991; Zaller 1992; Kinder and Sanders 1996; Nelson et al. 1997; Brewer and Gross 2005; Chong and Druckman 2007). This is the essential difference between framing and persuasion. As Chong and Druckman (2007) explain, per-suasion changes the content of beliefs while framing changes the weight assigned to different beliefs in a person's overall attitude. For instance, "In assessing a new housing project, framing takes place if a communication causes economic considerations to become more important relative to environmental considerations. Persuasion occurs if the communication alters one's evaluation of the proposal on one of those dimensions – e.g., by modifying one's beliefs about the project's economic consequences" (Chong and Druckman 2007: 115). Similarly, Tversky and Kahneman (1981) liken frames to "alternative perspectives on a visual scene" (453). The scene itself does not change, but a person may see and understand it differently depending on his or her vantage point.

For example, Sniderman and Theriault (2004) find that a majority of Americans support government spending on poverty alleviation when it is framed as enhancing the chances for poor people to get ahead, but oppose the same spending when it is framed as an increased tax burden. The details of the spending program do not change, but the "getting ahead" frame calls to mind a different set of considerations than the "higher taxes" frame. When people evaluate the program in these different lights, they come to different conclusions about its desirability, not because the content of their beliefs has changed, but because the weight they place on competing considerations has shifted. This example is particularly illuminating because it shows that the relationship between equality, a core value shared by many Americans, and support for poverty alleviation is contingent on how that program is framed. Many people who care about equality nevertheless oppose such spending when it is framed in terms of an increased tax burden, not because they have suddenly and capriciously abandoned their values, but because the "higher taxes" frame conjures up a different array of concerns about material self-interest and economic growth. The bottom line is that values are not, in themselves, determinative of public opinion. Rather, they are a latent influence that must be activated by political discourse (Hayes and Guardino 2013).

Frames that evoke shared values are a regular feature of political communication (Shah et al. 1996; Sniderman and Theriault 2004; Shen and Edwards 2005). Brewer (2001) defines a value frame as a frame that draws "an association between a value and an issue that carries an evaluative implication: it presents one position on an issue as being right (and others wrong) by linking that position to a specific core value" (46). Studies of value frames have shown that their impact is powerful but heterogeneous. In other words, value frames do not have the same effect on everyone (Entman 1993; Sniderman and Theriault 2004; Shen and Edwards 2005). Their effect depends on the importance that each individual places on the value being evoked. Consider the example of affirmative action. The more weight a person attaches to the value of equality, the more compelling he or she will find the framing of affirmative action as 'leveling the playing field' (Sniderman and Theriault 2004). Shen and Edwards (2005) refer to this as "value resonance," which occurs "when the frames used by political elites fit within the existing repertoire of individuals' values" (797). In other words, the power of value frames is contingent on the interaction between the frame and the value system of the receiver. The more important the value, the more likely it is to become accessible in the mind of the individual after exposure to a value frame, and the more likely he or she is to rely on that value as a heuristic, or decision-making shortcut, when called on to form an opinion.

Because of its potential to influence public opinion, framing is a source of political power for elites (Nelson and Kinder 1996; Edwards 2009), and they often compete with one another to establish the predominant framing of an issue because they know that winning the "war of frames" means winning the battle for public opinion (Nelson and Kinder 1996). According to Edwards (2009), framing has a number of advantages over direct persuasion when it comes to generating support for a policy proposal (66). To have an effect, framing does not require people to acquire any expertise, to learn the details of the policy proposal, or to process extensive information. Instead, the war of frames is a battle over which of the considerations that individuals already care deeply about will carry the most weight in their evaluations. Value frames are a particularly powerful and reliable weapon in this battle, especially when the value being evoked is widely shared. By appealing to these shared values, elites hope to sway a significant proportion of the populace to their side of the issue.

When it comes to the use of military force, I treat national leaders as the dominant influence over how the situation is framed, at least during the lead-up to war. I do so for several reasons. First, during times of crisis, citizens naturally turn to their leaders to explain what is happening and why, and leaders in turn have significant resources that they can devote to shaping the narrative of an unfolding crisis. National leaders also enjoy important advantages over other political elites who might seek to introduce competing frames. These advantages include privileged access to (and control over) information, command of the bully pulpit, and a superior ability to project a clear and consistent message, reinforced by other high-ranking members of the leaders' administration, party, or ruling coalition. The media have a crucial role to play in transmitting those frames to a wider audience, but they tend not to interject independent viewpoints into the political environment (Zaller and Chiu 1996; Bennett et al. 2006). As a result, the central organizing idea or story line that a leader chooses to present in his or her communication with the public will be the dominant frame that citizens encounter in the political environment. Once a conflict has begun, the leader's advantages become less potent as information about what is happening on the ground becomes more voluminous and harder to control (Baum and Groeling 2010). However, in the pre-war period, the leader's voice is often both the first and the loudest to reach the ears of the people.

Mine is certainly not the first theory to suggest that political elites play an important role in shaping popular support for war. Indeed, one of the main strands of research in the literature on public opinion and war has focused on the impact of elite cues, i.e., the positions taken by trusted political figures or entities, including elected officials (Zaller 1992, 1994; Berinsky 2007, 2009; Baum and Groeling 2009), military elites (Golby et al. 2013), and foreign voices such as allied leaders and international organizations (Chapman and Reiter 2004; Grieco et al. 2011; Chapman 2012; Hayes and Guardino 2013). There is substantial evidence that citizens use these cues as heuristics, or decision-making shortcuts, thereby outsourcing the work of arriving at a well-informed position.

I do not dispute the findings of these studies or the general importance of elite cues. Instead, my theory adds another layer to our understanding of how elites influence their citizens' attitudes toward war. The cues literature essentially reduces all elite communication to its direction. A cue is either a signal of support for the use of force or a signal of opposition. The content of that communication – i.e., *how* elites express their position – is not part of the theory. In contrast, my focus is on the content of leaders' rhetoric, and specifically on how they can frame the use of force in a way that activates their citizens' desire for revenge and channels it into support for war.

Framing the Use of Force as a Punishment

The logic of revenge suggests three key elements that are necessary to construct a narrative that activates the desire for revenge against a foreign adversary. First, because revenge is backward looking – the crime must come first in order for the punishment to be deserved – there must be a clear act of wrongdoing, i.e., an intentional action that causes undeserved harm to the victim (or victims). This act of wrongdoing may be a direct and immediate attack on the nation itself, but there are also many other possibilities. Historical transgressions, even reaching back centuries, can also be used as fodder for establishing an act of wrongdoing, as can transgressions against third parties or domestic human rights abuses. What matters is not the identity of the victim per se, but that the victim is innocent and has suffered undeservedly. Second, because the notion of desert requires a locus of responsibility, there must be a clear perpetrator (an individual, group, or state) who is responsible for that act of wrongdoing. In other words, the harm to the victim must be intentional and it must be attributed to a specific actor who can be targeted for punishment. Third, it must be clear that the proposed military action will cause some harm or injury to the perpetrator. While it may seem obvious that the use of military force will harm the target in some way, there are certain types of military action, such as establishing a no-fly zone or peacekeeping, that are not self-evidently destructive. In these cases, it is not apparent that the return of suffering for suffering has been achieved.

Going forward, I will refer to the combination of these three elements as a *punishment frame*. For individuals who hold revenge as a core value, framing the use of military force in this way renders a complex international crisis into a simple and familiar story – a bad guy who deserves to be punished – and transforms the use of military force into a righteous act, worthy of approbation. Seen from this perspective, punishing the bad guy is simply the right thing to do, regardless of the cost or future consequences. To be clear, the effect of the punishment frame is not to make anyone and everyone feel more vengeful. Rather, it is to increase the salience of revenge in the minds of people who already hold it as a core value.

At this point, a skeptic might reasonably ask whether the three elements of the punishment frame aren't simply matters of objective fact rather than elite framing. My answer to this question is threefold. First, when it comes to foreign affairs in general and international crises in particular, most ordinary people do not have direct access to the facts and rely on elites to tell them what is happening and why. Second, as I noted in the previous section, framing is a matter of choosing which information to emphasize and which to downplay or exclude altogether. In other words, frames are made up of facts (along with symbols, images, metaphors, etc.) – what matters is how those facts are selected and arranged to create a coherent story line. And third, international crises are complex and multifaceted, offering leaders a wealth of information with which to construct whatever narrative they believe will best serve their interests. Thus, the facts matter, but only insofar as they are the raw material out of which leaders construct the meaning of events for their citizens. Indeed, as I will discuss in more detail below, because they can draw on history as well as present-day events, leaders have a great deal of flexibility in choosing how to frame the use of military force.

To illustrate what both the presence and absence of a punishment frame look like in practice, and to highlight how leaders construct different frames by choosing which information to highlight, I will preview two cases of conflict that I examine in more depth in Chapter 4: the 2003 Iraq War and the 1999 NATO intervention in Kosovo.

Example 1: The 2003 Iraq War

Just a year after the September 11, 2001, terrorist attack, and just eleven months into the war in Afghanistan, President George W. Bush and his administration turned their sights to Iraq, a designated member of the "axis of evil" and alleged possessor of "the world's most destructive weapons." From the moment President Bush announced his intention to disarm Iraq in a speech to the UN General Assembly on September 12, 2002, up to the beginning of combat operations on March 20, 2003, he clearly and consistently framed the use of force against Iraq as a punishment.

In his rhetoric, President Bush regularly and rigorously laid out Iraq's criminal record, including the invasion of Kuwait in 1990, sheltering and supporting terrorist organizations, attempting to assassinate the former president George H. W. Bush in 1993, using chemical weapons against the Kurds in Iraq and against Iran during the Iran–Iraq War, and a long litany of domestic human rights violations, described in brutal detail (e.g., "International human rights groups have cataloged [the] methods used in the torture chambers of Iraq: electric shock, burning with hot irons, dripping acid on the skin, mutilation with electric drills, cutting out tongues, and rape"). This language clearly established the first necessary element of the punishment frame: an act of wrongdoing. The second element is a clear perpetrator who is held responsible for that act of wrongdoing, and on this count the Bush administration's Iraq War rhetoric was crystal clear. It was the Iraqi leader, Saddam Hussein, who was personally and solely responsible for the terrible crimes the world had witnessed in Iraq. More subtly, President Bush also consistently linked Saddam to al Qaeda, thereby encouraging the belief that he was at least partly culpable for the 9/11 terrorist attacks (Gershkoff and Kushner 2005). Finally, throughout the pre-war period, President Bush's statements made it plain that the aim of going to war with Iraq would be regime change. This fulfilled the third element of the punishment frame by making it clear that Saddam would personally pay the price for his crimes by losing his hold on power.

This example of a punishment frame in action illustrates two important points. First, it exemplifies three major strategies that leaders can use to establish the existence of an act of wrongdoing. The first and most obvious is to link the adversary, either directly or indirectly, to an attack on the nation's homeland or citizens. This was clearly the Bush administration's intent in fostering the alleged connection between Saddam and al Qaeda. The second is to highlight some transgression against another state, as demonstrated by the consistent references to Iraq's invasion of Kuwait and its use of chemical weapons against Iran. And the third is to focus on domestic atrocities and/or human rights abuses, such as the repression and torture that President Bush consistently described in harrowing language. In this case, all three strategies were used in combination; however, each alone would be sufficient to satisfy the first element of the punishment frame. This is part of what makes punishment framing such a flexible strategy. In constructing a victim–perpetrator narrative for their citizens, leaders are not limited to the adversary's transgressions against their own state, nor are they limited to the present day. With such diverse options at their disposal, leaders can employ a punishment frame in a wide variety of situations.

Second, the Iraq War case illustrates the difference between framing and explicit justifications for war. Framing is subtle. It is about emphasizing certain pieces of information and deemphasizing others in order to create a coherent picture of events. Explicit justifications, on the other hand, are direct and persuasive arguments that are intended to change people's minds by providing new information that causes them to update their beliefs. President Bush did not explicitly justify going to war in Iraq in terms of punishment or revenge. Rather, he consistently emphasized information about Saddam's past misdeeds and his links to al Qaeda and other terrorist organizations, and then allowed his audience to draw their own conclusions about Saddam's deservingness. At the same time, he offered an explicit justification for war that focused on Iraq's possession of weapons of mass destruction, arguing that if Saddam would not give them up voluntarily, then the United States must use military force to eliminate them before they could be used against us or our allies. These two elements of the rhetoric of war – framing and explicit justifications – are often interwoven in the statements of leaders, but they are conceptually distinct, and in the case of Iraq, there is evidence that they each had an independent effect on popular support for the war.[6]

---

[6] Liberman and Skitka (2017) find that the desire to avenge 9/11 had a substantial positive effect on support for expanding the War on Terror to Iraq and that the size of this effect was comparable to the effect of believing that Iraq possessed weapons of mass destruction.

The distinction that I have drawn between framing and explicit justifications for war naturally raises the question of whether national leaders ever use revenge as an explicit justification. In the modern era, this is a rare occurrence. There are several reasons why this is the case. First, as I will discuss in greater detail in the next section, the prevalence of revenge as a core value varies across countries, and thus, many leaders face a population in which attitudes toward revenge are mixed. For these leaders, citing revenge as an explicit justification for war may appeal to the vengeful segment of the population but provoke a backlash from the non-vengeful segment. Those who reject the idea that wrongs deserve to be repaid may turn against a leader who appears to wholeheartedly endorse it. Because framing is subtler and eschews any explicit talk of punishment or revenge, it represents a way for leaders to capture support from the vengeful segment of their population without paying the costs that are likely to accompany a naked call for revenge. In other words, the advantage of using a punishment frame over more explicitly vengeful rhetoric is that it is strong enough to resonate with those who endorse revenge but subtle enough not to trigger a backlash among those who do not. The punishment frame essentially acts like a dog whistle that can be heard only by those who will appreciate its appeal.

Second, when justifying the resort to war, leaders must also be aware of their international audience. Revenge is not considered a legitimate *causus belli* under international law and stating it as such risks provoking opposition from the international community and damaging the state's reputation in ways that may prove costly in the future. Furthermore, a leader may refrain from explicitly invoking revenge out of concern for how it will affect the position of key allies. For instance, had President Bush argued that the United States had the right to go to war against Iraq to avenge 9/11, he would likely have lost the support of the United Kingdom, which by all available measures has a significantly less vengeful population than the United States, and whose leaders have, in the past, rejected revenge as an appropriate or necessary response to acts of terrorism.[7]

---

[7] After a bomb brought down Pan Am Flight 103 over Lockerbie, Scotland, killing a total of 270 people, Prime Minister Margaret Thatcher sought to distance herself from the Reagan administration's vows to punish those responsible through the use of military force if necessary. "I do not think an eye for an eye or a tooth for a tooth is ever valid," she said in a television interview. "The most important thing to do is to try to get the cooperation of all nations to track down these people so that they are brought to justice." Sheila Rule, "Thatcher Opposes Revenge for Bomb," *New York Times*, January 2, 1989.

This is not to say that leaders never use revenge as an explicit justification for the use of military force. For instance, in February of 2015, the militant group known as the Islamic State (or ISIS or ISIL) released a graphic video showing Muath al-Kasasbeh, a Jordanian pilot who was taken hostage when his plane crashed in Syria, being burned to death inside a cage. At the time, Jordan was an important partner in the US-led military coalition opposing the Islamic State in Syria and was directly involved in the ongoing air campaign against the group. In response to the video, Jordanian leaders immediately vowed to seek revenge for al-Kasabeh's death. Jordan's King Abdullah promised to wage a "relentless" war against the Islamic State that would end only when his military ran out of fuel and bullets.[8] "Our punishment and revenge will be as huge as the loss of the Jordanians," said military spokesman Mamdouh al-Ameri.[9] These events appeared to transform how many ordinary Jordanians regarded their country's participation in the fight against the Islamic State, consolidating support for a sustained war effort.[10] Just a few days later the Jordanian air force carried out fifty-six airstrikes on Islamic State targets. According to Major General Mansour al-Jabour, "We achieved what we were looking for: revenge for Muath. And this is not the end. This is the beginning."[11] However, instances such as this are relatively rare, and as I will show in Chapter 4, such unvarnished language is not a necessary condition for mobilizing support for war among vengeful individuals.

Example 2: The 1999 NATO Intervention in Kosovo

I now turn to a case in which the use of force was not framed as a punishment: the 1999 NATO intervention in Kosovo. This intervention, the second major use of military force in NATO's history, was triggered by escalating violence between the Kosovo Liberation Army, an ethnic Albanian paramilitary group seeking independence for the Serbian province of Kosovo, and Serbian military forces under the direction of President Slobodan Milošević. After the breakdown of peace talks in Rambouillet, France, and with a major Serbian offensive imminent,

---

[8] Suleiman Al-Khalidi, "Jordanian King Vows 'Relentless' War on Islamic State's Own Ground," *Reuters*, February 4, 2015.

[9] Jared Malsin, "Jordan Vows Revenge for ISIS Burning of Pilot," *Time*, February 3, 2015.

[10] Martin Chulov, "Jordanians Turn Their Minds to Revenge after Isis Killing of Pilot," *The Guardian*, February 4, 2015.

[11] Mohammed Daraghmeh "Jordan Seeks Revenge in Pilot's Death," *Detroit Free Press*, February 8, 2015.

NATO commenced a bombing campaign, led by the United States and targeted at Milošević's military forces. After several months, Milošević withdrew from Kosovo, which was placed under the administration of the United Nations.

Prior to the start of the air war on March 24, 1999, President Bill Clinton's public statements on the situation in Kosovo regularly highlighted the toll the conflict had taken on innocent civilians, and while his language lacked the visceral impact of President Bush's descriptions of Iraq's rape rooms and torture chambers, it was sufficiently clear and consistent to satisfy the first element of the punishment frame (an act of wrongdoing). The major difference between the rhetoric of the two conflicts lies in the second element of the punishment frame, the attribution of responsibility. In contrast to Bush's single-minded focus on Saddam Hussein, Clinton crafted a narrative of shared responsibility for the conflict in Kosovo. Rather than casting one side or the other in the role of the villain, Clinton's speeches are full of statements that place both parties on equal footing in terms of both the legitimacy of their grievances and their role in bringing the violence to an end. Indeed, when set alongside the rhetoric of the Iraq War, it seems remarkable that Clinton never made a concerted effort to demonize Slobodan Milošević, even though the latter's actions in Kosovo, including the massacres at Prekaz and Račak and his previous role in the ethnic cleansing in Bosnia provided plenty of material with which to construct such a narrative. Instead, Clinton's language is studiously neutral (e.g., "You've got a part of Serbia which is 90 percent Albanian, and they want some kind of autonomy and to have their legitimate concerns addressed. The Serbs don't want to give up a big part of their country ... There are 50 different ways this could be worked out ... They don't have to kill each other to get this done"). Thus, although terrible things were obviously happening on the ground in Kosovo, NATO's intervention in the conflict was not framed as a punishment because Clinton's communication with the public never clearly established Milošević or Serbia as the perpetrator. Unlike Iraq, the main story line that the American people heard from Clinton regarding the situation in Kosovo was not one that featured an unambiguous evildoer getting his just deserts at the hands of US military forces.

The fact that Clinton did not frame NATO intervention in Kosovo as a punishment raises an important question: if using a punishment frame is an effective way to increase support for war, why would any leader choose not to do so? There are several possible answers to this question. First, perhaps some situations lend themselves more naturally to a punishment frame than others. In my view, this is unlikely to explain the non-use of a punishment frame in most cases. As I argued previously, international crises are complex and multifaceted. Many different kinds of transgressions can be used to construct a punishment frame, and they can be exaggerated, and sometimes even invented, if necessary. Thus, the facts on the ground do not seem likely to be the decisive factor determining how the use of force is framed. Indeed, the case of Kosovo clearly illustrates that framing is less a matter of the facts themselves than of the choices leaders make about which of those facts to emphasize in their rhetoric. Clinton could have framed the use of force in Kosovo as a punishment by highlighting Serbian atrocities on the ground and hearkening back to the ethnic cleansing in Bosnia, and by holding Milošević personally responsible for those terrible deeds. Yet he chose instead to focus on the long history of tension in the region and the legitimate grievances of both sides. These were all true facts, but by emphasizing the latter rather than the former, Clinton painted a picture of the crisis as a case of shared responsibility that would best be resolved by peaceful compromise.

A second possibility is that leaders' own dispositions play a role in how they chose to frame the use of force. A number of recent works suggest that leaders' cultural backgrounds, life experiences, and worldviews can profoundly shape their foreign policy choices (Saunders 2011; Horowitz and Stam 2014; Dafoe and Caughey 2016), and these attributes may also influence how they communicate with the public about those choices.

A final explanation concerns leaders' political calculus. Framing the use of force as a punishment provides a benefit to leaders in the form of increased support from the vengeful segment of their population. However, it also has some potential downsides. Most importantly, use of a punishment frame could make a negotiated settlement more difficult to achieve. For one thing, once a leader has stoked the fires of public support for war by demonizing the adversary, he or she may face political costs for backing down. For vengeful individuals in particular, the failure to follow through on the use of force may be perceived not only as weakness or incompetence but as a serious miscarriage of justice. Being perceived as 'letting the bad guy get away with it' could do serious damage to a leader's popularity and his ability to govern effectively. Thus, using a punishment frame may have the effect of tying leaders' hands and making it more difficult for them to accept an outcome short of war. Furthermore, as we saw in the case of Iraq, framing the use of force as punishment involves depicting the adversary in an extremely negative light. "If this is not evil, then evil has no meaning," President Bush said after describing Iraq's 'criminal record' in his 2002 State of the Union Address. Such rhetoric, even if only aimed at a domestic audience, will be observed by the adversary and could be interpreted as a signal of malign intent, thereby making it more difficult to strike a bargain that avoids war.

This last point seems the most likely explanation for Clinton's decision not to demonize Milošević during most of the Kosovo crisis. Clinton was highly motivated to broker a peaceful settlement between Milošević and the Kosovar Albanians, and he believed, at least until the final days of the crisis, that such an outcome was achievable. Thus, from Clinton's perspective, the costs of using a punishment frame likely outweighed the benefits, and he chose instead to employ a narrative of shared responsibility in order to maximize the chances of reaching a peaceful settlement. Only when negotiations at Rambouillet reached a standstill due to Milošević's intransigence did Clinton come to believe that the use of military force was likely to be the end result. And indeed, it was at that point, just a few days before the bombing commenced, that Clinton began to talk about Milošević with the kind of harsh language that Bush regularly used to talk about Saddam Hussein. This pattern suggests that for Clinton, the scales had tipped such that the benefits of demonizing Milošević in order to boost popular support for military intervention finally exceeded the costs of doing so.

In summary, both the historical record and contemporary scholarship tell us that revenge can be an important source of public support for war under a wide variety of circumstances. However, in most cases, people will connect their beliefs about revenge to debates about the use of military force only when political elites, and particularly national leaders, frame the use of force as a punishment that the adversary deserves to suffer. Like most political issues, international crises are complex and multifaceted, and ordinary people rely heavily on the information provided by their leaders to form a coherent picture of what is happening and why. Only when they have such a picture in their heads can they use their values to form a judgment about the wisdom of particular policies.[12] This means that for leaders, framing the use of military force as a punishment is a powerful and versatile tool that can help them sway public opinion in favor of the use of military force when it is in their interest to do so. In the

---

[12] According to Zaller (1991), "every opinion is the marriage of information and values – information to generate a mental picture of what is at stake and values to make a judgment of it" (1215).

next section, I explore how this dynamic systematically shapes the decisions that democratic leaders make about the use of military force.

PART 3: CROSS-NATIONAL VARIATION IN VENGEFULNESS AND CONFLICT INITIATION BY DEMOCRACIES

The Role of Public Opinion in Democratic Conflict Behavior

For democratically elected leaders, public support for war is highly consequential. Although early research cast doubt on the structure and stability of mass attitudes toward foreign policy and concluded that leaders had little incentive to attend to public opinion on international issues (Lippmann 1922; Almond 1950; Campbell et al. 1960; Converse 1964), there is now substantial evidence demonstrating that this pessimism was unwarranted (see Holsti 1996 for a review). Numerous studies have demonstrated that individuals have stable and coherent opinions about foreign policy (Achen 1975; Maggiotto and Wittkopf 1981; Hurwitz and Peffley 1987; Wittkopf 1990; Holsti 1992; Isernia et al. 2002), that changes in aggregate opinion are not erratic but occur in predictable ways in response to international events (Shapiro and Page 1988; Peffley and Hurwitz 1992), and that citizens consider their leaders' foreign policy records when evaluating their performance in office and casting their votes (Hurwitz and Peffley 1987; Aldrich et al. 1989; Krosnick and Kinder 1990; Karol and Miguel 2007).

Consequently, when it comes to the use of military force, democratic leaders make their decisions in the shadow of the next election, knowing that if they lose the support of too many of their citizens, there will be a price to pay. That price may come in the form of electoral punishment, i.e., getting voted out of office in the next election (Bueno de Mesquita and Siverson 1995; Goemans 2000; Croco 2015). However, this is not the only way in which embarking on an unpopular war can be politically costly. A leader who sends his military forces abroad against the will of the majority is likely see his overall popularity suffer (Mueller 1973), and as Krosnick and Kinder (1990) put it, "popularity is a vital political resource" (497). In general, popular leaders have more influence over the nation's political agenda and more leverage in bargaining over policy with other elites than do unpopular leaders (Edwards 1976; Ostrom and Simon 1985; Rivers and Rose 1985; Kernell 2007). A loss of popularity due to a military misadventure can thus deal a significant blow to a leader's overall ability to achieve his policy goals in both the domestic and international arenas. Hence, the decision to use military force can influence a leader's prospects for political survival even if citizens do not directly condition their vote on that issue.

It is therefore not surprising that leaders pay close attention to public opinion (Western 2005), drawing on a variety of sources to track the public mood (Steele 1974; Altschuler 1990; Hinckley 1992; Powlick 1995; Jacobs and Shapiro 1999), and there is now a veritable mountain of evidence indicating that public opinion shapes leaders' decisions about when and how to use military force (Arian et al. 1992; Powlick and Katz 1998; Foyle 1999; Morgan and Anderson 1999; Casey 2001; Sobel 2001; Baum 2004; Aldrich et al. 2006; Baum and Potter 2008). This is not to say that public opinion exerts a determinative effect on leaders' foreign policy choices. Public opinion will matter more under certain conditions and less under others (Risse-Kappen 1991; Cohen 1995; Foyle 1997). However, contrary to the early conventional wisdom, which viewed leaders as having a free hand in matters of foreign policy (Holsti 1992), we now know that leaders factor public opinion into their decision calculus in ways that systematically influence their behavior.

Indeed, theories of democracy and war have long held that elected leaders are constrained by their accountability to the mass public (Reiter and Tillman 2002), and this accountability is thought to be the source of much of what is distinctive about the conflict behavior of democracies as compared with autocracies. For instance, studies have found that democracies are more likely to win the wars they initiate (Siverson 1995; Bueno de Mesquita et al. 1999; Reiter and Stam 2002), that they are more likely to seek a negotiated settlement if victory is not achieved quickly (Reiter and Stam 2002; Filson and Werner 2004), and that their conflicts are shorter and less costly in terms of both civilian and military casualties (Bennett and Stam 1996; Slantchev 2004; Valentino et al. 2010). Caverley (2014) refers to this school of thought as "democratic exceptionalism."

Many of the theoretical arguments put forward in the democratic exceptionalism literature rest on a key assumption: that it is citizens and not leaders who pay the costs of war, and thus, "in most cases, it is not in the citizen's self-interest for the state to go to war" (Chernoff 2004, 54). The origins of this idea can be traced back to the philosopher Immanuel Kant, who argued that "if ... the consent of the citizens is required to decide whether or not war is to be declared, it is very natural that they will have great hesitation in embarking on so dangerous an enterprise. For this would mean calling down all the miseries of war" (1991, 100). This assumption is essential to understanding why public opinion is viewed as a *constraint* on the behavior of democratic leaders. Because the mass public is generally averse to war, leaders must exercise caution in when and how they employ their state's military forces. Knowing that they will pay a cost for straying too far outside the bounds of what the average voter is willing to accept, leaders will strive to produce only short, low-cost, and victorious wars that are unlikely to trigger any serious or sustained dissatisfaction on the part of their constituents. Thus, they will initiate a conflict only when they believe they are likely to win; they will spend less on defense in peacetime but try harder in wartime; they will try to minimize costs of fighting and use their resources efficiently; and they will try to exit wars that are getting too expensive via a negotiated settlement (Caverley 2014).

There is also a second assumption, often implicit, needed to support this view of public opinion as a constraint: that leaders cannot easily manufacture support for war. As Reiter and Stam (2002) put it, "if democratic leaders could manipulate public opinion into supporting military ventures, then of course, public opinion would provide little constraint on democratic foreign policy, as it could be actively molded to support the foreign policy aims of the leadership" (146). They argue that leaders will have a hard time manipulating public opinion because the "open marketplace of ideas" will quickly undercut any fallacious claims. Thus, they conclude that although democratic leaders may sometimes be able to shift public opinion on the margins, "it is more accurate to think of the public as controlling the actions of its elected leaders rather than dancing on strings pulled by the leadership as puppet master" (146). In other words, influence flows from the bottom up rather than the top down.

This second assumption rests on an overly simplistic picture of how elected leaders respond to public opinion. The opinions of the masses are not set in stone, and leaders do not behave as if they are. Instead, recognizing the importance of securing public support for war, leaders engage in what Rosenblatt (1998) terms "aggressive foreign policy marketing," a barrage of high-profile tactics, including prime-time television appearances and national speaking tours, designed to use the advantages of the bully pulpit to sway public opinion in their favor. This is not merely "waltzing before a blind audience," to use Aldrich et al.'s (1989) turn of phrase. In the realm of foreign affairs, leaders' public appeals routinely have an impact on their citizens' policy preferences (Sigelman 1980; Page et al. 1987; Rosenblatt 1998; Meernik and Ault 2001; Canes-Wrone 2010), and numerous studies have documented the influence that cues from political elites have on attitudes toward the use of military force (Zaller 1992, 1994; Berinsky 2007, 2009; Baum and Groeling 2009).

However, this does not mean that a leader can "simply obtain any foreign policy proposal he wants by promoting it over the airwaves" (Canes-Wrone 2010: 185). Leaders are neither slaves nor puppet masters when it comes to public opinion. Their ability to exercise "opinion leadership" depends on a number of factors, including their own popularity (Page et al. 1987), the baseline level of popular support for their proposed initiative (Rottinghaus 2008; Canes-Wrone 2010), and the public's basic goals and values (Rosenblatt 1998; Edwards 2009). Consequently, even leaders who are known for their skill at communication can fail to bring the public around to supporting their most important priorities (Edwards 2009). Thus, instead of viewing the relationship between leaders and public opinion as unidirectional, with influence flowing from either the top down or the bottom up, it is more accurate to conceptualize it as reciprocal (Page et al. 1987; Powlick and Katz 1998; Baum 2004).

Taken together, this evidence suggests that the degree to which public opinion constrains leaders' decisions about the use of military force should be treated as a variable rather than as a constant. Constraint will be strongest under conditions that make it difficult for leaders to sway public opinion, and it will become progressively weaker as their power to shape public opinion grows. The key question then becomes: what makes some leaders more effective at generating popular support for war than others? It is here that the relationship between revenge and support for war provides us with analytical leverage. As we saw in the previous section, framing the use of force as a punishment can be a powerful and versatile strategy for generating popular support for war. However, this strategy will work better for some leaders than for others because there is substantial cross-national variation in the prevalence of revenge as a core value.

Cross-National Variation in Vengefulness and Its Implications for Democratic Accountability

Revenge is a human universal in the sense that it has been found (in some form) in virtually every culture studied by ethnographers (Daly and Wilson 1988; McCullough 2008; Pinker 2011; McCullough et al. 2013). For instance, McCullough (2008) reports that 95% of cultures that have been examined show evidence of blood revenge, which refers to a situation in which the close kinsmen of a homicide victim seek revenge against the killer and his kin. At the same time, revenge varies across cultures in terms of its frequency, intensity, and form. This variation is evident in a variety of ways. First, there are both historical and contemporary differences among societies in the frequency of highly visible revenge behaviors, such as revenge-motivated homicides and familial or clan-based blood feuds (Otterbein and Otterbein 1965; Eriksen and Horton 1992; Schuman and Ross 2010). For example, according to McCullough et al. (2013), the percentage of homicides attributable to revenge ranges across societies from as low as 8% to as high as 45%. More broadly, numerous studies have documented cultural differences in norms of revenge and linked this variation to the frequency of various kinds of lethal violence (Boehm 1984; Chagnon 1988; Elster 1990; Nisbett and Cohen 1996; Hinton 1998; Figueredo et al. 2004). Finally, cross-country survey data show substantial national differences in attitudes toward revenge. I will delve into these data in more detail in Chapter 5, but the bottom line is that they show clearly that even in a highly globalized world, there are persistent differences in the prevalence of revenge as a core value across national populations.

Why does vengefulness vary across countries? This is not a fully settled question, but many scholars posit that this cultural variation has its roots in early economic and political conditions (Pitt-Rivers 1968; Posner 1980; Nisbett and Cohen 1996; Figueredo et al. 2004; Shackelford 2005). In places where property rights were highly insecure and central authorities were either incapable of enforcing those rights or entirely absent, strong norms of revenge emerged as a solution to the problem of social order.

As Posner (1980) cogently argues, all societies have a need for social order. Without it, they will either destroy themselves from within or be out-competed to the point of extinction by more orderly groups. In the absence of a central authority, social order can emerge if individuals take it upon themselves to enforce community rules by retaliating against those who violate them. The key question then becomes: what motivates individuals to punish rule breakers, often at significant cost to themselves? The most obvious answer is deterrence. By building a reputation as a "punisher," an individual can help to discourage future acts of wrongdoing directed at him- or herself and/or family.

However, these benefits alone are not sufficient to guarantee that punishment will take place. A reputation for vigorous retaliation against rule breakers is a good that will benefit the individual in the long term through its deterrent effect, but its value may be discounted in the short term. Thus, there will be circumstances under which the net benefit of punishing will be outweighed by its immediate costs. Recognizing this, potential rule breakers will be emboldened by the knowledge that they can discourage retaliation by making it very costly for the victim. Thus, without a way for victims to commit to punishing regardless of the short-term cost, it will be difficult to establish the kind of self-sustaining system of consistent punishment that is necessary for social order.

Norms of revenge represent a solution to this problem because they endow the punishment of wrongdoing with a moral imperative that is explicitly decoupled from any consideration of the costs and benefits. In a revenge system, the mere fact that a transgression has been committed is sufficient both to justify and to compel punishment. The rule of retaliation is inexorable and unconditional – wrongs must be repaid regardless of the cost. Indeed, studies of societies in which punishment is governed primarily by norms of revenge furnish numerous examples of individuals who are willing to pay any price, up to and including their lives, in order to exact the necessary punishment (Hallpike 1977; Boehm 1984; Chagnon 1988). At first glance this behavior might seem irrational; however, as Posner (1980) points out, "knowledge that a victim will retaliate when attacked without making a fresh cost–benefit analysis of retaliation will deter aggression more effectively than knowledge that the victim will respond 'rationally' to each act of aggression by weighing the costs and benefits of retaliation as they then appear" (77). In this way, a functioning system of deterrence can be established and social order can be achieved.

Thus, norms of revenge are thought to emerge initially under conditions of weak or absent authority because they serve a functional purpose in the provision of social order. Over time, strong norms of revenge will become internalized in the minds of individual members of the community as a set of core values governing the use of violence in response to transgressions. Once these values become embedded in the culture of a particular place, they can persist long after the conditions that originally gave rise to them, and their effects can still be observed after many generations and sometimes even after many centuries (Nisbett and Cohen 1996; Uslaner 2008; Fernandez and Fogli 2009; Algan and Cahuc 2010; Nunn and Wantchekon 2011; Voigtlander and Voth 2012). Scholars have identified a number of different mechanisms that contribute to this kind of long-term persistence.

The first mechanism operates at the level of the family. Vertical transmission from parents to children helps to maintain distinctive values and beliefs across generations (Doepke and Zilibotti 2008; Tabellini 2008; Voigtlander and Voth 2012). For instance, Nunn and Wantchekon

(2011) find that in Africa, mistrust is higher among individuals whose ancestors were more heavily raided during the slave trade in part because, "over the 400 years of insecurity generated by the slave trade, general beliefs or 'rules-of-thumb' based on mistrust evolved. These beliefs were then transmitted from parents to children over time, and they continue to manifest themselves today, more than 100 years after the end of the slave trade" (3249–50).

A second mechanism operates at the societal level, where symbolic cultural practices serve to perpetuate values and beliefs by weaving them into the fabric of social life and embedding them in the edifice of tradition. For example, Voigtlander and Voth (2012) suggest that this mechanism may have helped to sustain German anti-Semitism over several centuries: "Passion plays, for instance, often portrayed Jews as engaged in deicide. Anti-Semitic sculptures decorated churches and private houses, and book printing widely distributed the same demeaning images. In some towns, festivals commemorated pogroms; in the Bavarian town of Deggendorf, for example, the attack on the town's Jewish community was celebrated every year until 1968" (1341–42). Consequently, even in places where Jews were not physically present, hostility toward them was preserved in art, literature, and celebratory traditions that were passed from one generation to the next.

Finally, various types of institutions and civic organizations can play an important role in the long-term persistence of values and beliefs by communicating appropriate standards of behavior and by applying social stigma to those who transgress those standards. Cohen and Nisbett (1997) provide an illustration of this mechanism in a set of field experiments that form part of their seminal study of the Southern culture of honor and its proclivity toward honor-based violence (also see Nisbett and Cohen 1996). These experiments demonstrate that "violence related to honor is less stigmatized by institutions of the South ... than by those of the North" (1196). In particular, Southern newspapers portrayed honor-related killing as more "sympathetic, justified, or legitimately provoked" than their Northern counterparts, and Southern employers responded in a "warmer, more sympathetic, and more cooperative way" to a person convicted of an honor-related killing (1196–97).[13] Thus, these institutions provide important feedback – both to the specific individuals involved and to the wider community – about the legitimacy

---

[13] Cohen and Nisbett (1997) found no such differences for non-honor-related crime.

of violence in the name of honor, which in turn serves to reinforce and sustain the South's distinct culture.

Of course, there are also processes that can work against long-term cultural persistence, disrupting traditional values and beliefs and encouraging the evolution of new ones. These include factors such as economic interconnectedness with other groups and high geographical mobility, both of which can catalyze cultural change through repeated contact with outsiders (Voigtlander and Voth 2012). Thus, the existing literature, while not definitive, suggests that the present-day cross-national variation in vengefulness is the product both of early differences in economic and political conditions, which gave rise to cultures with different norms, values, and behaviors surrounding revenge, and of the long-term interplay between the social forces of cultural preservation and change that have been acting on those cultures ever since.

Due to these different cultural legacies, some democratic leaders face constituencies in which revenge is broadly endorsed, while others do not. This gives leaders with more vengeful populations a systematic advantage in generating popular support for war because they have a larger pool of citizens available to be mobilized through the use of a punishment frame. As a result, the constraining effect of accountability will be weaker for leaders with highly vengeful populations. Their superior ability to lead public opinion means that, on average, they will be less concerned about the potential political costs of an unpopular war and more likely to make use of military force as a tool of foreign policy. To be clear, my argument is not that a highly vengeful public will seize upon the slightest provocation to demand war from a reluctant leader. Rather, broad public endorsement of revenge is a latent source of support for war that leaders can activate by deploying strategically crafted rhetoric (Jacobs and Shapiro 2000).

This argument flows directly from the assumption, which I share with much of the existing literature on the domestic politics of international conflict, that leaders are rational actors who care first and foremost about retaining political power. Consequently, their decisions about the use of military force will be based on an assessment of how both the costs and benefits of fighting will impact their chances of staying in office. One implication of this assumption is that leaders will actively try to manage those costs and benefits.[14] Specifically, when faced with the prospect of

---

[14] I also assume that leaders do not initiate conflicts solely for personal or national revenge. However, even a leader who did desire war for these reasons would still need to convince the public to support his cause or risk paying a high political price.

using military force, they will use any means available to them in order to increase the expected benefits and decrease the expected costs.[15] An unpopular war can decrease the likelihood of maintaining power in a variety of ways, and leaders will therefore seek to generate as much public support as they can before a conflict begins.

This is not meant to suggest that framing the use of force as a punishment is the only strategy that leaders use to sway public opinion. Punishment framing is best thought of as one item in a toolbox of strategies that can be employed alone or in combination (Edwards 2009). Nor am I claiming that leaders have access to perfect information about their citizens' beliefs about revenge, that any and all potential conflicts can be framed as punishment with equal ease, or that leaders always use this frame when it would be advantageous to do so. In any specific case, the use of force can be framed in a variety of ways, and as I discussed earlier in my preview of the Kosovo case, whether or not a leader chooses to employ a punishment frame may be influenced by a number of factors, the most important of which is his or her assessment of the political costs and benefits of doing so. The benefit of using a punishment frame is an increase in support for the use of force among citizens who hold revenge as a core value. The cost of doing so is the possibility that demonizing the adversary could make a peaceful settlement more difficult to achieve. Thus, in deciding whether to use this kind of language, leaders must balance these considerations against one another in light of their expectations about the outcome of the crisis. In general, as a leader becomes more certain that war is in the offing, the more likely it is that the expected benefits of using a punishment frame will exceed the expected costs. However, because the evaluation of these variables is subjective and depends on the particulars of the situation, my theory cannot make predictions about whether or not a leader will employ a punishment frame in any specific case. Rather, my contention is that leaders with more vengeful publics will utilize a punishment framing strategy more often and with greater effect than leaders with less vengeful publics and that, on average, this advantage will result in a greater overall propensity to utilize force in international relations.

---

[15] This motivation also manifests itself in other ways. For instance, Valentino et al. (2010) find that democracies tend to adopt foreign and military policies that minimize the costs of war in terms of military and civilian fatalities.

Is Revenge a Cause of War?

Before moving on to the specific hypotheses that I test in the subsequent chapters, it is important to consider where revenge fits into the broader literature on the causes of war. The process that leads from peace to war involves factors that operate at many different levels of analysis (Senese and Vasquez 2008; Levy and Thompson 2009). In the theory that I have laid out in this chapter, the vengefulness of a country's population acts as a latent risk factor for war, meaning that it is a background condition that influences the likelihood of conflict only when other critical factors are present. Latent risk factors are distinct from what we might call proximate causes of war, which are acts or events that contribute directly to the conflict-generating process, and without which the conflict would not have occurred.

In order for two states to move from a peaceful status quo to a state of war, two key steps must occur. First, some conflict of interest must arise between them, and second, they must fail to reach a peaceful bargain. These are proximate causes of war, and a great deal of scholarly work has addressed the issues that give rise to disputes between states – such as unsettled borders (Huth 2009), natural resources (Colgan 2013), and spillovers from civil conflicts (Gleditsch et al. 2008) – and the reasons why they sometimes fail to find a peaceful bargain that both sides prefer to war (see Powell 2002 for a review). My theory does not seek to challenge the insights of these literatures, nor do I claim that vengefulness causes conflicts of interest to emerge or bargaining to break down. Rather, I posit that the vengefulness of a country's population enters into the equation by exacerbating the causes of bargaining failure.

The bargaining model of war assumes that war is ex post inefficient. In other words, because war is costly, there should always be a bargaining range – a set of peaceful bargains that would leave both sides better off than if they chose to fight. Consequently, any rational explanation for war must explain why states fail to reach one of these deals (Reiter 2003). Fearon's (1995) seminal article identified three such causes of bargaining failure: private information and incentives to misrepresent, commitment problems, and issue indivisibility. Most work that adopts the bargaining model treats the state as a unitary actor. However, this assumption can be relaxed to incorporate domestic politics by making individual leaders the primary actors in the bargaining process and translating the costs and benefits of using military force into the currency of domestic political power (Filson and Werner 2004, 2007; Tarar 2006).[16]

From this perspective, anything that increases a leader's expected utility from war will reduce the set of peaceful bargains that make him or her better off than fighting, thereby shrinking the bargaining range. In and of itself, this shrinking of the bargaining range does not cause war to break out because there still exist at least some peaceful bargains that both sides prefer to war. However, according to Fearon (1995), factors that narrow but do not completely eliminate the bargaining range will exacerbate the other causes of war:

> If for whatever reason the issues in dispute are hard to divide up, then war will be more likely the smaller the set of enforceable agreements both sides prefer to a fight. Alternatively, the problems posed by private information and incentives to misrepresent may be more intractable when the de facto bargaining range is small. (404)

Because popular disapproval represents an important cost of war for democratic leaders, the ability of those with more vengeful populations to generate a significant boost in popular support for war by using a punishment frame has the effect of both increasing the overall expected utility of war and narrowing the bargaining range, thereby making it more likely that bargaining will fail and that war will be the result.

Why Not Autocracies?

I do not expect the same logic to apply to autocratic leaders. While recent research has argued that autocratic leaders do in fact face a need to maintain support among their "selectorate," or the group of people who have a say in leadership selection, that selectorate tends to be both smaller and less diverse in terms of interests than the selectorate in democracies (Bueno de Mesquita et al. 2005; Weeks 2008). Weeks (2008) argues that for most autocratic leaders, the relevant selectorate is composed of regime insiders, individuals who hold power within the institutions of government, rather than the mass public, as is the case for democracies.

There are several reasons to believe that in autocracies, leaders' willingness to initiate the use of military force is unlikely to be conditional on

---

[16] These studies assume, as I do, that leaders' primary motivation is to maintain power.

the prevalence of vengeful attitudes in their selectorate. First, with a small selectorate, autocratic leaders can afford to maintain support by doling out rewards and punishments (Bueno de Mesquita et al. 2005). An autocratic leader facing a less vengeful selectorate has the ability to build sufficient support for war by paying off those who back him and eliminating those who do not, and he or she is therefore not at a disadvantage compared with an autocratic leader facing a more vengeful selectorate. In contrast, the reward and punishment strategy is too expensive for democratic leaders with large selectorates, and as a result, they must rely on cheaper but less certain methods of ensuring support, such as rhetorical persuasion.[17]

Second, given their status as political elites, regime insiders will rely less on their core values when evaluating the wisdom of going to war than will the average citizen. In general, they should have access to higher quality information about foreign policy than is available to the general public, combined with the experience and knowledge required to process that information and determine which policy is in their best interest. Thus, even without the payoffs and punishments provided by autocratic leaders, vengefulness should play no more than a minor role in shaping the opinions of well-informed regime insiders.

HYPOTHESES

In this section, I lay out the three main hypotheses that I test in the book's empirical chapters. Each hypothesis corresponds to one part of my theory. The first two hypotheses deal with the theory's individual-level micro-foundations, while the third concerns its international implications.

The Core Value Hypothesis

In part 1, I argued that at the individual level, revenge is best understood as a core value. I based this argument on insights gleaned from the growing body of empirical social science research on revenge. The existing evidence is strongest concerning the first two elements of the standard definition of core values: that revenge is a belief (element 1), and that it pertains to a desirable end state (element 2), namely that

---

[17] In a few autocracies, the selectorate may be so large that leaders cannot rely on reward and punishment strategies to secure support. In such cases, autocratic leaders should behave similarly to their democratic counterparts.

wrongdoers get the punishment they deserve. There is also substantial evidence consistent with the second two elements of the definition: that revenge transcends specific situations (element 3) and that it guides the selection or evaluation of behavior, people, and events (element 4).

However, because the existing literature is distributed across disciplines that rarely, if ever, acknowledge or communicate with one another, a skeptic might question the strength of the evidence on these last two points by asking whether such a diverse set of studies, each with its own methods, measures, and standards of research, are really investigating the same phenomena. If they are not, then what looks like evidence for revenge as a trans-situational evaluative standard may simply be the result of conceptual confusion. I do not find this concern particularly persuasive, as I discussed in greater detail in part 1. That said, because conceptualizing revenge as a core value represents a sharp departure from the conventional wisdom on revenge, additional testing is warranted to establish that it fulfills the third and fourth elements of the definition.

If revenge does transcend specific situations and guide the selection or evaluation of behavior, people, and events, then we should find empirically that endorsement of revenge as a general principle is an important predictor of individuals' attitudes toward punishment across various contexts, including situations in which the individual is not personally involved. Of particular importance for this study is the way that revenge shapes individuals' attitudes toward the use of punitive violence, i.e., violence that is used in response to a perceived transgression. To be clear, my argument is not that revenge is synonymous with violence. The principle that wrongs deserve to be repaid is equally applicable to situations involving both violent and non-violent forms of punishment, and acts of revenge can take a multitude of forms, from minor harms such as procrastinating or starting rumors (Ferrari and Emmons 1994; Jones 2009) to horrific acts of cruelty (Knoll 2010). However, because my theory is ultimately concerned with making the connection between individual vengefulness and war, the relationship between endorsement of revenge and attitudes toward violence is of particular importance.

As a core value, revenge should provide individuals with a useful shortcut for forming judgments about the various types of violence that they observe and experience over the course of their lives. It transforms what would otherwise be a complex process of weighing many different considerations into a much simpler decision. The crucial question is whether, by virtue of some prior act of wrongdoing, the target is perceived as deserving of punishment. If the answer is yes, the use of violence to punish the target is transformed, in the eyes of those who embrace revenge, into a righteous act that is worthy of approbation regardless of its cost or its consequences. This suggests the following hypothesis, which I test in Chapter 3:

Vengeful individuals will be more supportive of punitive violence than non-vengeful individuals across a wide variety of contexts, regardless of their personal involvement.

If the data support this hypothesis, it will further strengthen the case already made by the existing literature that revenge shares all the essential properties of a core value and that theorizing about revenge as a core value, as I do here, therefore rests on a solid empirical foundation.

The Framing Hypothesis

In part 2, I argued that revenge can be a powerful source of popular support for war, but that this relationship is conditional on how political elites, and particularly national leaders, frame the use of military force in their political communication. Specifically, I introduced the concept of a punishment frame, which has three key elements: (1) a clear act of wrongdoing, (2) a clear perpetrator, and (3) a proposed military action that will cause some harm to the perpetrator. All these elements are necessary to construct a narrative that will make citizens' beliefs about revenge salient, thereby causing them to rely on those beliefs when forming their attitudes toward the use of military force. This suggests the following hypothesis, which I test in Chapter 4:

Vengeful individuals will be more supportive of the use of force than non-vengeful individuals when (and only when) that use of force is framed as a punishment.

Put another way, endorsement of revenge should predict support for the use of force when it is framed as a punishment, but when one or more of the necessary elements of that frame is absent, there should be no significant difference between the attitudes of vengeful and non-vengeful individuals. In order for the evidence to support my theory, both of these predictions must be born out. This is why I use the somewhat awkward phrasing of "when (and only when)" in stating the framing hypothesis. The "when" implies that we should see a significant relationship between endorsement of revenge and support for the use of force under the circumstances specified, while the "and only when" implies that we should *not* see a significant relationship in the absence of those circumstances. Identifying the conditions under which vengeful-ness should not predict support for the use of force is critical because it allows me to rule out an alternative explanation that has dogged previous research, namely that individuals who express endorsement of revenge are not expressing a principled moral view but rather a general taste for violence that manifests itself in a predilection for harsh punishments both at home and abroad. I return to this point in Chapter 4.

The Conflict Initiation Hypothesis

In part 3, I argued that cross-national variation in the prevalence of revenge affects the degree of constraint that democratic leaders face and their propensity to use military force in international relations. Leaders who face more vengeful populations can regularly and reliably tap into a substantial pool of latent support for war by employing a punishment frame in their rhetoric, and they are therefore less likely to be deterred from using military force by the potential political costs of an unpopular war. This suggests the following hypothesis:

Democracies with more vengeful populations will be more likely to initiate the use of military force than democracies with less vengeful populations.

Why does my expectation concern conflict initiation rather than recip-rocation or escalation? The answer is that the advantage enjoyed by leaders with highly vengeful populations is largely eliminated once the adversary makes the first move. Consider a situation in which state A has initiated a conflict with state B. The leader of state B can now make the case for going to war on the basis of self-defense. Given the widespread legitimacy of self-defense as a justification for both interpersonal and interstate violence (Alexandrov 1996; Ramirez 2007), this is a potent argument that will most likely generate enough public support to over-come leader B's reticence about waging an unpopular war, regardless of the vengefulness of his or her constituents. However, if state A has not yet made the first move, then the self-defense argument becomes much more difficult to make, and leader B's ability to appeal to the public's desire for revenge becomes much more important in generating a sufficient level of public support. If leader B faces a highly vengeful population, he or she can generate support for initiating a conflict against state A by framing the use of force as a punishment for acts of wrongdoing that state A has committed against state B in the past, against a third state, or against its own people. Having this tool in his or her tool kit means that leader B has greater liberty to take military action against state A compared with a leader who must wait for a plausible case for self-defense to emerge in order to surmount public opposition.[18]

CONCLUSION

In this chapter, I argued that revenge plays an important role in fomenting international conflict and that it does so through the dynamic interaction between democratically elected leaders, who behave strategically in order to secure support for their policies and maintain their position in power, and their citizens, who rely on their core values to form their opinions about complex foreign policy questions.

The roots of this theory lie in the growing body of empirical social science research on revenge. Contrary to the pejorative view of revenge that has long been dominant in Western legal and philosophical thought, this emerging literature points to a new way to understand the nature of revenge and the role that it plays in the lives of individuals. Revenge is not an irrational, immoral, or pathological impulse; rather, it is best understood as a core value – rooted in the belief that wrongs deserve to be repaid – that shapes both personal conduct and political attitudes, including attitudes toward the use of military force.

Synthesizing this insight with existing theories concerning the role of core values and issue framing in the formation of public opinion, I argued that national leaders can mobilize and channel their citizens' desire for revenge into support for war under a wide variety of circumstances by using rhetoric that frames the use of military force as a punishment that the adversary deserves to suffer. For democratically elected leaders, and particularly those with highly vengeful populations, the ability to generate

---

[18] This argument assumes that the relationship between the level of popular support for the use of force and the likelihood that a leader will initiate a conflict is a logistic function. At very low and very high levels of support, the likelihood that a leader will use force is close to zero or one, respectively, and an increase in support is not likely to influence his or her decision. However, around the inflection point of the curve, an increase in support will have a substantial effect on a leader's willingness to employ military force. In the case of reciprocation or escalation, the level of popular support is more likely to fall toward the right tail of the curve due to the power of the self-defense justification. In this situation, vengefulness may increase public support for war, but the likelihood of reciprocation or escalation will not change markedly. When it comes to initiation, the level of popular support for war is more likely to fall near the inflection point where the effect of revenge can have a significant impact on the leader's calculus.

popular support for war in this way loosens the constraints of account-ability to the public, making the use of military force a relatively less costly (and therefore more attractive) tool of foreign policy.

Unlike prior approaches, which have identified either leaders or states themselves as the locus of the desire for revenge, my theory places the values and opinions of ordinary people at the center of the story. As such, it does not purport to explain specific conflicts, but rather a behav-ioral tendency: on average, democracies with more vengeful populations will exhibit a greater propensity to use force in international relations. This is the central prediction of my theory, but in the subsequent empir-ical chapters, I place equal weight on testing its individual-level micro-foundations. This provides a more rigorous test of the theory's logic than would be the case if I focused solely on its observable implications at the international level.

By building my theory of war and revenge from the ground up, I arrive at an understanding of the relationship between leaders and citizens that differs from the prevailing view in much of the existing literature on democratic conflict behavior. I contend that by assuming that public opinion imposes a constraint on leaders that they cannot escape or loosen, existing theories have missed an important source of variation in the conflict behavior of democracies. In democracies, regular, free, and fair elections make leaders accountable to the mass public and give them an incentive not to stray beyond the bounds of what their citizens are willing to accept. However, in order to predict how that accountability will affect leaders' choices, we need to understand the beliefs and preferences of the people to whom they are accountable. Attitudes toward war are not the same in all democracies. Different cultural legacies have left their imprint on the core values that citizens rely on to form their opinions about the use of military force, and as I will show, these differences are crucial for understanding why some democracies are more warlike than others.

3

Wrongs Must Be Repaid

Revenge as a Core Value

Unlike previous efforts to incorporate revenge into International Relations, my theory begins with the role that revenge plays in the lives of ordinary individuals. Thus, establishing the theory's individual-level micro-foundations is just as important as exploring its international implications. In this chapter, I test the *core value hypothesis*, which predicts that vengeful individuals will be more supportive of punitive violence than non-vengeful individuals across a wide variety of contexts, regardless of their personal involvement. To do so, I use both contemporary and historical data from the United States to examine how vengefulness shapes Americans' attitudes toward various kinds of punitive violence in the domestic sphere, including corporal punishment, vigilante justice, lethal police violence, capital punishment, and torture.

Consistent with the *core value hypothesis*, I find that Americans who believe strongly that wrongs deserve to be repaid are consistently more supportive of punitive violence in all of the diverse scenarios that I examine. Together with the existing empirical literature on revenge, which I reviewed in Chapter 2, this evidence makes a strong case that revenge shares the essential properties that define core values and that in spite of the conventional wisdom to the contrary, revenge is properly conceptualized as a core value rather than a pathological aberration. By firmly establishing that revenge transcends the realm of the personal to influence how individuals evaluate the use of punitive violence by other actors, including their own government, this chapter takes the first step toward demonstrating the validity of the mechanism that links individual-level vengefulness with state-level violence.

REVENGE AND ATTITUDES TOWARD PUNITIVE VIOLENCE IN THE CONTEMPORARY UNITED STATES [1]

Data and Measures

In this section, I explore the relationship between revenge and attitudes toward punitive violence using data from an original survey conducted in 2010 and administered to a nationally representative sample of American adults (*N* = 1,000).[1]

Dependent Variables

On this survey, I asked respondents to evaluate the use of punitive violence in six different scenarios. By punitive violence, I mean violence that is being used in response to some kind of transgression. The first scenario involved a man who punched a stranger after seeing the stranger slap his own wife in public (*Punch stranger*). The second scenario involved a parent who killed the man responsible for raping his or her child (*Kill rapist*). The third scenario involved the use of physical punishment by parents to discipline their children (*Parental punishment*). The fourth scenario involved the use of physical punishment by teachers to discipline their students (*School punishment*). The fifth scenario asked about capital punishment for the crime of murder (*Death penalty*), and the sixth scenario asked about torturing a terrorism suspect (*Torture*).[2] After reading about each scenario, respondents were asked whether they approved or disapproved with five response options ranging from "approve strongly" to "disapprove strongly."

I coded support for the use of violence in each scenario as a dichotomous variable equal to one if the respondent approved either somewhat or strongly. Support is highest in the *Death penalty* (62%) and *Punch stranger* (53%) scenarios, followed by *Parental Punishment* (49%), *Kill rapist* (47%), *Torture* (43%), and *School punishment* (25%).

---

[1] This survey was part of a team module on the 2010 Cooperative Congressional Election Study. The CCES is a large multi-investigator study, which allows researchers to combine a module containing their own content with a set of common content questions that are available to all researchers participating in the study. The survey was administered online by YouGov using a matched random sample. The first wave of the study was in the field during October 2010, and the second wave was in the field during November 2010.

[2] The precise wording of these items is available in the Appendix.

Several aspects of these scenarios are worth highlighting here. First, none of them is personal in the sense that they explicitly ask respondents to pass judgment on the conduct of others rather than asking them to say how they would behave in the same situation. Second, the scenarios vary in the type of actor involved (individuals vs. government authorities) and the relationships that those actors have with one another. Third, they vary substantially in the severity of the violence involved. What they all have in common is the use of violence in response to a perceived act of wrongdoing or injustice. Thus, if revenge is a core value that individuals rely on to form judgments about issues beyond their own sphere of personal concern, then endorsement of revenge should have a positive relationship with approval of punitive violence across all six scenarios.

Measuring Revenge

To measure endorsement of revenge, I asked respondents whether they agreed or disagreed with the following statement: "In order for justice to be served, violence must be repaid with violence." The distribution of responses is as follows: 6% agree strongly, 17% agree somewhat, 22% neither agree nor disagree, 22% disagree somewhat, and 34% disagree strongly. This distribution shows a population that skews toward the disagree end of the spectrum with the plurality of responses falling in the strongly disagree category. At the same time, there is a substantial segment of the population that accepts this principle to at least some degree, and there is significant variation among individuals in the strength of their endorsement. This will be my main independent variable in the analyses presented in the remainder of this section. In all statistical models, I treat it as a continuous variable (*Vengefulness*) ranging from one (least vengeful) to five (most vengeful).[3] My expectation is that the more strongly an individual agrees with the idea that violence must be repaid with violence, the more likely he or she will be to approve of the use of violence in each of the six scenarios.

Control Variables

I also include in my analyses a number of control variables that are known (or suspected) to be correlated with individual differences in vengefulness and that may also be related to attitudes toward violence.

---

[3] The mean of this variable is 2.40 with a standard deviation of 1.27.

- *Gender*: A number of studies have found that men are more likely than women to hold vengeful attitudes and to engage in vengeful behaviors (Stuckless and Goranson 1992; Wiesenthal et al. 2000; Cota-McKinley et al. 2001; Hennessey and Wiesenthal 2002).
- *Age*: Younger people appear to be more likely to hold vengeful attitudes and to engage in vengeful behaviors (Wiesenthal et al. 2000; Cota-McKinley et al. 2001).
- *Race*: Existing research suggests that African Americans are less likely to endorse revenge than whites (Baker et al. 2005).
- *Education*: According to Kohlberg (1981), more education is related to higher stages of "moral development" and a rejection of revenge as a basis for punishment (Kohlberg and Elfenbein 1975).
- *Political ideology*: Gollwitzer et al. (2014) find a positive correlation between vengefulness and conservative ideology.
- *Party identification*: There is no extant research linking party identification to individual differences in vengefulness. However, the significant partisan gap in support for the death penalty, which research indicates is driven primarily by the desire for revenge, suggests a correlation.[4]

Including measures of *Gender* (a dummy variable for male), *Age* (in years), *Race* (a dummy variable for non-Hispanic white), *Education* (an ordinal variable with six levels ranging from high school to post-graduate degree), *Political ideology* (measured on a five-point scale ranging from very liberal to very conservative), and *Party identification* (measured on a seven-point scale ranging from strong Democrat to strong Republican) helps to ensure that any observed relationship between endorsement of revenge and support for punitive violence is not spurious.

Analysis and Results

I examine the relationship between *Vengefulness* and support for the use of punitive violence in a series of logistic regression models.[5] The results are reported in Table 3.1. Consistent with the *core value hypothesis*, *Vengefulness* is a positive and significant predictor of support in all six

---

[4] In 2014, 76% of Republicans favored capital punishment compared with 49% of Democrats. Jeffrey M. Jones, "Americans' Support for Death Penalty Stable," *Gallup .com*. October 23, 2014. www.gallup.com/poll/178790/americans-support-death-penalty-stable.aspx.

[5] As a robustness check, I replicated this analysis using ordered logistic regression models. The overall pattern of results does not change.

TABLE 3.1 *Predictors of support for punitive violence*

	Punch stranger	Kill rapist	Parental punishment	School punishment	Death penalty	Torture
Vengefulness	0.40***	0.61***	0.460***	0.30**	0.77***	0.64***
	(0.10)	(0.10)	(0.11)	(0.10)	(0.15)	(0.11)
Gender	0.03	0.50*	0.57*	0.28	0.06	0.10
	(0.21)	(0.22)	(0.23)	(0.25)	(0.28)	(0.25)
Age	-0.01	-0.02*	0.02*	0.01	0.03**	0.02
	(0.01)	(0.01)	(0.01)	(0.01)	(0.01)	(0.01)
Race	-0.01	0.69*	-0.83*	-0.33	0.62	-0.21
	(0.30)	(0.31)	(0.34)	(0.34)	(0.35)	(0.37)
Education	-0.07	-0.12	-0.04	0.07	-0.05	0.01
	(0.08)	(0.08)	(0.08)	(0.09)	(0.10)	(0.08)
Pol. ideology	0.00	0.02	0.44*	0.50**	0.19	0.45**
	(0.15)	(0.14)	(0.17)	(0.18)	(0.18)	(0.17)
Party ID	-0.00	0.00	0.06	0.12	0.15	0.24**
	(0.08)	(0.07)	(0.08)	(0.09)	(0.10)	(0.08)
Constant	-0.17	-1.31	-3.15***	-4.70***	-4.06***	-5.14***
	(0.63)	(0.67)	(0.70)	(0.74)	(0.82)	(0.85)
N	929	926	929	925	928	926

Note: All models are logistic regression models with standard errors in parentheses.
Significance: * $p < 0.05$, ** $p < 0.01$, *** $p < 0.001$.

scenarios, even when controlling for potential confounders. The more strongly a person endorses the idea that violence must be repaid with violence, the more likely he or she is to approve of vigilante justice (in the *Punch stranger* and *Kill rapist* scenarios), corporal punishment (both at home and in school), capital punishment, and torture. In fact, *Vengefulness* is the only predictor that has a consistent effect across all these different contexts. The desire to see the wrongdoer get his or her just deserts is the common thread that links attitudes toward all six scenarios together.

Just how big is the effect of *Vengefulness* on support for the use of punitive violence in these scenarios? One way to answer this question is to depict the results graphically. Figure 3.1 plots the predicted probability of supporting punitive violence in each scenario as *Vengefulness* increases from its minimum to its maximum. This figure shows that *Vengefulness* has the biggest impact on attitudes in the *Kill rapist, Death penalty*, and *Torture* scenarios. In the case of a parent who kills his or her child's rapist, moving *Vengefulness* from its minimum to its maximum produces a 52.1 percentage point increase in the predicted probability of approval (from 26.1% to 78.2%). In the *Death penalty* scenario, that figure is 49.7 percentage points (from 42.6% to 92.3%), and in the *Torture* scenario it is 48.7 percentage

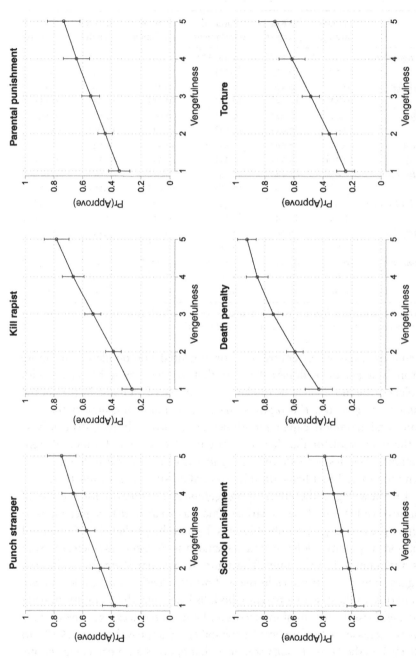

FIGURE 3.1 The effect of vengefulness on support for punitive violence. Note: Predicted probabilities were calculated based on the models reported in Table 3.1, with all other variables set at their means. Error bars represent 95% confidence intervals.

points (from 24.5% to 73.2%). In the *Parental punishment* and *Punch stranger* scenarios, moving *Vengefulness* from its minimum to its maximum increases the predicted probability of approval by 38.7 percentage points (from 34.6% to 73.3%) and 36.7 percentage points (from 38.0% to 74.7%), respectively. Finally, the effect of *Vengefulness* is smallest, although still quite substantial, in the *School punishment* scenario. There, moving *Vengefulness* from its minimum to its maximum increases the predicted probability of approval by 21.0 percentage points (from 17.5% to 38.5%). By looking at the results this way, it becomes clear that there is a profound difference in the attitudes of individuals who reject the idea that wrongs must be repaid and individuals who strongly endorse it.

Overall, these are very large and meaningful differences. For instance, the size of the *Vengefulness* effect exceeds the gender gap, which refers to the well-known finding that women are, generally speaking, less willing to endorse the use of violence than men (Gallagher 1993; Nincic and Nincic 2002; Brooks and Valentino 2011). The results reported in Table 3.1 show that there is a significant gender gap in the *Kill rapist* and *Parental punishment* scenarios. In the *Kill rapist* scenario, the difference in predicted support between men and women is 10.3 percentage points (49.7% vs. 39.4%), compared with the 52.1 percentage point difference between the most and least vengeful individuals. Similarly, in the *Parental punishment* scenario, men are 11.7 percentage points more likely to express approval than women (54.6% vs. 42.9%), compared with the gap of 38.7 percentage points that separates the most and least vengeful individuals. Indeed, comparing the average marginal effect[6] of *Vengefulness* with the other significant predictors for each scenario shows that *Vengefulness* is a more powerful driver of support for punitive violence than many of the socioeconomic and political variables that are often used to predict attitudes toward violence.

REVENGE AND ATTITUDES TOWARD LETHAL POLICE VIOLENCE AND CRIMINAL JUSTICE IN THE 1960S

Data and Measures

In this section, I provide an additional test of the *core value hypothesis* using data from the Justifying Violence Survey (JVS), which was conducted in 1969 by Monica D. Blumenthal, Robert L. Kahn, and Frank

---

[6] The change in the predicted probability of support caused by a one unit increase in *Vengefulness*.

M. Andrews through the University of Michigan's Survey Research Center.[7] The original aim of the JVS was to study Americans' attitudes toward violence during a period of substantial social unrest in the United States, including a rising tide of primarily black-led violent protests that catapulted the issue of "social control" to the top of the national agenda.

As far as I am aware, the JVS is the only publicly available national opinion survey to include a direct measure of revenge as an abstract and general principle. As such, it offers a unique opportunity to demonstrate that the findings presented in the previous section are not an artifact of the particular questions asked on the survey or of the particular time period in which the survey was conducted. Moreover, the JVS includes a number of questions that capture other facets of the respondents' attitudes toward violence, including their beliefs about the efficacy of using violence to solve social problems and their general orientation (positive or negative) toward violence. Including these items as control variables in my analysis allows me to test whether endorsement of revenge has a distinct and independent effect on support for the use of punitive violence.

The main limitation of the JVS is that its sample was restricted to men. Men tend to be more vengeful than women, but I have found no evidence to suggest that the relationship between vengefulness and attitudes toward punitive violence varies by gender. Thus, there is little reason to expect that the results of this analysis would differ markedly if the sample included both genders.

Dependent Variables

The *core value hypothesis* predicts that endorsement of revenge will be associated with greater support for the use of punitive violence across a wide variety of contexts. I test this prediction using two sets of questions from the JVS. The first set of questions measured respondents' support for lethal police violence in response to various types of social unrest. The second set of questions captured their more general attitudes toward the criminal justice system.

Support for Lethal Police Violence

To probe respondents' attitudes toward lethal police violence, they were presented with three different scenarios. The first scenario involved

---

[7] These data were made available by the Inter-University Consortium for Political and Social Research (ICPSR). Neither the original collectors of the data nor the archive bears any responsibility for the analyses or interpretations presented here.

"gangs of hoodlums" who had "gone into a town, terrified people, and caused a lot of property damage." The second scenario concerned "big city riots involving Negroes and the police," and the third dealt with "student disturbances on campuses and elsewhere, which involve a lot of property damage." After each scenario, respondents were asked how the police should handle the situation, including whether or not they should employ lethal violence (i.e., shoot to kill). I code support for lethal police violence in each of these scenarios as a dichotomous variable, equal to 1 for respondents who said that the police should "sometimes" or "almost always" shoot to kill, and 0 for respondents who said either "never" or "hardly ever." These variables are labeled as *Shoot to kill hoodlums, Shoot to kill rioters,* and *Shoot to kill students.*

In the *Shoot to kill hoodlums* scenario, approximately one in three respondents (32.1%) expressed support for the use of lethal police violence. Similarly, 30.1% of respondents endorsed a shoot to kill policy in the *Shoot to kill rioters* scenario. Approval was somewhat lower in the *Shoot to kill students* scenario (18.6%). However, it is clear that even in this case, there are many Americans who support the use of violence to respond to social unrest. This may be a minority viewpoint, but it is by no means a negligible minority.

Note that in each of the three scenarios, it is clear that the miscreants' activities have caused serious harm. In the scenarios involving hoodlum gangs and student protesters, property damage is explicitly mentioned. This is not the case in the big city riots scenario, but in the context of the late 1960s, with memories of cataclysmic events like the 1965 Watts riots in Los Angeles fresh in people's minds, the use of the word "riots" clearly telegraphs images of violent destruction. Thus, if the *core value hypothesis* is correct, we should observe a positive relationship between endorsement of revenge and support for lethal police violence in these scenarios.

Attitudes toward Criminal Justice

The JVS also included a number of questions intended to capture respondents' general attitudes toward the criminal justice system. If the *core value hypothesis* is correct, then endorsement of revenge should predict support for harsh criminal penalties and for giving civil authorities the necessary power to deliver those penalties to those who deserve them. To test whether this is the case, I look at four different dependent variables:

- *Death penalty support*: Respondents were asked whether they agreed or disagreed with the following statement: "People who commit murder deserve capital punishment." The response options were: agree a great deal, agree somewhat, disagree somewhat, or disagree a great deal. In the analyses that follow, I treat this as a dichotomous variable equal to 1 if the respondent chose one of the agree options, and 0 otherwise.

- *Courts too easy*: Respondents were asked whether they agreed or disagreed with the following statement: "Courts nowadays are much too easy on criminals." The response options were: agree a great deal, agree somewhat, disagree somewhat, or disagree a great deal. I code this as a dichotomous variable equal to 1 if the respondent chose one of the agree options, and 0 otherwise.

- *More police power*: Respondents were asked whether they agreed or disagreed with the following statement: "Police nowadays should have more power to enforce the law adequately." The response options were: agree a great deal, agree somewhat, disagree somewhat, or disagree a great deal. I treat this as a dichotomous variable equal to 1 if the respondent chose one of the agree options, and 0 otherwise.

- *Empathy with policeman*: Respondents were presented with the following scenario: "A policeman is giving a ticket to a man for reckless driving. The driver takes the ticket, begins to swear, and calls the policeman a pig." They were then told that the policeman reacted by punching the driver in the nose and knocking him down. The question asked: "How likely is it that you could feel like that policeman if a similar thing happened to you?" Respondents could answer very likely, somewhat likely, not too likely, or not likely at all. I code this as a dichotomous variable equal to 1 if the respondent said very or somewhat likely, and 0 otherwise.

Overall, substantial majorities of respondents voiced support for capital punishment (70.8%) and increased police power (75.1%), agreed that the courts are too easy on criminals (78.8%), and expressed empathy with the policeman who punched the driver (71.8%).

Measuring Revenge

To measure endorsement of revenge, I constructed a vengefulness scale from the following three agree/disagree items: (1) "violence deserves violence," (2) "'an eye for an eye and a tooth for a tooth' is a good rule for living," and (3) "when someone does wrong he should be paid back for it." The scale ranges from 1 to 4 (mean = 2.32, std. dev. = 0.72), with higher scores indicating greater endorsement of revenge.[8]

---

[8] Cronbach's alpha for this scale is 0.537.

Control Variables

As in the previous section, I include *Age*, *Race*, and *Education* as control variables (I do not include *Gender* because the sample does not include any women).[9] Unfortunately, the survey did not contain items related to political ideology or party identification, so I cannot control directly for those variables. However, I do include controls for a number of other sociodemographic factors that are likely to be related to attitudes toward lethal police violence and criminal justice.

- *Neighborhood unsafe*: a dichotomous variable equal to 1 if the respondent reported that his or her neighborhood was "not safe at all" or "not too safe," and equal to 0 if the respondent reported that his or her neighborhood was "usually safe" or "completely safe."
- *Rural residence*: a dichotomous variable equal to 1 if the respondent reported living in a rural area or a small town with population below 5,000, and 0 otherwise.
- *Income*: family income, an interval variable with eight levels ranging from under $2,000 to more than $16,000 in increments of $2,000.
- *Southern*: a dichotomous variable equal to 1 for respondents living in the "solid South" (Alabama, Arkansas, Florida, Georgia, Louisiana, Mississippi, North Carolina, South Carolina, Texas, Virginia), and 0 otherwise.
- *Conservative Protestant*: a dichotomous variable equal to 1 if the respondent belonged to a conservative Protestant denomination as defined by Ellison et al. (2003), and 0 otherwise.[10]
- *Regular church attendance*: a dichotomous variable equal to 1 if the respondent reported attending church once a week or more, and 0 otherwise.
- *Veteran*: a dichotomous variable equal to 1 if the respondent reported having served in the armed forces, and 0 otherwise.

---

[9] The coding of these variables is the same as for the 2010 survey described in the previous section.

[10] The category of conservative Protestant was first introduced by Roof and McKinney (1987) to describe a group of denominations that share certain historical, theological, and sociopolitical orientations. Ellison et al. (2003) summarizes the basic beliefs that characterize conservative Protestantism: "(a) the Bible is without error, is the authoritative source of wisdom regarding human affairs, and/or should be interpreted literally; (b) God intervenes in the lives of individuals; (c) humans are fundamentally sinful and are subject to judgment at the hands of a righteous, punitive god; (d) morality is often clear-cut and dichotomous, consisting of black/white judgments rather than many shades of gray; and (e) personal salvation through faith is the only escape from eternal damnation" (331). A number of studies have shown that conservative Protestant religious beliefs are associated with punitiveness (Grasmick et al. 1991; Grasmick et al. 1993; Grasmick 1994; Ellison et al. 1996).

In addition to these sociodemographic variables, I include two measures that capture respondents' general attitudes toward race and the police.

- *Black social change*: a dichotomous variable equal to 1 if the respondent agreed that "social change is needed to improve the lives of blacks," and 0 if the respondent disagreed.[11]
- *Trust police*: a dichotomous variable equal to 1 for respondents who indicated that they believe "most policemen can be trusted," and equal to 0 for respondents who said that "you can't be too careful when dealing with [the police]."

Analysis and Results

I begin by examining the relationship between *Vengefulness* and support for lethal police violence. My three dependent variables, *Shoot to kill hoodlums*, *Shoot to kill rioters*, and *Shoot to kill students*, are coded as dichotomous variables and I therefore employ logistic regression models. I report the results in columns 1–3 in Table 3.2. As the *core value hypothesis* predicts, *Vengefulness* is a positive and significant predictor of support for lethal police violence in all three scenarios. The more vengeful an individual is, the more likely he or she is to say that the police should regularly shoot to kill when confronted with social unrest involving hoodlum gangs, big city riots, and student protesters.

The magnitude of these effects is substantial. Figure 3.2 shows how the predicted probability of support for lethal police violence in each scenario changes as *Vengefulness* increases from its minimum of 1 to its maximum of 4. In the *Shoot to kill hoodlums* scenario, moving revenge from its minimum to its maximum increases the predicted probability of support by 28.9 percentage points (from 20.4% to 49.3%), meaning that the most vengeful individuals are almost two and a half times as likely as the least vengeful individuals to view lethal violence as an appropriate response to this kind of social unrest. Similarly, as *Vengefulness* increases over its range, the predicted probability of support in the *Shoot to kill rioters* scenario rises by 35.9 percentage points (from 15.8% to 51.7%). Finally, in the *Shoot to kill students* scenario, the predicted probability of support increases by 23.0 percentage points (from 9.9% to 32.9%) as

---

[11] The JVS did not contain any direct measures of racial prejudice or antipathy, so I use this measure as a proxy for those attitudes. I assume that individuals who agree that social change is needed to improve the lives of blacks have lower levels of prejudice/antipathy than individuals who disagree with that statement.

TABLE 3.2 *Predictors of attitudes toward police violence and criminal justice in the 1960s*

	Shoot hoodlums	Shoot rioters	Shoot students	Death penalty	Courts too easy	Police power	Empathy w/ police
Vengefulness	0.46***	0.60***	0.52***	1.14***	0.52***	0.41***	0.46***
	(0.10)	(0.10)	(0.12)	(0.12)	(0.12)	(0.12)	(0.11)
Age	0.01	0.01	0.01	-0.00	0.03***	0.01*	-0.00
	(0.01)	(0.01)	(0.01)	(0.00)	(0.01)	(0.01)	(0.01)
Race	0.26	0.56*	0.29	0.27	0.88***	1.04***	0.39
	(0.21)	(0.22)	(0.25)	(0.20)	(0.21)	(0.20)	(0.21)
Education	-0.05	-0.03	-0.04	-0.034	-0.07*	-0.11***	-0.07*
	(0.03)	(0.03)	(0.03)	(0.03)	(0.03)	(0.030)	(0.03)
Neighborhood unsafe	-0.13	-0.03	0.05	-0.21	-0.26	-0.42*	-0.02
	(0.17)	(0.18)	(0.21)	(0.20)	(0.21)	(0.20)	(0.19)
Rural residence	0.29	0.22	0.31	0.51**	0.06	0.17	0.23
	(0.16)	(0.16)	(0.19)	(0.19)	(0.21)	(0.19)	(0.18)
Income	0.08	-0.02	-0.07	0.07	0.16**	-0.01	-0.03
	(0.04)	(0.04)	(0.05)	(0.04)	(0.05)	(0.05)	(0.04)
Southern	0.13	0.03	0.14	0.13	0.30	0.36	0.23
	(0.17)	(0.18)	(0.20)	(0.19)	(0.20)	(0.19)	(0.18)
Conservative Protestant	0.32*	0.36*	0.41*	0.20	0.15	0.20	0.29
	(0.16)	(0.17)	(0.19)	(0.18)	(0.20)	(0.19)	(0.17)
Regular church attend.	0.05	-0.07	0.09	-0.03	0.41*	0.13	-0.03
	(0.15)	(0.16)	(0.18)	(0.16)	(0.18)	(0.17)	(0.15)

(*continued*)

TABLE 3.2 (continued)

	Shoot hoodlums	Shoot rioters	Shoot students	Death penalty	Courts too easy	Police power	Empathy w/ police
Veteran	0.49**	0.22	0.34	0.25	-0.04	0.11	-0.04
	(0.15)	(0.15)	(0.18)	(0.15)	(0.16)	(0.16)	(0.15)
Black social change	-0.345	-0.68**	-0.45	-0.96*	-0.11	0.04	-0.03
	(0.24)	(0.25)	(0.27)	(0.38)	(0.34)	(0.32)	(0.28)
Trust police	0.10	0.22	0.53*	0.65**	0.07	1.31***	-0.13
	(0.21)	(0.23)	(0.27)	(0.20)	(0.22)	(0.21)	(0.21)
Constant	-2.41***	-2.54***	-3.10***	-1.45*	-1.71*	-1.01	0.58
	(0.55)	(0.58)	(0.69)	(0.67)	(0.72)	(0.66)	(0.62)
N	1,257	1,255	1,256	1,263	1,252	1,260	1,255

Note: All models are logistic regression models with standard errors in parentheses. Significance: * $p < 0.05$, ** $p < 0.01$, *** $p < 0.001$.

78

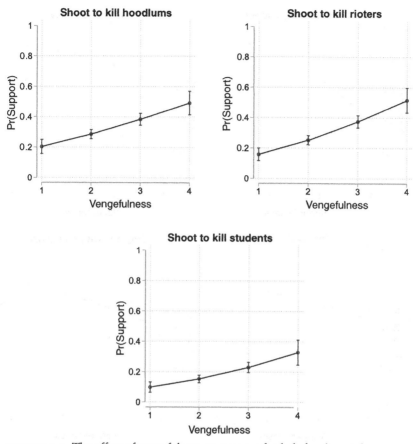

FIGURE 3.2 The effect of vengefulness on support for lethal police violence. Note: Predicted probabilities were calculated based on the models reported in Table 3.2 (columns 1–3), with all other variables set at their means. Error bars represent 95% confidence intervals.

Vengefulness moves from its minimum to its maximum. It is clear from these results that individuals' attitudes toward the use of lethal violence by the police are shaped by their beliefs about revenge.

I now turn to my second set of dependent variables: *Death penalty support, Courts too easy, More police power,* and *Empathy with policeman.* These are dichotomous variables and I employ logistic regression models in my analysis. The results are reported in columns 4–7 in Table 3.2. According to the prediction of the *core value hypothesis, Vengefulness* should have a positive relationship with each of these variables, and this is exactly what we see. The higher an individual scores on

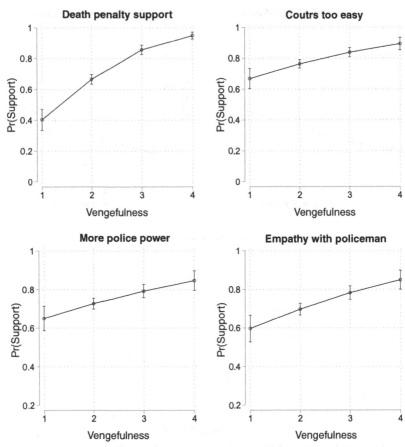

FIGURE 3.3 The effect of vengefulness on support for harsh criminal justice. Note: Predicted probabilities were calculated based on the models reported in Table 3.2 (columns 4–7), with all other variables set at their means. Error bars represent 95% confidence intervals.

the *Vengefulness* scale, the more likely he or she is to support capital punishment and increased police power, to say that the courts are too easy on criminals, and to express empathy with the policeman who punched a driver in the face.

The effect of *Vengefulness* on support for capital punishment is particularly strong, as shown in Figure 3.3. At the low end of the *Vengefulness* scale the predicted probability of support for capital punishment is 40.3%, while at the high end of the *Vengefulness* scale, the predicted probability of support for capital punishment is nearly unanimous at 94.5%, an increase of 54.2 percentage points. Figure 3.3 also shows that *Vengefulness* has a substantial effect on the three other dependent variables. Moving *Vengefulness* from its minimum to its maximum increases the probability of saying that the courts are too easy by 22.5 percentage points (from 66.9% to 89.4%). For *More police power*, that increase is 19.5 percentage points (from 65.1% to 84.6%), and for *Empathy with policeman* it is 25.2 percentage points (an increase from 59.7% to 84.9%).

Taken together, the results presented in Table 3.2 show that even in the late 1960s, a time when American society and politics looked very different from the world we know today, endorsement of revenge was a powerful and consistent predictor of attitudes toward the use of punitive violence in a variety of forms and contexts, as well as toward the criminal justice system more generally. This lends additional support to the *core value hypothesis* and confirms that the relationship between endorsement of revenge and support for punitive violence is not simply the product of some unique feature of the contemporary social and political environment.

In addition, the JVS offers the opportunity to test whether this relationship is robust to the inclusion of other measures of individuals' attitudes toward violence. First, one might be concerned that endorsement of revenge simply reflects an overall positive orientation toward violence. To measure the latter, I created a scale (*Positive orientation*) using three items from the JVS that asked respondents to choose how they would describe violence from a pair of words: (1) bad vs. good, (2) unnecessary vs. necessary, and (3) worthless vs. valuable. I assume that individuals who tend to describe violence as bad, unnecessary, and worthless have a generally negative orientation toward violence, while individuals who tend to describe violence as good, necessary, and valuable have a generally positive orientation toward violence. The resulting scale ranges from 1 to 7 with lower numbers indicating a more negative orientation toward violence and higher numbers indicating a more positive orientation.[12]

Second, one might be concerned that individuals who endorse revenge also have a strong belief in the utility of violence for solving problems, and that it is this belief, rather than commitment to the principle that wrongs must be repaid, that is driving the relationship between vengefulness and support for punitive violence. To control for beliefs about the utility of violence, I use two items from the JVS. The first item (*Learn through violence*) asked respondents whether they agreed or disagreed

---

[12] Cronbach's alpha for this scale is 0.77. The mean is 2.24 with a standard deviation of 1.34.

that "some people learn only through violence." Responses ranged from
1 (disagree a great deal) to 4 (agree a great deal).[13] The second item
(*Violence prevents violence*) asked respondents whether they agreed or
disagreed that "often violence is needed to prevent violence." Responses
again ranged from 1 (disagree a great deal) to 4 (agree a great deal).[14]
These two items are not highly correlated (0.24) and yield a low scale
reliability coefficient (0.39) when combined into an additive scale. I therefore include them in the analysis separately, treating them as continuous variables so that their coefficients can be directly compared with
Vengefulness, which also ranges from 1 to 4.

Table 3.3 replicates the analyses reported in Table 3.2 with the addition of *Learn through violence*, *Violence prevents violence*, and *Positive
orientation* in all models. The first thing to note is that across the board,
Vengefulness continues to be a positive and significant predictor of both
support for the use of punitive violence and a general preference for harsh
criminal justice. Compared with the models without *Learn through violence*, *Violence prevents violence*, and *Positive orientation*, the coefficients
on *Vengefulness* in Table 3.2 are somewhat reduced in size, but even so,
the magnitude of these effects remains substantial, with the difference
between the least and most vengeful individuals ranging from 52.2 percentage points (for *Death penalty support*) to 13.0 percentage points (for
More police power).

Moreover, *Vengefulness* is the only variable in the model that has a
consistent effect across all seven scenarios. *Learn through violence* has no
significant effects, either positive or negative. The belief that some people
learn only through violence does not appear to influence individuals'
attitudes toward lethal police violence or the criminal justice system. In
contrast, *Violence prevents violence* is a positive and significant predictor
of approval of lethal police violence against hoodlums, rioters, and student protesters, as well as empathy with the policeman who punched a
driver. However, this variable has no significant effect on support for the
death penalty, nor does it predict either the desire to give the police more
power or the belief that the courts are too easy on criminals. Surprisingly,
the effect of *Positive orientation* is negative in all seven scenarios and is
significant for *Shoot to kill hoodlums*, *Shoot to kill rioters*, *Courts too
easy*, and *Empathy with policeman*. It seems that individuals who generally describe violence as good, necessary, and valuable are actually less

---

[13] The mean of this item is 2.48 with a standard deviation of 0.99.
[14] The mean of this item is 3.68 with a standard deviation of 0.97.

TABLE 3.3 *Models with additional controls for attitudes toward violence*

	Shoot hoodlums	Shoot rioters	Shoot students	Death penalty	Courts too easy	Police power	Empathy w/ police
Vengefulness	0.36***	0.44***	0.41**	1.08***	0.42**	0.27*	0.39***
	(0.10)	(0.11)	(0.13)	(0.13)	(0.13)	(0.13)	(0.11)
Learn through violence	-0.02	0.01	-0.10	0.05	0.14	0.14	-0.12
	(0.07)	(0.08)	(0.09)	(0.08)	(0.08)	(0.09)	(0.07)
Violence prevents violence	0.19*	0.37***	0.31**	0.09	0.15	0.19	0.16*
	(0.08)	(0.08)	(0.10)	(0.08)	(0.09)	(0.10)	(0.08)
Positive orientation	-0.19**	-0.21***	-0.13	-0.09	-0.13*	-0.22***	-0.05
	(0.06)	(0.06)	(0.08)	(0.06)	(0.06)	(0.06)	(0.06)
Age	0.01	0.01	0.01	-0.01	0.03***	0.01	-0.00
	(0.01)	(0.01)	(0.01)	(0.01)	(0.01)	(0.01)	(0.01)
Race	0.15	0.47*	0.23	0.21	0.84***	0.94***	0.35
	(0.21)	(0.24)	(0.25)	(0.21)	(0.22)	(0.20)	(0.21)
Education	-0.03	-0.02	-0.04	-0.03	-0.06*	-0.10***	-0.07*
	(0.03)	(0.03)	(0.03)	(0.03)	(0.03)	(0.03)	(0.03)
Neighborhood unsafe	-0.13	0.01	0.07	-0.20	-0.20	-0.41*	0.00
	(0.18)	(0.18)	(0.21)	(0.20)	(0.21)	(0.20)	(0.19)
Rural residence	0.29	0.20	0.34	0.47*	0.02	0.19	0.27
	(0.16)	(0.17)	(0.19)	(0.19)	(0.21)	(0.19)	(0.18)
Income	0.06	-0.04	-0.08	0.05	0.15**	-0.01	-0.04
	(0.04)	(0.04)	(0.05)	(0.04)	(0.05)	(0.05)	(0.05)

(*continued*)

TABLE 3.3 (continued)

	Shoot hoodlums	Shoot rioters	Shoot students	Death penalty	Courts too easy	Police power	Empathy w/ police
Southern	0.09	-0.06	0.08	0.14	0.29	0.32	0.23
	(0.17)	(0.18)	(0.21)	(0.20)	(0.20)	(0.19)	(0.19)
Conservative Protestant	0.27	0.28	0.41*	0.18	0.09	0.12	0.25
	(0.17)	(0.17)	(0.19)	(0.19)	(0.20)	(0.20)	(0.18)
Regular church attend.	0.10	0.02	0.18	-0.03	0.43*	0.24	0.02
	(0.15)	(0.16)	(0.18)	(0.16)	(0.18)	(0.17)	(0.16)
Veteran	0.50***	0.21	0.34	0.29	-0.03	0.16	-0.07
	(0.15)	(0.16)	(0.19)	(0.15)	(0.17)	(0.16)	(0.15)
Black social change	-0.29	-0.62*	-0.39	-0.95*	-0.08	0.11	0.00
	(0.24)	(0.25)	(0.28)	(0.38)	(0.34)	(0.32)	(0.29)
Trust police	0.02	0.11	0.43	0.61**	0.01	1.26***	-0.19
	(0.22)	(0.24)	(0.26)	(0.21)	(0.23)	(0.21)	(0.22)
Constant	-2.08***	-2.48***	-3.04***	-1.35	-1.91*	-0.91	0.80
	(0.59)	(0.63)	(0.74)	(0.72)	(0.75)	(0.69)	(0.67)
N	1,229	1,229	1,228	1,234	1,223	1,232	1,226

Note: All models are logistic regression models with standard errors in parentheses. Significance: * $p < 0.05$, ** $p < 0.01$, *** $p < 0.001$.

likely to approve of lethal police violence and to express a preference for a harsher criminal justice system. This is contrary to my initial expectation and represents something of a puzzle. That said, the main finding of this table is that the relationship between *Vengefulness* and support for punitive violence is not simply the product of a generally positive orientation toward violence or of beliefs about the efficacy of violence for solving social problems.

TESTING THE CROSS-CULTURAL VALIDITY OF THE CORE VALUE HYPOTHESIS

In the previous sections, I found strong support for the *core value hypothesis* using data from two surveys of attitudes toward the use of violence in the United States, one from 2010 and one from 1969. Should we expect these results to generalize across countries? According to my theory, countries should vary in terms of the vengefulness of their populations (i.e., the percentage of the population that endorses revenge as a general principle), while at the individual level, the effect of vengefulness on support for punitive violence should remain consistent. Testing this proposition is challenging because of the paucity of non-US surveys that include both a direct measure of vengefulness and questions about punitive violence. For instance, in Chapter 5, I document the range of cross-national variation in vengefulness using data from a Gallup International survey conducted in fifty-nine countries. This is the only multi-country survey I have been able to find that includes a reasonable measure of endorsement of revenge, but unfortunately, it does not include any questions about attitudes toward violence. Even so, it is possible to gain some analytical leverage on the cross-cultural validity of the *core value hypothesis* by exploiting long-standing cultural differences between regions within the United States itself.

From the earliest days of its history, the American South has been home to a distinct culture, which Nisbett and Cohen (1996) have termed a "culture of honor." Cultures of honor are found in many places around the world (Peristany 1966; Pitt-Rivers 1968; Black-Michaud 1975; Daly and Wilson 1988; Stewart 1994). They are defined as cultures in which men cultivate a reputation for toughness and display a willingness to respond immediately and forcefully to any threat to that reputation, including seemingly minor slights and insults. In such places, honor is defined not by virtuous conduct but by precedence or status. In other words, a man's honor is not his good character but his "strength and power to enforce his will on others" (Nisbett and Cohen 1996: 4). Honor is thus a zero-sum game. One can gain honor only at another's expense, and violence is the primary means by which honor is both won and lost.

Historians have argued that the culture of honor was imported into the South by Scots-Irish immigrants, who brought along with them the norms and traditions that had long governed life in the British borderlands. The culture of honor's long-term impact on life in the South has been well documented (Fischer 1989). In particular, the Southern culture of honor has manifested itself in chronically higher levels of interpersonal violence compared with the rest of the country (Cash 1941; Bruce 1979; Ayers 1984; Wyatt-Brown 1986; Fischer 1989; Nisbett and Cohen 1996). Even in the present day, the attitudes and behavior of Southerners remain distinctive, especially when it comes to aggression and violence (Cohen et al. 1996; Nisbett and Cohen 1996; Vandello and Cohen 2004; Hayes and Lee 2005).

Revenge is an important part of the culture of honor. A man who has been wronged or insulted must be prepared to seek revenge at all costs or else he will lose his honor. Moreover, in cultures of honor, this behavior is embedded in a system of norms and community moral standards that defines revenge as a righteous and legitimate response to wrongdoing. Consequently, members of the community will look favorably on acts of revenge even if the individuals involved are total strangers (Montell 1986). According to Vandello and Cohen (2004), the norms of the Southern culture of honor have become internalized as a set of core values that define when the use of violence is justified and that set Southerners apart from individuals who were born and raised outside the region. Thus, if we revisit the surveys that I analyzed in the previous sections, we should find that endorsement of revenge as a general principle is stronger among Southerners than among non-Southerners.

To test whether this is the case, I define the South as the eleven states of the former Confederacy (Alabama, Arkansas, Florida, Georgia, Louisiana, Mississippi, North Carolina, South Carolina, Texas, Tennessee, Virginia) plus Kentucky and Oklahoma. According to the sociologist John Shelton Reed (1972, 1982), this is the geographic region in which individuals generally think of themselves as culturally Southern and are therefore likely to have internalized the norms of the culture of honor. In the 1969 Justifying Violence Survey, I find that Southerners score significantly higher on the revenge scale than non-Southerners.[15] Similarly, in

---

[15] For this analysis, I define someone as a Southerner if he or she grew up (i.e., spent at least the first ten years of his or her life) in the South. I exclude non-whites because they are not

my original 2010 survey, I find that Southerners are significantly more likely to agree that "in order for justice to be served, violence must be repaid with violence."[16]

Thus, if we engage in a little revisionist history, we can imagine the South and the non-South as two separate countries, one of which has a population that is (on average) more vengeful than the other due to its distinct cultural heritage. From the perspective of my theory, it would be problematic if endorsement of revenge predicted support for punitive violence only in the South, or if it predicted support for some subset of my dependent variables in the South and a completely different subset outside the South. Either of these outcomes would suggest that not only does the prevalence of revenge vary across cultures, but that the process whereby it influences individuals' attitudes toward the use of punitive violence varies as well.

Table 3.4 reports the average marginal effect of *Vengefulness* for all thirteen dependent variables from both surveys, split between Southerners and non-Southerners. To produce these results, I divided the sample for each survey into Southerners and non-Southerners and then replicated the models from Tables 3.1 and 3.2 in each sample. For each dependent variable, the average marginal effect of *Vengefulness* tells us the percentage point change in the probability of support for punitive violence that is produced by a one-point increase in *Vengefulness* (recall that on both surveys, I measured *Vengefulness* on a four-point scale).

Overall, the results look very similar for Southerners and non-Southerners. With few exceptions, *Vengefulness* has a positive and statistically significant effect on support for punitive violence among both groups. In many cases, these effects are quite large. Take the *Torture* scenario from my 2010 survey as an example. Among both Southerners and non-Southerners, a one-point increase in *Vengefulness* increases the likelihood of supporting the use of torture for terrorism suspects by 11.4 percentage points. The main difference between Southerners and non-Southerners concerns corporal punishment. Among Southerners,

---

generally viewed as part of the Southern culture of honor and should not, therefore, have internalized its norms and values. The mean of the revenge scale for Southerners is 2.40, while the mean for non-Southerners is 2.32. This difference is statistically significant at $p = 0.046$.

[16] On this survey, I asked respondents whether or not they identified as Southern rather than relying on geographical location. Among those who said yes, the mean of my revenge measure is 2.70 compared with 2.35 among those who said they did not identify as Southern. This difference is statistically significant at $p = 0.0006$. Again, I limited this analysis to whites only.

TABLE 3.4 *Average marginal effects of vengefulness for*
Southerners and non-Southerners

	Southerners	Non-Southerners
Punch stranger	7.7**	12.4***
	(2.8, 12.6)	(6.6, 18.1)
Kill rapist	8.6**	13.3***
	(2.2, 14.9)	(9.9, 16.8)
Parental punishment	6.1	10.6***
	(-1.2, 13.4)	(7.0, 14.2)
School punishment	9.8**	3.3
	(3.6, 16.0)	(-0.4, 7.0)
Death penalty (2010)	8.0*	15.7***
	(1.5, 14.5)	(12.1, 19.4)
Torture	11.4***	11.4***
	(5.8, 17.1)	(8.0, 14.9)
Shoot to kill hoodlums	6.8*	8.4***
	(1.8, 13.5)	(4.1, 12.7)
Shoot to kill rioters	6.5*	10.0***
	(1.3, 13.0)	(5.9, 14.1)
Shoot to kill students	6.3*	6.1**
	(4.5, 12.1)	(2.6, 9.5)
Death penalty (1969)	18.2***	18.9***
	(12.4, 24.0)	(15.0, 22.9)
Courts too easy	7.5*	5.9**
	(1.7, 13.3)	(2.0, 9.8)
More police power	3.3	6.4**
	(-2.2, 8.9)	(2.2, 10.6)
Empathy with policeman	6.9*	8.6***
	(1.0, 12.8)	(4.1, 13.1)

Note: This table reports the average marginal effect of *Vengefulness*
with 95% confidence intervals in parentheses. Significance: * $p < 0.05$,
** $p < 0.01$, *** $p < 0.001$.

Vengefulness predicts support for *School punishment* but not for *Parental
punishment*, while the reverse is true among non-Southerners. For a
number of the other dependent variables, the marginal effect of *Vengefulness* appears to be somewhat smaller among Southerners, but none of
these differences is statistically significant. The main story of this table
is that in spite of their cultural differences, both Southerners and non-
Southerners appear to draw on their beliefs about revenge to evaluate
the use of punitive violence across a wide variety of contexts. A highly

vengeful person in the South seems to think about punitive violence in much the same way as a highly vengeful person outside the South.

This evidence lends support to my argument that revenge is a basic human value, which serves a similar function for the individuals who subscribe to it even in diverse cultural contexts. The key difference between the South and the non-South, and between more and less vengeful cultures in general, is not how their individual members think about revenge but how prevalent that value is in the population as a whole.

CONCLUSION

The purpose of this chapter was to provide evidence for my claim that revenge should be conceptualized as a core value. Core values are beliefs about desirable behavior or outcomes that transcend specific situations and are used as evaluative criteria for forming judgments and selecting actions. If revenge shares these properties, we should be able to observe its influence on individuals' attitudes and opinions across a wide variety of contexts, regardless of their personal involvement in the situation. Previous studies have linked revenge to support for capital punishment (Ellsworth and Ross 1983; Bohm 1992; Cotton 2000; Carlsmith et al. 2002) and torture (Carlsmith and Sood 2009), but these studies have not generally conceptualized revenge as a core value, nor have they shown that endorsement of revenge is a common thread that links these attitudes together.

I began by examining the relationship between endorsement of revenge and attitudes toward punitive violence in the contemporary United States using data from an original nationally representative survey conducted in 2010. I then supplemented this analysis with data from a unique historical survey, which probed Americans' attitudes toward lethal police violence and criminal justice in 1969, a time when the country was wracked by social unrest. In both surveys, I find strong support for the *core value hypothesis*: endorsement of revenge is a powerful predictor of whether or not an individual will approve of the use of punitive violence in a diverse set of scenarios. Moreover, I find that this relationship is robust to the inclusion of controls for respondents' general orientations toward violence and their beliefs about the utility of violence for solving social problems, indicating that the effect of vengefulness cannot be reduced to these other attitudes. Revenge is a distinct value with an independent effect on individuals' attitudes toward punitive violence. I also find that even in populations that differ in their average level of vengefulness, such as Southerners versus non-Southerners in the United States, individual differences in endorsement of revenge have a strong and consistent effect on support for punitive violence.

Taken together, these results paint a clear picture. Individuals who believe strongly that wrongs deserve to be repaid view the world in a fundamentally different way from those who reject that principle. In general, highly vengeful people see the use of punitive violence as good and right. It is giving wrongdoers their just deserts by repaying suffering with suffering. In a world populated only by these highly vengeful types, large majorities would support corporal punishment, vigilante killing, the death penalty, and torture of terrorism suspects. The view that courts are too easy on criminals and that the police should be given more power would be nearly unanimous. Approximately one out of every two people would support the regular use of deadly force by the police to quell social unrest caused by gangs and rioters, and approximately one in three would do so in the case of student protesters. In contrast, a world populated only by low vengefulness types would be a very different place. Support for corporal punishment, vigilante killing, the death penalty, and torture would all be minority viewpoints. The desire for stricter courts and more powerful police forces would be far less unanimous and support for deadly repression of unrest would be confined to the fringes. The acceptance or rejection of revenge fundamentally colors how individuals think about the right way to deal with transgressions.

It is particularly important to note that the impact of revenge is not limited to situations in which the individual has a personal stake. For those who endorse revenge as a general principle, the belief that wrongs deserve to be repaid provides a basis for evaluating the conduct of others, even in situations that do not touch their immediate sphere of concern. Furthermore, these individuals do not seem to make a stark distinction between the actions of private individuals and the actions of the state. Endorsement of revenge underlies support for the use of punitive violence in both the private and public spheres. For instance, vengefulness is a powerful predictor of support for the parent who killed his or her child's rapist and for state-sanctioned capital punishment for the crime of murder. While the vigilante parent has clearly committed a serious crime, from the perspective of someone who strongly endorses revenge, the parent's act is justified because it gives the rapist his or her just deserts, just as capital punishment carried out by the state gives murderers their just deserts. What matters is that wrongs get repaid, not the identity of the agent who delivers the punishment.

Violence is something that many people regularly observe and experience in the course of their everyday lives. It is a staple of both the news cycle and popular culture. It happens frequently in families, schools, and workplaces, as well as on the streets. And it is wielded regularly by governments as a tool of social control. Questions about when the use of violence is justified are complex and multifaceted, and it is therefore no surprise that ordinary people draw on their core values when confronted with such questions. This is precisely why core values play such an important role in human psychology, because they help individuals make straightforward judgments and form opinions about issues that would otherwise be forbiddingly complex. However, revenge has generally not been recognized as a core value, thanks in large part to the long tradition of "anti-vengeance" discourse in Western thought (Miller 1998). Setting normative judgments aside, the evidence presented in this chapter, along with the growing empirical literature on revenge that I reviewed in Chapter 2, makes a compelling case that revenge is an important core value that, for many people, anchors judgments about both public and private violence. Thus, with the cornerstone of my theory firmly established, I move on in Chapter 4 to elucidate the relationship between revenge and support for the use of military force.

4

Framing War as Punishment

Rhetoric, Revenge, and Public Support for War

Having established in Chapter 3 that revenge is a core value that individuals use to form judgments about a range of personal and political issues, I now turn to the relationship between revenge and support for the use of military force. In this chapter, I test the *framing hypothesis*, which predicts that vengeful individuals will be more supportive of the use of force than non-vengeful individuals when (and only when) that use of force is framed as a punishment. Crucially, this effect should not be limited to cases in which there has been a direct attack on the nation's homeland or citizens.

As I argued in Chapter 2, a punishment frame comprises three key elements: (1) a clear act of wrongdoing that causes undeserved harm to a victim or victims, (2) a clear perpetrator (an individual, group, or state) who is responsible for that act of wrongdoing, and (3) a proposed military response that will cause some harm or injury to the perpetrator. For individuals who endorse revenge, framing the use of military force in this way renders a complex international crisis into a simple and familiar story – a bad guy who deserves to be punished – and transforms the use of military force into a righteous act, regardless of the identity of the victim.

I use a three-pronged empirical strategy to evaluate this argument. First, I exploit differences in question wording on public opinion surveys to show that endorsement of revenge predicts support for the use of force only on those questions that include all three necessary elements of the punishment frame. Second, I present the results of a survey experiment in which I manipulate the framing of a hypothetical conflict scenario in order to show that the relationship between revenge and support for war is conditional on the use of a punishment frame even when all the other details of the scenario are held constant. Third, I compare two recent cases of conflict involving the United States: Iraq (2003), which was framed as a punishment, and Kosovo (1999), which was not. This comparison allows me to illustrate what punishment framing looks like in practice and to address concerns about the external validity of my experimental results. As my theory would lead us to expect, endorsement of revenge (as proxied by support for capital punishment) predicts support for the Iraq War but has no effect on support for intervention in Kosovo.

Alone, each strategy has its advantages and its limitations. Taken together, the evidence presented in this chapter provides strong support for the *framing hypothesis*. Vengefulness can be an important source of support for war in a variety of contexts, including those that do not involve a direct attack on the nation's homeland or citizens, but its salience in any particular case depends on how leaders frame the conflict in their political rhetoric.

PART 1: SUPPORT FOR THE USE OF FORCE IN PUNITIVE AND NON-PUNITIVE SCENARIOS

Questions about the use of military force that appear on public opinion surveys often vary in their framing due to differences in question wording (Zaller 1992; Borelli and Lockerbie 2008). Consequently, some questions will contain all three elements of the punishment frame, while others will not. In this section, I take advantage of this variation to conduct an initial test of the *framing hypothesis*.

What should we expect to see in the data if the *framing hypothesis* is correct? Framing the use of force as punishment works by increasing the salience of revenge, causing individuals who hold that value to rely on it when forming their opinions about the wisdom of going to war. Thus, on questions that use a punishment frame, endorsement of revenge should be a positive and significant predictor of support for the use of force. In contrast, on questions that do not use a punishment frame, revenge will not be a salient consideration, and there should therefore be no significant difference in the attitudes of vengeful and non-vengeful people.

To be clear, I am not looking for differences in the overall level of support for the use of force between questions that use a punishment frame and questions that do not. The questions that I analyze in this section ask about a diverse set of scenarios, and there are many differences between them that could have an impact on the overall level of support.[1] Rather, I am looking for differences in the salience of revenge as reflected by the predictive power of my measure of vengefulness. The bottom line is that if my hypothesis is correct, this measure should predict support for military action only on those questions that frame the use of force as a punishment the adversary deserves to suffer.

Data and Measures

Dependent Variables

For this analysis, I analyze nine questions about the use of military force from two nationally representative surveys conducted in 2010 and 2011.[2] These questions cover a range of different issues, from terrorism and nuclear weapons to humanitarian intervention and democracy promotion, and they represent various styles and formats in which such questions are frequently asked in national public opinion polls. I evaluated each question to determine whether the use of force was framed as a punishment. Three of the nine questions clearly established all three necessary elements: (1) a clear act of wrongdoing that causes undeserved harm to a victim or victims, (2) a clear perpetrator (an individual, group, or state) who is responsible for that act of wrongdoing, and (3) a proposed military response that will cause some harm or injury to the perpetrator. For the other six questions, at least one of those elements was ambiguous or absent. As a shorthand, I refer to the former as punitive scenarios and the latter as non-punitive scenarios.[3]

---

[1] The experiment that I present in Part 2 of this chapter allows me to evaluate the effect of punishment framing on aggregate support without concern about these confounding factors.

[2] The first survey was part of a Stanford University team module on the 2010 Cooperative Congressional Election Study (CCES). The CCES is a large multi-investigator study, which allows researchers to combine a module ($N = 1,000$) containing their own content with a set of common content questions that are available to all researchers participating in the study. The survey was administered online in two waves by YouGov using a matched random sample recruited from YouGov's proprietary opt-in panel. The first wave was in the field during October 2010, and the second wave was in the field during November 2010. The second survey was an independent study with 1,000 respondents administered online by YouGov in July 2011.

[3] The exact wording of all the scenarios can be found in the Appendix, along with a detailed explanation of how I classified them as punitive vs. non-punitive.

For example, consider the following two questions, both of which ask about a military response to terrorism. The first question informed respondents that "A foreign terrorist group has attacked the United States, killing dozens of people," and then asked them, "Would you favor or oppose using US military forces to attack the foreign terrorist group?" The wording of this question clearly establishes an act of wrongdoing (an attack on the United States), a clear perpetrator (a foreign terrorist group), and a military response that will cause the perpetrator to suffer (using US military forces to attack the foreign terrorist group). I therefore classify this as a punitive scenario. The second question asked respondents, "Would you favor or oppose the use of US military troops to destroy a terrorist camp?" This question establishes the existence of a terrorist camp, but it does not specify whether the camp is associated with a particular group, nor whether that group has been responsible for any attacks. It is therefore ambiguous with respect to the first two elements of the punishment frame, and I therefore classify it as a non-punitive scenario.

In addition to the above question about a terrorist attack on the United States (*Terrorist attack*), the other punitive scenarios include a question about the killing of Osama bin Laden (*Kill bin Laden*), and a question about whether the United States should use its nuclear weapons to retaliate against a foreign country that has launched a nuclear attack on its neighbor (*Nuclear strike*). Support for the use of force in these scenarios was measured on a five-point scale ranging from "approve/favor strongly" to "disapprove/oppose strongly." In the subsequent analyses, I treat these as ordinal variables. Overall, support was quite high in both the *Terrorist attack* and the *Kill bin Laden* scenarios, with over 80% of respondents saying they either somewhat or strongly approved, while 38% of respondents favored the use of force in the *Nuclear strike* scenario.

The six non-punitive questions concern the use of US troops for the following purposes: to ensure the supply of oil (*Oil supplies*), to destroy a terrorist camp (*Terrorist camp*), to intervene in a region where there is genocide or civil war (*Intervention*), to assist the spread of democracy (*Spread democracy*), to protect US allies under attack by foreign nations (*Protect allies*), and to help the United Nations uphold international law (*Uphold law*). These questions were asked in a yes or no format and I code them as dichotomous variables. The *Protect allies* scenario received the highest level of popular support at 71%, followed by the *Terrorist camp* scenario at 68%, the *Uphold law* scenario at 45%, the *Intervention* scenario at 33%, the *Oil supplies* scenario at 25%, and the *Spread democracy* scenario at 19%.

Measuring Revenge

To measure endorsement of revenge, I asked respondents whether they agreed or disagreed that "In order for justice to be served, violence must be repaid with violence." Response options ranged on a five-point scale from "agree strongly" to "disagree strongly." See Chapter 3 for more information about the distribution of responses to this question. In all statistical models reported later, I treat *Vengefulness* as a continuous variable ranging from 1 (least vengeful) to 5 (most vengeful).

Control Variables

I also include the following control variables that are known (or suspected) to be correlated with individual differences in vengefulness and that may also be related to attitudes toward the use of violence: *Gender* (a dummy variable for male), *Age* (in years), *Race* (a dummy variable for non-Hispanic white), *Education* (six levels ranging from no high school to a post-graduate degree), *Political ideology* (measured on a five-point scale ranging from extremely liberal to extremely conservative), and *Party identification* (measured on a five-point scale ranging from strong Democrat to strong Republican). See Chapter 2 for a more in-depth discussion of the selection of these variables.

Analysis and Results

To begin, I report the results of a simple bivariate analysis in which I divided respondents into a high vengefulness group (those who somewhat or strongly agreed that violence must be repaid with violence) and a low vengefulness group (everyone else). Consistent with the *framing hypothesis*, the high vengefulness group is substantially more likely to approve of military action in each of the punitive scenarios. In the *Kill bin Laden* scenario, about 76% of the low vengefulness group approved (either somewhat or strongly), while 92% of the high vengefulness group approved. In the *Terrorist attack* scenario, 79% of the low vengefulness group approved, and nearly 99% of the high vengefulness group approved. Finally, 35% of the low vengefulness group approved of the *Nuclear attack* scenario compared with 50% of the high vengefulness group. The differences between the two groups are statistically significant at conventional levels in all three punitive scenarios. In contrast, there are

TABLE 4.1 *Predictors of support for the use of military force in punitive scenarios*

	Kill bin Laden	Terrorist attack	Nuclear attack
Vengefulness	0.32**	0.45***	0.24**
	(0.10)	(0.10)	(0.08)
Gender	0.87***	1.23***	0.44*
	(0.24)	(0.22)	(0.20)
Age	0.02**	0.03***	0.01
	(0.01)	(0.01)	(0.01)
Race	0.32	0.03	−0.64**
	(0.29)	(0.25)	(0.22)
Education	−0.10	0.00	−0.04
	(0.08)	(0.08)	(0.07)
Party identification	0.04	0.07	0.08
	(0.07)	(0.07)	(0.06)
Political ideology	0.35*	0.50***	0.25
	(0.15)	(0.15)	(0.14)
N	454	441	452

Note: All models are ordered logistic regression models with standard errors in parentheses. Cut points not reported. Significance: * $p < 0.05$, ** $p < 0.01$, *** $p < 0.001$.

no statistically significant differences between the high and low vengefulness groups in four of the six non-punitive scenarios. The exceptions are the *Intervention* and *Uphold law* scenarios, where support for the use of force is actually lower in the high vengefulness group.

Next, I analyzed the relationship between endorsement of revenge and support for the use of force in the punitive scenarios using multivariate ordered logistic regression models. Table 4.1 shows that even when controls for key demographics and political attitudes are included, *Vengefulness* remains a robust positive predictor of support across all three punitive scenarios.[4] Its effect is largest in the *Terrorist attack* scenario, followed by the *Kill bin Laden* scenario and the *Nuclear attack* scenario. Among the control variables, being male has a consistent positive association with increased support for the use of force, as does increasing age and conservative ideology (although the latter two variables do not attain

[4] The punitive scenarios were asked of half the sample, hence the lower N for the models reported in Table 4.1.

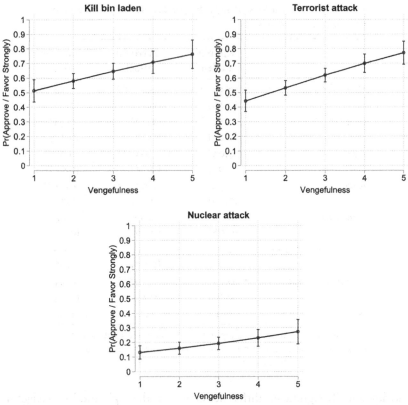

FIGURE 4.1 The effect of vengefulness on support for the use of military force in punitive scenarios. Note: Predicted probabilities were calculated based on the models reported in Table 4.1, with all other variables set at their means. Error bars represent 95% confidence intervals.

statistical significance in the *Nuclear attack* scenario). None of the other control variables has a significant effect with the exception of *Race* (non-Hispanic white), which is negatively associated with support for the *Nuclear attack* scenario.

How large is the effect of *Vengefulness* on support for the use of force in these scenarios? Figure 4.1 illustrates the magnitude of this effect by plotting the predicted probability that a respondent will express the highest level of support ("approve/favor strongly") as *Vengefulness* increases from its minimum of one to its maximum of five. In the *Terrorist attack* scenario, strong support for the use of force increases by 32.8 percentage points (from 44.4% to 77.2%) over the range of *Vengefulness*. This is similar to the difference in support between the most liberal and

TABLE 4.2 *Predictors of support for the use of military force in non-punitive scenarios*

	Oil supplies	Terrorist camp	Intervention	Spread democracy	Protect allies	Uphold law
Vengefulness	0.06	−0.01	−0.14	0.10	−0.09	−0.28**
	(0.11)	(0.13)	(0.09)	(0.12)	(0.13)	(0.10)
Gender	0.27	0.79**	0.12	−0.04	0.38	0.29
	(0.26)	(0.27)	(0.23)	(0.27)	(0.28)	(0.23)
Age	0.00	0.01	−0.01	−0.01	0.02**	−0.00
	(0.01)	(0.01)	(0.01)	(0.01)	(0.01)	(0.01)
Race	−0.19	−0.41	−0.37	−0.14	0.27	−0.43
	(0.35)	(0.33)	(0.32)	(0.37)	(0.33)	(0.32)
Education	−0.03	0.21*	0.26***	0.08	0.21*	0.13
	(0.09)	(0.11)	(0.07)	(0.10)	(0.10)	(0.08)
Party ID	0.17	0.19*	0.03	0.27**	0.14	−0.08
	(0.09)	(0.09)	(0.08)	(0.10)	(0.10)	(0.08)
Pol. ideology	0.29	0.33	−0.11	0.10	0.38*	−0.15
	(0.19)	(0.18)	(0.16)	(0.20)	(0.19)	(0.15)
Constant	−2.87***	−2.07*	−0.01	−2.97***	−2.60***	1.23
	(0.85)	(0.81)	(0.64)	(0.76)	(0.78)	(0.69)
N	778	778	778	778	778	778

Note: All models are logistic regression models with standard errors in parentheses. Significance: * $p < 0.05$, ** $p < 0.01$, *** $p < 0.001$.

the most conservative respondents (37.1% and 74.5%, respectively), and larger than the difference between men and women (68.6% and 45.5%, respectively). The gap between the least and most vengeful respondents is somewhat reduced in the *Kill bin Laden* scenario (24.9 percentage points) and the *Nuclear attack* scenario (14.1 percentage points), but even in the latter scenario, there remains a meaningful difference between the attitudes of those who believe strongly that violence deserves to be repaid with violence and those who reject that idea.

This is not the case in the six non-punitive scenarios. Table 4.2 reports the results of a series of multivariate logistic regression models, with support for the use of force in the *Oil supplies, Terrorist camp, Intervention, Spread democracy, Protect allies*, and *Uphold law* scenarios as the dependent variables. As the *framing hypothesis* predicts, there is no statistically significant relationship between endorsement of revenge and support for the use of force in five of the six scenarios. The exception is the *Uphold law* scenario, where *Vengefulness* has a significant negative effect on support for the use of force.

One possible explanation for this unexpected result is that when respondents think about what it means to "help the United Nations uphold international law," they are thinking of the peacekeeping and peace-building missions that have become increasingly common since the end of the Cold War (Diehl et al. 1998). If those missions are seen as alternatives to more decisive military actions that would visit pain and suffering on the wrongdoer, then we might expect highly vengeful individuals to oppose them. Alternatively, individuals who hold revenge as a core value may have a negative view of international law in general because they view it as a restriction on the punitive use of military force by the United States.

Overall, these results provide strong support for the *framing hypothesis*. When questions about the use of force are worded in a way that establishes all three necessary elements of the punishment frame, endorsement of revenge is a statistically significant and substantively important predictor of support for military action. This is precisely what we should observe if the use of a punishment frame causes revenge to become a salient consideration in the minds of individuals who hold it as a core value. Moreover, we can be confident that (1) this effect is not due to basic demographic, partisan, or ideological differences between vengeful and non-vengeful individuals, and (2) it holds in situations that involve an attack on the United States (as was the case in the *Kill bin Laden* and *Terrorist attack* scenarios) and also in situations in which the United States has not suffered any direct harm (as was the case in the *Nuclear attack* scenario). In contrast, when questions about the use of military force lack at least one of the necessary elements of the punishment frame, we do not find any meaningful differences between the least and most vengeful individuals, indicating that revenge is not a salient consideration in the absence of a punishment frame. Thus, it is not the case that vengeful individuals are simply more bloodthirsty or militaristic than non-vengeful individuals. Their endorsement of revenge translates into increased support for the use of military force only when revenge is made salient by contextual cues that frame the use of force as a punishment that the bad guy deserves to suffer.

That said, one potential concern with the empirical approach taken in this section is that the questions I examined vary not only in their framing but also in a variety of other ways. Is framing what is really doing the work of making revenge salient in some scenarios but not others? I address this question in the next section using experimental evidence.

PART 2: EXPERIMENTAL EVIDENCE

The main advantage of an experimental approach to testing the *framing hypothesis* is that it allows me to manipulate the framing of a scenario while holding all other information constant, thereby isolating the causal effect of framing on the salience of revenge. The experiment that I present in this section was designed to manipulate the first element of the punishment frame, the act of wrongdoing. It was fielded as part of a nationally representative survey in 2011.[5]

If my theory is correct that the use of a punishment frame causes individuals who hold revenge as a core value to rely on that value as a heuristic when forming their opinions about the use of force, then we should find that vengeful individuals are more supportive of military action only in the version of the scenario that has all three elements of the punishment frame in place.

Design of the Experiment

In this experiment, respondents were assigned to one of two treatment groups.[6] One group received the following question: "A foreign country has invaded one of its neighbors and taken over a piece of the neighbor's territory. Would you favor or oppose using US military forces to attack the invader?" I refer to this as the non-punitive invasion scenario because while the question identifies a clear perpetrator (the foreign country) and proposes a military action (an attack) that will cause harm to the perpetrator, it does not clearly establish the invasion as an act of wrongdoing. Instead, it leaves open the possibility that the foreign country was justified in invading its neighbor. For example, the invasion might have been a preemptive strike meant to counter an imminent attack, or it might have been a retaliatory response to some prior transgression committed by the neighbor. Without additional information about *why* the foreign country decided to invade its neighbor, the wording of the scenario leaves significant ambiguity around the first element of the punishment frame.

---

[5] The survey was administered online by YouGov using a matched random sample recruited from YouGov's proprietary opt-in panel.

[6] Respondents were not randomized into the different treatments when they entered the study. Instead, the survey was conducted in two waves. The first 500 respondents received one treatment, while the subsequent 500 received the other treatment. There are no significant differences in demographics or political attitudes between the two waves.

Consequently, it fails to establish the narrative of an evildoer who deserves to be punished, which is necessary to trigger a desire for revenge among those who believe that wrongs deserve to be repaid. Thus, I expect that in this treatment group, there will be no difference between the attitudes of vengeful and non-vengeful individuals, and endorsement of revenge will therefore not be a significant predictor of support for the use of force.

The second group received the same question with an additional piece of information clarifying that the invasion was not a provoked response: "A foreign country has invaded one of its neighbors and taken over a piece of the neighbor's territory. The neighbor was innocent and did not do anything to provoke the invasion. Would you favor or oppose using US military forces to attack the invader?" I refer to this as the punitive invasion scenario because it removes the uncertainty around the foreign country's motive for invading its neighbor. The invasion is now clearly an act of unprovoked aggression against an innocent victim and is therefore an unambiguous act of wrongdoing. The essential narrative elements are in place to make revenge salient to individuals' attitudes toward the use of force in this scenario, and I therefore expect that in this treatment group, endorsement of revenge will be a positive and significant predictor of support for the use of force.

Analysis and Results

Using the same measure of vengefulness as described in the previous section, Table 4.3 compares the effect of this variable on support for the use of force in the punitive and non-punitive invasion scenarios. Support for the use of force was measured on a five-point scale ranging from "oppose strongly" to "favor strongly." I treat this as an ordinal variable and employ ordered logistic regression models. As in the previous section, I include controls for *Gender* (a dummy variable for male), *Age* (in years), *Race* (a dummy variable for non-Hispanic white), *Education* (six levels ranging from no high school to a post-graduate degree), *Political ideology* (measured on a five-point scale ranging from extremely liberal to extremely conservative), and *Party identification* (measured on a five-point scale ranging from strong Democrat to strong Republican).

Consistent with my expectation, *Vengefulness* is a positive and significant predictor of support for the use of force in the punitive invasion scenario. Among the most vengeful individuals, the model predicts that a total of 50.4% will either somewhat or strongly support using US military

TABLE 4.3 *Invasion experiment*

	Punitive invasion scenario	Non-punitive invasion scenario
Vengefulness	0.19*	−0.05
	(0.09)	(0.08)
Gender	0.43*	0.47*
	(0.20)	(0.21)
Age	−0.00	−0.01
	(0.01)	(0.01)
Race	−0.14	−0.26
	(0.21)	(0.25)
Education	−0.07	−0.11
	(0.07)	(0.08)
Party identification	0.01	0.08
	(0.06)	(0.06)
Political ideology	0.26	0.14
	(0.14)	(0.13)
N	439	454

Note: All models are ordered logistic regression models with standard errors in parentheses. Cut points not reported. Significance: $* p < 0.05$, $** p < 0.01$, $*** p < 0.001$.

forces to attack the invading country, whereas among the least vengeful individuals, the model predicts that 32.7% will either somewhat or strongly support the use of force. In contrast, *Vengefulness* has no significant effect on support for the use of force in the non-punitive invasion scenario. Because the framing of that scenario did not clearly establish the invasion as an act of wrongdoing, revenge was not a salient consideration in the formation of individuals' attitudes toward the use of force, and there is therefore no statistically significant difference between the least and most vengeful individuals.

Due to its design, this experiment also provides an opportunity to test whether the use of a punishment frame produces a backlash among individuals who do not hold revenge as a core value. In other words, is the difference between vengeful and non-vengeful individuals that emerges in the punitive invasion scenario due to an increase in support for the use of force among the vengeful (as my theory predicts) or a decrease in support among the non-vengeful (a backlash effect), or both? To answer this question, I dichotomized the *Vengefulness* variable such that respondents who somewhat or strongly agreed that "In order for

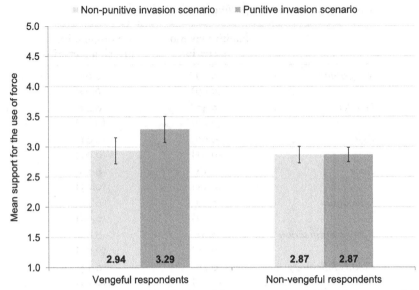

FIGURE 4.2 Mean support for the use of force among vengeful and non-vengeful respondents in the invasion experiment. Note: Error bars represent 95% confidence intervals. The different between the punitive and non-punitive invasion scenarios is statistically significant for vengeful respondents but not for non-vengeful respondents.

justice to be served, violence must be repaid with violence" are coded as vengeful and everyone else is coded as non-vengeful. Figure 4.2 depicts the mean support for the use of force (as measured on a five-point scale) among vengeful and non-vengeful respondents for both versions of the invasion scenario.

The results in Figure 4.2 clearly show that for the non-vengeful respondents, there is no difference in support for the use of force between the punitive and non-punitive invasion scenarios. Thus, there does not appear to be a backlash effect. The addition of information about the perpetrator's motive in the punitive invasion scenario does not have a negative effect on the attitudes of non-vengeful individuals. Instead, it is vengeful individuals who increase their support for the use of force in the punitive invasion scenario. They are the ones who hear the 'dog whistle' of the punishment frame and respond accordingly. This pattern is consistent with my theoretical argument that revenge will become a salient consideration only when the use of force is framed as a punishment, and that when this framing is used, its effect will be an increase in support for the use of force among those who most strongly endorse revenge as a core value.

Finally, because the design of the invasion experiment holds constant all the substantive features of the scenario except its framing, we can attribute any difference in the overall level of support between the two treatment groups to the use of a punishment frame and the attendant increase in support for using force among those who hold revenge as a core value. The overall level of support – i.e., the percentage of respondents who said they either somewhat or strongly favored the use of force – is nearly eight percentage points higher in the punitive invasion scenario than in the non-punitive invasion scenario (39.4% vs. 31.8%).[7] This increase illustrates the benefit that national leaders can achieve by employing a punishment frame in their rhetoric. By constructing a narrative that makes revenge salient, they can gain support for the use of force from the vengeful segment of their population without any backlash from the non-vengeful segment, thereby boosting the overall level of support for war.

Overall, the results of the invasion experiment provide further evidence that framing is indeed the key to forging a connection between endorsement of revenge and support for war. In the non-punitive invasion scenario, we saw that without all three elements of the punishment frame in place, vengeful individuals were no more enthusiastic about the use of force than non-vengeful individuals. In the punitive invasion scenario, the addition of information about the neighbor's innocence made it clear that the invasion was an act of wrongdoing and not a justified response to some kind of provocation. For vengeful individuals, this narrative resonated strongly with their core belief that wrongs deserve to be repaid, resulting in a significantly higher level of support for military action, even though all the other details of the scenario were held constant. Thus, individual differences in endorsement of revenge become consequential when (and only when) the use of force is framed as a punishment.

The results presented in this section also support my contention that revenge can be a source of support for war even when the adversary has not directly threatened or attacked the nation's homeland or citizens. In both versions of the invasion scenario, the United States is cast in the role of third-party enforcer, intervening in a conflict between two other states. It is the neighbor state that is the victim in this scenario, not the United States, and yet we still observe that when the use of force is framed as a punishment, Americans who endorse revenge express views that are

---

[7] This difference is statistically significant at $p = 0.02$.

substantially more hawkish than those of their fellow non-vengeful citizens. This is consistent with my conceptualization of revenge as a core value that shapes individuals' attitudes toward punishing evildoers regardless of the identity of the victim.

Finally, the design of this experiment should not be taken as an accurate representation of how national leaders actually frame the use of force as punishment in their political communication. The invasion scenario was constructed to provide a precise test of the minimal information necessary to make revenge salient, and it therefore employs largely neutral language rather than the dramatic and evocative rhetoric that national leaders often use when demonizing an adversary. In the next section I examine two recent cases of conflict involving the United States: the 2003 Iraq War and the 1999 NATO intervention in Kosovo. These cases serve to illustrate what both the presence (Iraq) and absence (Kosovo) of a punishment frame look like in practice, and they lend external validity to the results reported in this section and the previous section, which have dealt primarily with hypothetical scenarios. By turning to real-world cases, I show that even amid the noise of an ongoing international crisis – when citizens are bombarded by information from a variety of sources – endorsement of revenge still emerges as a powerful predictor of support for the use of military force, provided that it is framed as a punishment.

PART 3: PRESIDENTIAL RHETORIC AND THE FRAMING OF WAR IN IRAQ AND KOSOVO

In this section, I present a final test of the *framing hypothesis* by comparing the effect of vengefulness on support for two real world cases of conflict. The first case is the 2003 Iraq War, which I argue was consistently framed as a punishment in the rhetoric of President George W. Bush. The second case is the 1999 NATO intervention in Kosovo, which I argue was not framed as a punishment primarily because President Bill Clinton repeatedly attributed responsibility for the growing humanitarian crisis in Kosovo to both sides of the conflict, thereby failing to establish a clear perpetrator. This analysis serves to demonstrate the external validity of my previous findings and provides a detailed illustration of how a punishment frame is constructed, and what it looks like when that frame is absent.

Because I rely on contemporary survey data for each conflict, I cannot use my own measure of endorsement of revenge. Instead, following Liberman (2006), I use support for the death penalty as a proxy for vengefulness.

This strategy is supported by the large body of literature demonstrating that death penalty support is driven primarily by the desire for revenge (Ellsworth and Ross 1983; Bohm 1992; Cotton 2000; Carlsmith et al. 2002; McKee and Feather 2008). The choice of cases was determined by the availability of public opinion surveys that include both a death penalty item and questions about the use of military force. Although this is not the ideal case selection method, surveys that include both types of questions are exceedingly rare, and Iraq and Kosovo are the only major post–Cold War uses of force for which there are sufficient data to conduct the analysis.

My theory does not predict that aggregate support for the use of force will necessarily be higher for Iraq than for Kosovo. Because these are real-world cases and not tightly controlled experimental scenarios, there are many differences between the two conflicts that could influence the aggregate level of support (Eichenberg 2005). What my theory does predict is that the framing of the Iraq War will make revenge a salient consideration, and support for the use of force will therefore be higher among people who hold revenge as a core value. Or, to put it another way, endorsement of revenge (as proxied by death penalty support) should be a significant predictor of support for the use of force in the case of Iraq but not in the case of Kosovo.

Framing War with Iraq (2003)

Background

The 2003 Iraq War was the culmination of a series of clashes between the United States and Iraq that began with the 1991 Gulf War, in which a US-led coalition reversed Iraq's invasion and occupation of neighboring Kuwait. In order to remain in power after the Gulf War, President Saddam Hussein agreed to destroy Iraq's existing weapons of mass destruction and to allow UN inspectors to monitor the disarmament process. However, the inspectors' efforts were consistently thwarted by the regime, and in 1998, Saddam ejected them from Iraq. The United States and Britain retaliated with four days of intensive air strikes, focused on targets that military planners believed would damage Iraq's stockpiles of weapons.

Iraq next rose to prominence on the US foreign policy agenda in January 2002, when President George W. Bush identified it as one of the three members of the "axis of evil" in his State of the Union Address, declaring that the United States "will not permit the world's most dangerous regimes to threaten us with the world's most destructive weapons." However, it was not until September of that year that Bush announced to the world that Iraq would be the next target in America's War on Terror. That announcement came in the form of a speech to the UN General Assembly in which he called on the UN to enforce its demands for disarmament or the United States would take matters into its own hands. Less than a month later, Congress authorized the president to use military force against Iraq.

In the shadow of this threat, the UN passed Resolution 1441, which imposed a tough new regime of weapons inspections on Iraq, and inspectors returned to the country on November 18, 2002. Unsatisfied with Iraq's limited cooperation with the inspectors, the Bush administration conducted a concerted campaign for a second UN resolution, this time authorizing the use of military force. At the same time, in his 2003 State of the Union Address, Bush declared that the United States was ready to take military action with or without UN approval. Failing to gain the requisite votes in the Security Council, Bush delivered a final ultimatum to Saddam on March 17, 2003, giving him forty-eight hours to leave the country. He refused to comply, and on March 19, Bush announced to the American people that the United States was once again at war with Iraq.

The Rhetoric

To analyze how President Bush framed the conflict with Iraq, I collected all of the public statements in which he made more than a passing mention of Iraq in the period from September 12, 2002 (the date of his address to the UN General Assembly), to March 19, 2003 (the initiation of hostilities with Iraq). These statements include major national addresses, speeches or remarks, interviews, press conferences, and off-the-cuff exchanges with reporters. Altogether, this collection includes 124 separate documents, which are available online from the American Presidency Project at the University of California, Santa Barbara. I assigned each document a unique code, which I use to refer to them below. A full list of these documents is available in the Appendix.

Based on this corpus, I assessed the degree to which Bush's rhetoric established the three necessary elements of a punishment frame: (1) a clear act of wrongdoing, (2) a clear perpetrator, and (3) a proposed military action that will cause some harm to the perpetrator. To make these assessments, I looked for information relevant to each element of the punishment frame that consistently appeared in the president's statements on Iraq across all the different forums in which such statements are typically made. For instance, I would not consider a single mention of

Iraq's prior invasion of Kuwait to be sufficient to establish the first element of the punishment frame, even though it constitutes an act of wrongdoing. Instead, I endeavored to identify those pieces of information that formed part of a coherent and recurrent story line in the president's rhetoric. Thus, while I quote from specific speeches for the purpose of illustration, my conclusions are based on an evaluation of the general patterns and consistencies in the entire corpus of Bush's statements on Iraq.

I take this approach for two important reasons. First, by definition, a frame is "a central organizing idea or story line that provides meaning to an unfolding strip of events" (Gamson and Modigliani 1994: 376). When we are looking at a single survey question or a simple survey experiment (such as the invasion experiment described in the previous section), a single piece of information can alter that central organizing idea or story line because people have very little information available to them. However, when we are looking at an ongoing international crisis, the volume of information is much greater. In this case, the 124 separate statements that I examined totaled more than 27,000 words over the course of more than six months on the subject of Iraq. In this context, a single, isolated piece of information is unlikely to be sufficient to shape the central organizing idea or story line of the president's rhetoric. Second, most people will not be exposed to every single statement that the president makes about an unfolding crisis. The statements themselves will get varying amounts of media coverage, and individuals themselves vary in the amount of media they consume and the sources they prefer. Therefore, elements of the president's rhetoric that are regularly repeated are more likely to reach the ears of average citizens and to influence their understanding of the situation.

Is There a Clear Act of Wrongdoing?

From the very beginning, President Bush's rhetoric emphasized Iraq's long history of crimes against its own people, its neighbors, and the international community. The president's speech to the UN General Assembly on September 12, 2002, introduced many of the charges that he would return to regularly in his public statements as the confrontation with Iraq escalated. These included Iraq's invasion of Kuwait, its record of domestic human rights violations and repression, its support for terrorist organizations targeting Israel and the West, its failed assassination attempt on former President George H. W. Bush, and its use of chemical weapons against Kurdish villages in Iraq and against Iran during the Iran–Iraq War.

Indeed, throughout the pre-war period, Bush hammered home this litany of horrors, often providing extremely graphic detail. For example, in one speech he described reports from Iraqi refugees, who "tell us how forced confessions are obtained, by torturing children while their parents are made to watch. International human rights groups have cataloged other methods used in the torture chambers of Iraq: electric shock, burning with hot irons, dripping acid on the skin, mutilation with electric drills, cutting out tongues, and rape" (B012803). In another speech he describes the effects of a chemical weapons attack on the Iraqi village of Halabja: "Whole families died while trying to flee clouds of nerve and mustard agents descending from the sky. Many who managed to survive still suffer from cancer, blindness, respiratory diseases, miscarriages, and severe birth defects among their children" (B031503). The consistency and frequency with which these and other atrocities appear in the president's rhetoric make it clear that Iraq has long been the locus of not one, but many terrible acts of wrongdoing committed against a variety of victims, both domestic and international.

Is There a Clear Perpetrator?

President Bush's statements on Iraq are marked by an intense focus on Saddam Hussein's personal responsibility for Iraq's record of atrocities. Bush frequently referred to the Iraqi leader by name (and often by first name alone), labeling him "a homicidal dictator" and "a coldblooded killer" and attributing many of the worst horrors to his personal agency (B091402, B100402). In Bush's narrative, Saddam is a man consumed by hatred, obsessed with following in the footsteps of Stalin, who orders his own people to be poisoned and his political opponents to be decapitated with their heads displayed outside their homes (B091902, B102020a). His evil is so inveterate that he has "used murder as a tool of terror and control" not only within his own cabinet and army but also within his own family (B102020a). Indeed, the rhetoric of the Iraq War is unrelenting in its depiction of Saddam as the incarnation of evil. "If this is not evil," Bush said in his 2003 State of the Union Address, "then evil has no meaning" (B102803).

Bush's indictment of Saddam also took on a second, and subtler, incarnation. In his statements, Bush consistently linked Saddam to al Qaeda, describing him as "a man who loves to link up with al Qaida [*sic*]," asserting that "the regime has longstanding and continuing ties to terrorist organizations, and there are al Qaida [*sic*] terrorists inside Iraq," and concluding that "you can't distinguish between al Qaida [*sic*] and

Saddam when you talk about the war on terror" (B092502a, B092502a). It is true that Bush never directly said that Saddam played a role in the events of 9/11; however, the way his speeches switched seamlessly from discussing Iraq to discussing "the enemy" that attacked the United States on 9/11 left the door wide open for this interpretation. According to Gershkoff and Kushner (2005), this strategy was quite successful in forging a link between Saddam and the 9/11 attacks in the minds of many Americans, thereby adding the deaths of 2,977 people, many of them American citizens, to the long list of crimes for which Saddam was personally responsible.

Will the Proposed Military Action Cause Harm to the Perpetrator?

Throughout the pre-war period, President Bush's statements made it abundantly clear that the aim of going to war with Iraq would be regime change and that when the time came to knock Saddam Hussein off his pedestal, "the full force and fury of the United States" would be unleashed (B100802). By explicitly stating regime change as the goal, Bush's rhetoric left no doubt that Saddam would personally pay the price for his crimes by losing his hold on power.

Overall, this examination of President Bush's rhetoric leads me to conclude that the use of force against Iraq was clearly and consistently framed as a punishment. All three essential elements of the punishment frame were established early on in the pre-war period and were reiterated regularly over the following months. Therefore, endorsement of revenge should be a positive and significant predictor of support for the war in Iraq.

Data and Measures

To test this prediction, I use data from two nationally representative public opinion surveys conducted during the pre-war period. Both surveys were conducted by Time Magazine/CNN/Harris. The first was conducted on October 23–24, 2002.[8] In the remainder of this section, I will refer to this survey as the Time October survey. The second was conducted on January 15–16, 2003, and I will therefore refer to it as the Time January survey.[9] Each survey includes several questions about the use of military

---

[8] National adult sample (N = 1,007). Data provided by the Roper Center for Public Opinion Research.

[9] National adult sample with an oversample of women 18–39 years old (N = 1,111). Data provided by the Roper Center for Public Opinion Research.

force against Iraq. I report the full text of each question below, along with the variable names that I will use to reference them in the subsequent analyses. Response options for each question are in parentheses.

Questions about the use of force against Iraq from the Time October survey:

- *Ground troops 1*: Do you think the US should or should not use military action involving ground troops to attempt to remove Saddam Hussein from power in Iraq? (Should / Should not)
- *Remove Saddam*: Which do you think should be a more important goal for the US, removing Saddam Hussein from power or eliminating Saddam Hussein's ability to produce weapons of mass destruction whether he is removed from power or not? (Removing Saddam Hussein from power / Eliminating Saddam Hussein's ability to produce WMDs)

Questions about the use of force against Iraq from the Time January survey:

- *Ground troops 2*: Do you think the US should or should not use military action involving ground troops to attempt to remove Saddam Hussein from power in Iraq? (Should / Should not)
- *Morally justified*: Regardless of whether you think the US should or should not use ground troops to remove Saddam Hussein from power, do you think the US would be morally justified or morally unjustified if it sends troops into Iraq to remove Saddam Hussein from power? (Morally justified / Morally unjustified)
- *Act now*: If you could choose, how long would you wait until the US took action against Iraq? (End of January / March / Sometime during the summer / Sometime during the winter / Longer than that / Never)
- *Right pace*: Do you think President Bush is moving too quickly toward a war with Iraq, or don't you think so? (Yes, too quickly / No, don't think so)

I coded both questions about ground troops (*Ground troops 1* and *Ground troops 2*) as dichotomous variables equal to one if the respondent answered that the United States should use ground troops to remove Saddam Hussein from power. I coded *Remove Saddam* as a dichotomous variable equal to one if the respondent said removing Saddam from power should be a more important goal than eliminating his WMD capabilities. *Morally justified* is also coded as a dichotomous variable equal to one if the respondent said sending troops to remove Saddam from power

TABLE 4.4 *Support for the use of military force in Iraq (2003)*

Question	Support (%)
Time October survey	
Ground troops 1	53.2
Remove Saddam	32.3
Time January survey	
Ground troops 2	58.2
Morally justified	64.0
Act now	31.0
Right pace	53.9

would be morally justified. I coded *Act now* as a dichotomous variable equal to one if the respondent said that he or she would choose to take military action at the end of January, and I coded *Right pace* as another dichotomous variable equal to one if the respondent said that Bush was not moving too quickly toward a war with Iraq. Thus, each of these six variables indicates some dimension of support for military action against Iraq. Table 4.4 reports the percentage of people who indicated support for each item. There is significant variation in support across the items, ranging from 31% support for taking action immediately to 64% support for the idea that removing Saddam Hussein from power would be morally justified.

As discussed previously, I use support for the death penalty as a proxy for endorsement of revenge. The Time October survey included a question about the death penalty that specifically referenced the then recent Beltway sniper attacks, a shooting spree carried out by two men, that killed ten people over the course of three weeks in Maryland, Virginia, and Washington, DC. The question asked: "As you know, there are two people who are suspects in the sniper attacks – one is an adult; the other is 17 years old. If the adult is found guilty of murder, do you think he should be sentenced to death or get life in prison without parole?" Based on this question, I coded *Death penalty support* as a dichotomous variable equal to one if the respondent said he or she favored the death penalty over life in prison. The Time January survey asked a standard question about the death penalty: "Do you favor or oppose the death penalty for individuals convicted of serious crimes, such as murder?" Based on this question, I coded *Death penalty support* as a dichotomous variable equal to one if the respondent said he or she favored the death penalty in general.

The analyses presented below also include the following control variables: *Gender* (a dummy variable for male), *Age* (seven levels ranging from 18–24 to 65 or older), *Race* (a dummy variable for non-Hispanic white), *Education* (six levels ranging from eighth grade or less to postgraduate study), *Political ideology* (measured on a five-point scale ranging from extremely liberal to extremely conservative), *Party identification* (measured on a five-point scale ranging from strong Democrat to strong Republican), the president's job approval (*Bush job approval*, a dummy variable equal to one if the respondent approved of the way President Bush was handling his job as president), concerns about terrorism (*Terror fear*, a dummy variable equal to one if said the United States was very likely to suffer an act of terrorism within the next year), and perceptions of success in Afghanistan (*Afghanistan success*, a dummy variable equal to one if the respondent said US military action in Afghanistan was successful).[10]

Why control for these particular variables? First, recent surveys show that gender, race, party identification, and ideology are all major correlates of Americans' attitudes toward capital punishment. Support for the death penalty tends to be significantly higher among men, non-Hispanic whites, Republicans, and those who identify themselves as conservative. There are also smaller differences by education and age, with the older and less educated more likely to favor capital punishment.[11] At the same time, these variables are also associated with hawkishness in matters of foreign policy, at least in certain contexts (Holsti 1996; Nincic and Nincic 2002; Burris 2008; Brooks and Valentino 2011). It is therefore important to control for them in order to ensure that if there is a significant relationship between *Death penalty support* and attitudes toward the use of force, it is not merely a reflection of the basic demographic and political differences between supporters and opponents of the death penalty.

Second, I control for the president's job approval to guard against the possibility that individuals' willingness to endorse capital punishment and the use of military force abroad are both influenced by their feelings about the current occupant of the White House. It is possible that

[10] Due to variation in the contents of the two surveys, *Terror fear* and *Afghanistan success* are available only on the Time January Survey.

[11] Joseph Carroll, "Who Supports the Death Penalty?," *Death Penalty Information Center*, November 16, 2004, https://deathpenaltyinfo.org/gallup-poll-who-supports-death-penalty; Baxter Oliphant, "Support for Death Penalty Lowest in More than Four Decades," *Pew Research Center*, September 29, 2016, www.pewresearch.org/fact-tank/2016/09/29/support-for-death-penalty-lowest-in-more-than-four-decades/.

individuals who generally approve of the president's performance are simply more likely to express support for any policy they associate with him or her. As commander in chief of the armed forces, the president will obviously be associated with any proposed use of military force. The connection is less straightforward when it comes to capital punishment, which is carried out at both the state and federal levels and is not under the direct control of the president. Nevertheless, given that every sitting president in the post-Furman era[12] (1972 to present) has publicly endorsed the death penalty, it is possible that at least some people associate the incumbent president with a pro–death penalty stance. If this is indeed the case, then failing to control for the president's job approval could produce a spurious relationship between *Death penalty support* and attitudes toward the use of force.

Finally, it is important to take into account the broader foreign policy context of the Iraq case, namely the War on Terror. The concern here is that support for the wider War on Terror could be driving both hawkish attitudes toward Iraq, which the Bush administration clearly framed as the next front in the war between "freedom and fear," and increased endorsement of capital punishment at home. As with many aspects of domestic policy, the death penalty became linked to terrorism in the aftermath of the 9/11 attacks, specifically as a punishment for terrorists who might be captured or extradited and tried in American courts. Unsurprisingly, large majorities of Americans favored the death penalty when asked what the appropriate penalty would be if high-profile terrorists like Osama bin Laden and Khalid Sheikh Mohammed were ever tried and found guilty.[13] Consequently, any opposition to capital punishment could be portrayed as "soft on terrorism," as evidenced by the 2004 presidential election in which the Democratic nominee John Kerry felt it

---

[12] The post-Furman era began in 1972 when a Supreme Court decision in the case of *Furman v. Georgia* placed a moratorium on the use of capital punishment in the United States due to the court's finding that the death penalty, as currently practiced, violated the Constitution's protections against cruel and unusual punishment. In response, many states enacted reformed death penalty statutes, and the moratorium was lifted just four years later in the *Gregg v. Georgia* decision.

[13] Jeffrey M. Jones, "Seven in 10 Americans Would Favor Death Sentence for Bin Laden," *Gallup*, December 19, 2001, www.gallup.com/poll/5128/Seven-Americans-Would-Favor-Death-Sentence-bin-Laden.aspx; Lydia Saad, "Americans at Odds with Recent Terror Trial Decisions," *Gallup*, November 27, 2009, www.gallup.com/poll/124493/Americans-Odds-Recent-Terror-Trial-Decisions.aspx.

necessary to clarify that his long-time opposition to capital punishment did not apply to terrorists (even though he had expressed the opposite view before 9/11).

This raises the possibility that at least for some Americans, the 9/11 attacks and their political aftermath reframed capital punishment as a tool for fighting terrorism, causing those individuals who strongly supported the War on Terror to express a greater enthusiasm for the death penalty, not only for specific individual terrorists, but also as a general matter. As described above, I measure support for the War on Terror in two ways – fear of an imminent terrorist attack and perceptions of success in Afghanistan – based on the questions available in the surveys I selected for analysis. Respectively, these variables serve as indicators of two important facets of support for the War on Terror: the degree to which terrorism is perceived as a serious threat to the United States (therefore necessitating a War on Terror in the first place), and the degree to which the Bush administration's strategy is perceived as successful and therefore worth continuing. Controlling for these variables helps to ensure that any relationship that emerges between death penalty attitudes and support for military action in Iraq is not simply the product of factors unique to the post-9/11 context.

Analysis and Results

Table 4.5 presents the results of a series of multivariate logistic regression models for both the Time October and Time January survey questions. Consistent with my expectation, *Death penalty support* is a positive and statistically significant predictor for all six dependent variables. Death penalty supporters are more likely to say they support the use of ground troops to remove Saddam Hussein from power and that doing so is a more important goal than eliminating his ability to produce weapons of mass destruction. They are more likely to say that removing Saddam from power would be morally just, that the United States should begin its military operations as soon as possible, and that Bush is not moving too quickly toward war with Iraq.

To illustrate these effects, Figure 4.3 shows the predicted level of support among death penalty proponents versus death penalty opponents for each of the six questions (based on the models reported in Table 4.5). We see the biggest gap between these two groups on the *Remove Saddam* question from the Time October survey. Here, the model predicts that preference for removing Saddam from power over eliminating weapons of mass destruction is 19.4 percentage points higher among death penalty

TABLE 4.5 *Predictors of support for the use of military force in Iraq (2003)*

	Ground troops 1	Remove Saddam	Ground troops 2	Morally justified	Act now	Right pace
Death pen. support	0.92***	1.02***	0.62***	0.49**	0.59**	0.60**
	(0.25)	(0.26)	(0.18)	(0.18)	(0.21)	(0.19)
Gender	0.28	0.08	0.39*	0.02	0.02	0.18
	(0.23)	(0.22)	(0.17)	(0.18)	(0.18)	(0.18)
Age	−0.12*	0.02	−0.12*	0.00	−0.06	−0.11*
	(0.06)	(0.06)	(0.05)	(0.05)	(0.05)	(0.05)
Race	−0.03	−0.12	0.19	0.06	−0.09	0.23
	(0.28)	(0.29)	(0.21)	(0.22)	(0.23)	(0.23)
Education	−0.15	−0.04	−0.25***	−0.26***	−0.20**	−0.16*
	(0.10)	(0.09)	(0.07)	(0.07)	(0.07)	(0.07)
Party ID	0.17*	−0.05	0.01	0.10	0.18**	0.09
	(0.07)	(0.07)	(0.06)	(0.06)	(0.06)	(0.06)
Political ideology	0.04	0.14	0.26**	0.17	−0.09	0.12
	(0.13)	(0.14)	(0.10)	(0.10)	(0.09)	(0.10)
Bush job approval	1.16***	0.99***	1.14***	1.26***	0.34	1.81***
	(0.25)	(0.28)	(0.19)	(0.21)	(0.21)	(0.19)
Terror fear	0.24	0.15				
	(0.23)	(0.23)				
Afghan. success	0.78**	0.29				
	(0.25)	(0.25)				
Constant	−1.02	−2.46***	−0.10	−0.02	−0.55	−0.85
	(0.71)	(0.62)	(0.52)	(0.541)	(0.50)	(0.50)
N	531	531	886	886	773	886

Note: All models are logistic regression models with standard errors in parentheses.
Significance: * $p < 0.05$, ** $p < 0.01$, *** $p < 0.001$.

supporters than death penalty opponents. The difference between death penalty supporters and opponents is smallest, at 9.5 percentage points, for the *Morally justified* question from the Time January survey.[14] Across all six questions, the average difference between death penalty supporters and death penalty opponents is 13.9 percentage points.

These results provide important evidence in support of the *framing hypothesis*. In his pre-war rhetoric, President Bush consistently emphasized information that framed the use of force against Iraq as a punishment that Saddam Hussein deserved to suffer by virtue of his long history

---

[14] For comparison, the difference between those who approve of the job Bush is doing as president and those who do not ranges from 7.1 percentage points (on the *Act now* question from the Time January survey) to 39.8 percentage points (on the *Right pace* question from the Time January survey).

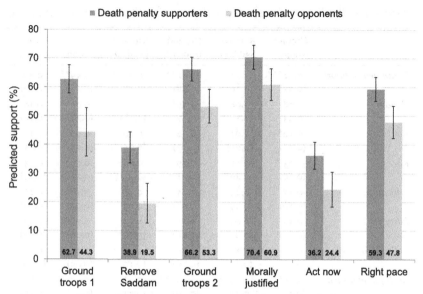

FIGURE 4.3 Comparing support for the use of military force in Iraq among death penalty supporters and opponents. Note: Predicted support was calculated based on the models reported in Table 4.5, with all other variables set at their means. Error bars represent 95% confidence intervals.

of criminality. According to my theory, this narrative should have resonated strongly with vengeful individuals, thereby increasing the salience of revenge and making their opinions about the use of force distinctly more hawkish. The data show this pattern very clearly: across two different surveys and six different measures of support for military action, vengeful individuals (as proxied by death penalty support) expressed a significantly greater willingness to see the United States go to war with Iraq for the second time in a generation.

In the next section, I compare these results with a similar analysis of the 1999 NATO intervention in Kosovo. As I will show, President Bill Clinton did not clearly frame the use of force in Kosovo as a punishment. It is critical to examine a negative case because the *framing hypothesis* predicts that vengeful individuals will be more supportive of the use of force than non-vengeful individuals when (and only when) that use of force is framed as a punishment. If we find a significant relationship between vengefulness and support for military action in the absence of a punishment frame, we will need to reconsider the role of framing in making revenge salient to individuals' attitudes toward the use of military force.

Framing Intervention in Kosovo (1999)

Background

The crisis that precipitated NATO's intervention in Kosovo in 1999 had its origins a decade earlier when Serbia was one of the six republics that made up the Socialist Federal Republic of Yugoslavia. Kosovo was a province of Serbia that had enjoyed considerable autonomy since 1974. In 1989, Serbian President Slobodan Milošević instituted changes to the Serbian constitution that stripped Kosovo of much of its autonomy. When the collapse of the Soviet Union triggered the breakup of Yugoslavia, ethnic Albanians in Kosovo declared their independence alongside the Republics of Slovenia, Croatia, and Bosnia. However, Kosovo's declaration of independence received little recognition from the international community, which soon became preoccupied with the conflict in neighboring Bosnia (1992–95). In 1996, the Kosovo Liberation Army was formed and began carrying out attacks against the Serb authorities in Kosovo, to which Serbia responded with increasingly harsh repression.

On March 31, 1998, the UN Security Council passed Resolution 1160, which condemned the growing violence in Kosovo and imposed an arms embargo on Serbia and Montenegro, then known as the Federal Republic of Yugoslavia. US diplomats attempted to foster a dialogue between Milošević and Kosovo's president, Ibrahim Rugova, but this effort proved unsuccessful. Throughout the summer, attacks by Serbian forces intensified, driving thousands of refugees into the hills where they faced serious danger from the approaching winter weather. In response to this approaching nascent humanitarian crisis, the Security Council passed Resolution 1199 on September 23, demanding a cease-fire and the immediate withdrawal of Serbian forces. It also called for "additional measures" if Serbia did not comply, thereby broaching the possibility of a military response. On October 12, NATO approved an "activation order," which authorized preparations for a limited bombing campaign. The next day, Milošević agreed to a cease-fire and troop withdrawals, followed by elections and greater autonomy for Kosovo. By the end of October, Serbia had withdrawn most of its forces and the refugees had come down safely from the hills.

However, the peace achieved by the "October Agreement" was short lived. Border clashes and skirmishes in Kosovo resumed in December of 1998. The violence continued to escalate, and on January 30, 1999, NATO reapproved its activation order, thereby renewing its threat of air strikes against Serbia. In an effort to resolve the conflict peacefully,

peace talks began in early February in Rambouillet, France. With no
agreement forthcoming, and Serbian forces massing on the Kosovo
border, the CIA issued a warning on March 16, stating that a Serbian
offensive was imminent. Under intense pressure, the Kosovar Albanians
finally agreed to a deal on March 18, but Milošević continued to reject the
terms of the agreement. The United States issued a final ultimatum to
Milošević on March 22, but he offered no concessions, and on March 24,
NATO's air war began.

The Rhetoric

Following the same procedure that I used in the case of Iraq, I collected
and examined all of the public statements in which President Clinton
made more than a passing mention of the situation in Kosovo during
the period from March 31, 1998 (the date of the first UN Security Council
resolution on Kosovo), to March 24, 1999 (the beginning of the bombing
campaign). I identified a total of thirty-three separate documents, which
are listed in the Appendix. Based on this corpus, I assessed the degree to
which each of the three elements of the punishment frame was present in
Clinton's rhetoric. I use specific quotes for the purpose of illustration, but
my conclusions are based on general patterns and consistencies in the
corpus as a whole.

Is There a Clear Act of Wrongdoing?

Compared with President Bush's often visceral account of Saddam Hussein's criminal record, President Clinton employed far less gruesome
specificity in describing the situation in Kosovo. Nevertheless, he regularly discussed what was happening in Kosovo in morally loaded terms –
repression, atrocities, slaughter, and bloodshed – and most importantly,
he made it clear that many of the victims of that violence were civilians.
For instance, in one speech, Clinton explained that "The escalation of
tension in Kosovo inflicts heavy suffering on innocent civilians. Over
200,000 people were forced to leave their homes as the result of armed
clashes. The situation is aggravated by large-scale destruction of houses,
food shortages, and the risk of epidemic disease" (C090298). The
involvement of civilians is crucial because they are innocent victims who
have done nothing to deserve the suffering visited on them. It is wrong to
inflict harm upon the innocent, and Clinton's regular emphasis on the
suffering of innocents in Kosovo clearly establishes the first essential
element of the punishment frame.

Is There a Clear Perpetrator?

On this dimension, there is a profound difference between how President Bush framed the Iraq War and how President Clinton framed the US-led NATO intervention in Kosovo. In contrast to Bush's single-minded focus on Saddam Hussein as the epitome of all evil, Clinton did not employ demonizing rhetoric against Slobodan Milošević. Instead, throughout nearly the entire crisis period, Clinton consistently held both sides responsible for causing the suffering in Kosovo (C060298, C090298, C021999). Indeed, he spent a great deal of time and effort trying to explain the origins of the conflict in Kosovo to the American people in the most academic and diplomatic terms possible. For instance:

> You've got a part of Serbia which is 90 percent Albanian, and they want some kind of autonomy and to have their legitimate concerns addressed. The Serbs don't want to give up a big part of their country which they believe and is legally part of their country ... There are 50 different ways this could be worked out in a humane, legitimate way. They don't to have to kill each other to get this done, and they should not do that. (C050698)

This kind of language put both sides of the conflict on equal footing. It created a narrative in which both sides have legitimate aims that they want to attain; both sides have resentments that have prevented them from reaching a peaceful compromise; both sides are guilty of doing "injuries and harms" to the other; and both sides must stop fighting in order to end the conflict.

During the refugee crisis in the fall of 1998, Clinton did shift his apportionment of responsibility toward Milošević and Serbia, but this was usually couched as a responsibility to help prevent the looming humanitarian disaster rather than as an unambiguous assignment of blame for creating that disaster in the first place. Overt attribution of intentional wrongdoing to either Milošević or Serbia was a rare occurrence in Clinton's rhetoric until just a few days before the bombing began. Only then did Clinton single out Serbia as having committed atrocities such as "shelling civilians and torching their houses" and dragging innocent people from their homes to be "lined up and shot in cold blood" (C032499).

Indeed, one of the most remarkable aspects of Clinton's rhetoric on Kosovo, especially in comparison to the Iraq case, is the near total absence of any concerted effort to demonize Milošević, in spite of the fact that the latter provided him with abundant opportunity to do so. For example, during the course of the crisis, Serb forces massacred large numbers of civilians in the Kosovar villages of Prekaz and Račak. Yet Clinton mentioned these events less than a handful of times, and never in any kind of detail. Furthermore, Clinton almost never reminded the American people about the role that Milošević personally played in the ethnic cleansing in Bosnia several years earlier (and for which he was later charged with the crime of genocide).

It is true that Clinton mentioned Bosnia frequently when discussing the situation in Kosovo. However, he used it almost exclusively as an object lesson about the consequences of failing to take decisive action in Kosovo and about the efficacy of humanitarian intervention in the Balkans. Repeatedly, Clinton warned that, "our experience ... in Bosnia ... teaches us a sobering lesson: where you have these smoldering ethnic hatreds, where you know they can get out of hand and destabilize millions and millions of other people, violence begets violence" (C020499). The conflict in Kosovo should be stopped immediately, he argued, before the situation worsened and the price of intervention rose too high. In this narrative, the culprit that the world faced in Bosnia, and was facing again in Kosovo, was "smoldering ethnic hatreds," language that again suggests a shared culpability (C020499). It was not until the day before the bombing campaign began that Clinton finally played the Bosnia card against Milošević:

This is not the first time, let me remind you, this is not the first time we've faced this kind of choice. When President Milošević started the war in Bosnia seven years ago, the world did not act quickly enough to stop him. Let's don't forget what happened: Innocent people were herded into concentration camps. Children were gunned down by snipers on their way to school. Soccer fields and parks were turned into cemeteries. A quarter of a million people – in a country with only six million population – were killed, and a couple of million refugees were created – not because of anything they had done but because of who they were and because of the thirst of Mr. Milošević and his allies to dominate, indeed to crush people who were of different ethnic and religious affiliations. (C032399)

This is a powerful story that clearly identifies Milošević as a perpetrator of evil on par with Saddam Hussein, but is it sufficient to establish clearly the second element of the punishment frame? If the American people had heard this indictment of Milošević every time Clinton made the case for intervention in Kosovo, the answer would clearly be yes. However, given that this kind of language was both rare *and* heavily outweighed by assertions of shared responsibility for the crisis – of "injures and harms ... that have come from both sides" (C021999) – it seems highly unlikely that after months of exposure to that shared responsibility narrative, Clinton's late in the game shift toward demonizing Milošević would have had much of an influence on how most Americans understood the situation in Kosovo.

When trying to determine how a situation or issue is being framed in political communication, we are looking for the "central organizing idea or story line that provides meaning to an unfolding strip of events" (Gamson and Modigliani 1994: 376). In the context of a complex international crisis, rhetorical elements that occur rarely and intermittently are unlikely to provide a "central organizing idea" for most people, especially when there is a much more prevalent story line available, as was the case for Kosovo. Moreover, because individuals consume varying amounts of media coverage, and because the content of different sources will vary, individuals are much more likely to be exposed to (and therefore reliant on) the heavily recurrent elements of the president's rhetoric.

Overall, in my assessment of President Clinton's Kosovo speeches, I found shared responsibility to be a consistent and central part of the narrative that the president presented to the American people, while statements that clearly pinned responsibility for the current crisis on Slobodan Milošević or detailed his past atrocities were few and far between. I therefore conclude that in the case of Kosovo the second element of the punishment frame was ambiguous at best.

Will the Proposed Military Action Cause Harm to the Perpetrator?

Over the course of the crisis in Kosovo, two military options were regularly discussed: air strikes and ground troops. On the question of troops, President Clinton was adamant in his public statements that the United States would put boots on the ground in Kosovo only as part of a multinational peacekeeping force. For the average American, the word "peacekeeping" is not likely to invoke any kind of military action that would inflict serious damage on Slobodan Milošević or his military forces.

In terms of the air strikes, Clinton's rhetoric made it clear that they would be targeted at Serbia, but he introduced some ambiguity when discussing what they were intended to achieve. Clinton repeatedly explained the aim of the air strikes as "reducing" or "limiting" Milošević's capacity to wage war and engage in ethnic cleansing. This language could be interpreted in a variety of ways. To some people it might mean that the air strikes would inflict harm on Milošević by destroying some of his military forces and forcing him to make a humiliating retreat from Kosovo. However, for others it might mean that the air strikes would be aimed at blocking or destroying road and transportation networks in order to limit troop movements or used to establish a no-fly zone, neither of which would clearly cause any harm to Milošević or his forces. Clinton never offered more specific information about the consequences of the air strikes for Milošević, leading me to conclude that the third element of the punishment frame is also somewhat ambiguous.

Overall, this analysis of President Clinton's rhetoric shows that the intervention in Kosovo was not clearly framed as a punishment. While Clinton's rhetoric established an act (or acts) of wrongdoing in Kosovo by focusing on the suffering of innocent civilians, he placed too much emphasis on shared responsibility to firmly establish Serbia and/or Slobodan Milošević as the perpetrator, and there was significant uncertainty about whether the air strikes are going cause any real harm to Milošević in return for the suffering he had inflicted in Kosovo. Therefore, I expect that vengefulness will not be a significant predictor of support for the use of military force in Kosovo.

Data and Measures

To test this prediction, I use data from two nationally representative surveys, one conducted by Yankelovich/Time Magazine/CNN on March 25, 1999,[15] and one conducted by Opinion Dynamics/Fox News on April 21–22, 1999.[16] For the sake of brevity, I will refer to them respectively as the Yankelovich survey and the Opinion Dynamics survey. Each survey provides several questions about military intervention in Kosovo, the full text of which is presented below along with the variable names that I will use to reference each question in the subsequent analyses. Response options for each question are in parentheses.

Questions about Kosovo from the Opinion Dynamics survey:

- *Involved*: All things considered, do you think the United States should be involved in Kosovo or should we have stayed out of it? (Should be involved / Should have stayed out)
- *Continue bombing*: President Clinton has requested six billion dollars of emergency funding to pay for US military and humanitarian operations in the Balkans. Which of the following do you think is the best way to spend six billion dollars? (Use it to continue bombing / Pay it to

---

[15] National adult sample (N = 1,049). Data provided by the Roper Center for Public Opinion Research.

[16] National registered voter sample (N = 942). Data provided by the Roper Center for Public Opinion Research.

Serbian President Slobodan Milošević to leave the Kosovar Albanians alone / Use it to give Americans a tax break and just forget about the Balkans)

- *Ground troops*: If NATO decides to send ground troops to Kosovo, do you favor or oppose sending US ground troops as part of the NATO forces? (Favor / Oppose)
- *Escalate*: Which of the following would be the better way to end the war? (Send in ground forces / Call a cease-fire and negotiate)
- *Loss of life*: Do you think winning the war in Kosovo is worth the loss of even a single American life? (Yes / No)

Questions about military intervention in Kosovo from the Yankelovich survey:

- *Air strikes*: Do you approve or disapprove of the NATO airstrikes against Serbian targets in Yugoslavia and Kosovo? (Approve / Disapprove)
- *Moral imperative*: Do you think the United States has a moral imperative to stop Serbian actions in Kosovo or don't you feel that way? (Yes / No)
- *Peacekeeping*: If the Yugoslavia government signs a peace agreement in Kosovo, would you favor or oppose sending in US and NATO peace-keeping forces to enforce it? (Favor / Oppose)

I coded each of these variables as a dichotomous indicator equal to one if the respondent favored or approved of the military action in question and zero otherwise.[17] Table 4.6 reports the percentage of all respondents who indicated support for these seven items. Support ranges from just under 22% of people who think that sending in ground forces would be the best way to end the war to a 59% majority who favor sending US and NATO peacekeeping forces to enforce a peace agreement between the two sides.

The Opinion Dynamics survey included a question about the death penalty for juveniles, and I use this question as a proxy for endorsement of revenge. Specifically, the question asked: "Do you think teens who kill other teens should face the possibility of the death penalty?" Based on this question, I coded *Death penalty support* as a dichotomous variable equal to one if the respondent answered yes, and equal to zero if he or she answered either no or unsure. On this survey, 75% of respondents said

---

[17] For *Continue bombing*, I coded respondents as equal to one if they said the six billion dollars of emergency funding should be used to continue bombing and zero otherwise. For *Escalate*, I coded respondents as equal to one if they said that sending in ground forces would be the better way to end the war.

TABLE 4.6 *Support for the use of military force in Kosovo (1999)*

Question	Support (%)
Yankelovich survey	
Air strikes	44.5
Moral imperative	51.8
Peacekeeping	59.0
Opinion Dynamics survey	
Involved	49.0
Continue bombing	34.5
Ground troops	37.9
Escalate	21.7
Loss of life	37.3

they thought teens who kill other teens should face the possibility of the death penalty.

Unfortunately, the Yankelovich survey did not include a question about the death penalty, but it did ask a series of questions about respondents' willingness to forgive someone who committed an act of wrongdoing. Prior studies have found that vengefulness is negatively associated with the willingness to forgive (McCullough et al. 2001), and I therefore treat these forgiveness questions as an alternative proxy for endorsement of revenge, although the results should be treated with some caution as the relationship between revenge and forgiveness is less well established than the relationship between revenge and support for the death penalty.

Respondents were asked: "For each of the following circumstances, please tell me whether you would definitely forgive someone who did that to you, probably forgive them, probably not forgive them, or definitely not forgive them." I used the following four items to construct an index: (1) someone slapped or punched you in the face; (2) someone murdered a person in your community; (3) someone murdered your child; and (4) someone raped a member of your family. This variable, which I label *Unforgiving*, ranges from 1 to 4 with a mean of 3.04.[18] Higher values on the scale indicate that the respondent is more unforgiving.

In addition to these measures of endorsement of revenge, I include the same set of demographic and political control variables that I used in my

---

[18] Cronbach's alpha for this scale is 0.83.

analysis of the Iraq case: gender, age, race, education, political ideology, party identification, and presidential job approval (subject to the availability of appropriate questions on each survey).[19] For both surveys, *Gender* is coded as a dummy variable for male and party identification is coded as separate dummy variables for *Republican* and *Democrat* (with independents as the excluded category). For age and race there are some minor differences in coding due to how the questions were asked. On the Yankelovich survey, *Age* has seven levels ranging from 18–25 to 65+, and *Race* is a dummy variable for non-Hispanic white. On the Opinion Dynamics survey, *Age* has eight levels ranging from 18–25 to 71+, and *Race* is a dummy variable for white (the survey did not include a Hispanic question). *Education* (six levels ranging from eighth grade or less to postgraduate study) is available only on the Yankelovich survey. *Political ideology* (a five-point scale ranging from very liberal to very conservative) and *Clinton job approval* (a dummy variable equal to one if the respondent approves of the way President Clinton is handling his job as president) are available only on the Opinion Dynamics survey.

Analysis and Results

Table 4.7 presents the results of a series of multivariate logistic regression models for both the Opinion Dynamics and Yankelovich survey questions. If the *framing hypothesis* is correct, then *Death penalty support* and *Unforgiving* should have no significant effect on support for intervention in Kosovo, and this is precisely what we see. Across all eight independent variables, the coefficients on my measures of vengefulness are small and statistically insignificant. In other words, highly vengeful individuals are not significantly more likely to favor military action in Kosovo, whether that be in the form of air strikes, ground troops, or a peacekeeping mission. Nor are they more likely to say that the United States should be involved in Kosovo, that it has a moral imperative to stop Serbian actions, or that doing so would be worth the cost of even a single American life. Instead, the two most consistent predictors of support for intervention in Kosovo are *Gender*, with men significantly more likely to express support than women, and *Clinton job approval*, with those who approve of the president's performance in office significantly more likely to favor taking some kind of military action.

---

[19] There is no need to control for attitudes toward the War on Terror since NATO's intervention in Kosovo pre-dates the 9/11 era.

TABLE 4.7 *Predictors of support for the use of military force in Kosovo (1999)*

	Air strikes	Moral imperative	Peace-keeping	Involved	Continue bombing	Ground troops	Escalate	Loss of life
Unforgiving	-0.04 (0.10)	0.00 (0.10)	0.13 (0.10)	0.02 (0.17)	0.22 (0.18)	-0.25 (0.17)	0.15 (0.20)	-0.25 (0.17)
Death penalty support								
Gender	0.72*** (0.15)	0.37* (0.15)	-0.19 (0.15)	0.51*** (0.15)	0.54*** (0.15)	0.48*** (0.15)	0.79*** (0.17)	0.66*** (0.15)
Age	0.03 (0.04)	0.03 (0.04)	-0.14*** (0.04)	-0.04 (0.03)	0.09* (0.03)	0.02 (0.03)	0.06 (0.04)	-0.03 (0.03)
Race	0.32 (0.20)	-0.03 (0.19)	-0.14 (0.20)	0.34 (0.20)	0.55* (0.21)	0.22 (0.20)	0.68** (0.26)	0.52* (0.21)
Education	0.04 (0.06)	0.13* (0.06)	0.07 (0.06)					
Republican	-0.40* (0.19)	-0.29 (0.19)	-0.01 (0.18)	0.01 (0.19)	0.31 (0.21)	0.57** (0.20)	0.50* (0.25)	0.33 (0.20)
Democrat	0.71*** (0.18)	0.57** (0.18)	0.48* (0.19)	0.45* (0.19)	0.35 (0.19)	0.46* (0.19)	0.88*** (0.23)	0.53** (0.19)
Political ideology				-0.05 (0.07)	-0.04 (0.07)	-0.11 (0.07)	0.02 (0.08)	-0.02 (0.07)
Clinton job approval				1.33*** (0.17)	1.32*** (0.19)	1.06*** (0.18)	0.67** (0.21)	1.00*** (0.18)
Constant	-1.08* (0.48)	-0.82 (0.46)	0.42 (0.48)	-1.20** (0.39)	-2.88*** (0.42)	-1.53*** (0.39)	-3.69*** (0.49)	-1.84*** (0.40)
N	907	907	907	895	895	895	895	895

Note: All models are logistic regression models with standard errors in parentheses. Significance: * $p < 0.05$, ** $p < 0.01$, *** $p < 0.001$.

Overall, there is no meaningful difference in the attitudes of vengeful and non-vengeful individuals on the question of whether or not the United States should use military force in Kosovo. Unlike the case of Iraq, President Clinton's emphasis on shared responsibility for the crisis and his lack of clarity about the consequences of intervention for Milošević and Serbia failed to construct the narrative of an evildoer getting his just deserts that would make individuals' beliefs about revenge salient to their attitudes toward intervention in Kosovo.

The absence of this narrative in Clinton's rhetoric was not due to some inherent difference between the situation in Iraq and the situation in Kosovo. The raw materials for a victim/perpetrator/punisher story line were all there. Had Clinton made a concerted effort to demonize Milošević with his prior record of atrocities in Bosnia or the massacres of civilians that Serb forces were perpetrating in Kosovo, and had he made it clear that the bombing campaign would do some real damage to Milošević's power and prestige, all the essential elements of the punishment frame would have been clearly established. Yet Clinton chose not to employ this rhetorical strategy. Why?

In Chapter 2, I discussed several factors that might explain why leaders sometimes choose not to use a punishment frame even though doing so would help them gain popular support in the polls. In this case, the answer seems to be rooted in Clinton's political goals for Kosovo. In contrast to Iraq, where regime change appears to have been the ultimate goal from the beginning,[20] and where Saddam Hussein was given an ultimatum rather than an invitation to the negotiating table, Clinton preferred a negotiated settlement to the conflict over regime change and communicated as much to Milošević through intermediaries.[21] Clinton doggedly pursued such a settlement through multiple rounds of negotiation and only fully committed to the military option at the very last

---

[20] This decision is often attributed to the influence of neo-conservatism within the Bush administration, and particularly to the belief that establishing a Western-style democracy in Iraq would pave the way for the transformation of the entire Middle East (Fukuyama 2004). According to administration insiders, the decision to remove Saddam Hussein from power was taken in early 2002, many months before President Bush's speech to the UN General Assembly set the ball rolling. For instance, Spencer Ackerman and Franklin Foer report that in March of 2002, "Bush interrupted a meeting between National Security Adviser Condoleezza Rice and three senators to boast, 'Fuck Saddam. We're taking him out.'" Spencer Ackerman and Franklin Foer, "The Radical," *New Republic.* December 1, 2003.

[21] Peter Baker, "Blunt Political Assessments in Bill Clinton Transcripts," *New York Times*, January 7, 2016.

minute, when it became clear that while the Kosovar Albanians were willing to concede all that could be expected of them, Milošević remained unwilling to budge while simultaneously massing his forces along the Kosovo border.

Prior to the breakdown of the final negotiations in Rambouillet, it seems likely that Clinton refrained from demonizing Milošević because doing so would have made a negotiated settlement more difficult to achieve. Antagonizing your adversary by denouncing him as the epitome of evil is not a strategy that is likely to make him more inclined to offer concessions at the bargaining table or to trust your assurances. Moreover, employing inflammatory rhetoric to rouse public support for war might have made it more difficult for Clinton to sell a negotiated settlement at home, should one be forthcoming. Compromising with an adversary who has been consistently portrayed as an irredeemable villain might well be viewed by a significant segment of the public as a sign of weakness or incompetence, which would in turn provide grist for the mill of domestic political opponents. At the very least, harsh criticism from these opponents could deal a significant blow to the president's overall popularity, thereby diminishing his political capital in both domestic and foreign affairs.

Indeed, it is telling that Clinton raised the specter of Milošević's crimes in Bosnia only after he had lost all hope of securing a deal that would put an end to the conflict. Once Clinton viewed himself as squarely on the road to war, the need to hold back on provocative rhetoric so as not to upset the negotiations was gone, and he was free to depict Milošević as a villain, motivated by the will to "dominate, indeed to crush people who were of different ethnic and religious affiliations," rather than by legitimate goals and grievances. However, by that point it was too late for a single speech to alter how most Americans understood the nature of the conflict in Kosovo.

Alternative Explanations

The main finding that emerges from these case studies is that, as predicted by my theory, endorsement of revenge had a significant effect on support for war in Iraq but not in Kosovo. In this section, I address possible alternative explanations for this pattern of results.[22]

---

[22] I thank the three anonymous reviewers for calling my attention to these alternative explanations.

First, could the results of my analysis be due to some unobserved difference between the two presidents rather than how they chose to frame the use of force? To be clear, the issue here is not whether differences between President Bush and President Clinton affected the overall level of support for the use of force in these cases. The issue is whether there is some difference between them that can explain why vengefulness predicts support for the use of force by Bush in Iraq but not by Clinton in Kosovo. The most obvious possibility is that Bush was simply a more vengeful person than Clinton. Some news reporting has suggested that Bush might have been motivated to go to war in Iraq by the desire to avenge his father, the former President George H. W. Bush, who was the target of a (failed) assassination attempt orchestrated by Saddam Hussein. This speculation was sparked by a press conference in which Bush said of Saddam, "After all, this is a guy that tried to kill my dad at one time."

While experts are still debating why the United States ultimately went to war in Iraq, they have not generally given much credence to personal revenge as an explanation for the decision itself. It is possible that Bush's desire for revenge might help to explain why he employed a punishment frame in his rhetoric about Iraq while Clinton did not do so with Kosovo. However, given how strategically the Bush administration managed its political communications regarding Iraq (Gershkoff and Kushner 2005), it seems unlikely that a personal desire for revenge was solely or even primarily responsible for Bush's rhetorical strategy. Moreover, even if a personal desire for revenge did drive Bush's framing of the Iraq war, with the exception of that single press conference, his public statements carried no hint of a personal motivation. Therefore, it is very unlikely that this is what people were responding to rather than the use of a punishment frame.

Second, could the death penalty support variable be picking up on some difference in how people felt about Bush versus Clinton, rather than their beliefs about revenge? This seems like a remote possibility because any difference in how respondents felt about the two presidents will be captured largely by the job approval variable, which I include as a control in my analysis of both cases. The job approval question is widely used on public opinion surveys, reported on by the media, and tracked by presidents themselves, because it does a good job of indexing how positively or negatively Americans feel about their president at a given moment in time. Unsurprisingly, job approval is a large and significant predictor of support for the use of force in both the Iraq and Kosovo cases. Thus, the effect of death penalty support that we observe in the Iraq case exists above and beyond how the respondents felt about Bush as a president.

Relatedly, could the effect of death penalty support be reflecting the impact of ideology in the case of Iraq (with a Republican president) but not in the case of Kosovo (with a Democratic president)? It is true that both Republicans and self-professed conservatives are more likely to express support for capital punishment, which is why I controlled for both political ideology and party identification in my analysis of both cases. The inclusion of these controls should eliminate the concern that ideology is driving the results in the Iraq case.

Overall, none of these potential alternative explanations provides a compelling account of the results of the Iraq and Kosovo case studies, and there is therefore little reason to doubt that the fundamental difference driving those results is the way in which the two conflicts were framed for the American people.

Summary of the Cases

Overall, the cases of Iraq and Kosovo provide another compelling piece of evidence in favor of the *framing hypothesis*. Even in the context of two complex and lengthy international crises, endorsement of revenge emerges as an important predictor of support for the use of military force when it is framed as a punishment the adversary deserves to suffer, as was the case with the Iraq War. However, in the absence of that frame, as was the case with NATO intervention in Kosovo, the most vengeful individuals are no more enthusiastic about the prospect of war than the least vengeful individuals. In other words, individuals who hold revenge as a core value are not automatically more likely to favor war. However, they can be mobilized to do so by rhetoric that makes revenge salient in their minds, causing them to rely on that value as a useful heuristic for forming an opinion about the wisdom of going to war.

Furthermore, like the invasion experiment presented in the previous section, these cases also demonstrate that a direct attack on the nation's homeland or its citizens is not necessary to make revenge salient. Neither conflict involved such an attack, yet in the case of Iraq, President Bush was able to successfully construct a narrative that would resonate with vengeful individuals by emphasizing Saddam Hussein's crimes against his own people, his neighbors, and the international community. Furthermore, the fact that President Clinton did not employ similar rhetoric in the case of Kosovo was not due to the lack of any direct harm to the

United States, but to his own persistent belief that a negotiated settlement to the conflict could be achieved.

On a more practical note, this analysis suggests that when elected leaders use the kind of demonizing rhetoric that Bush employed during the run-up to the Iraq War, it may signal that they have, at least in their own minds, committed themselves to a course of action that is likely to lead to war. Because inflammatory rhetoric increases the expected political costs of backing down or accepting an outcome short of war, only leaders who are willing to accept that outcome if necessary should invest heavily in demonizing their enemy. Thus, the frequent use of such rhetoric on one or both sides of a crisis may be a useful signal that the window for diplomatic resolution has begun to close and escalation to the use of military force is close at hand.

CONCLUSION

The purpose of this chapter was to test the *framing hypothesis*, which predicts that vengeful individuals will be more supportive of the use of force than non-vengeful individuals when (and only when) that use of force is framed as a punishment, i.e., when there is a clear act of wrongdoing, a clear perpetrator who is responsible for that act of wrongdoing, and a proposed military response that will cause some harm or injury to the perpetrator.

I presented three types of evidence in support of this hypothesis. First, I examined a set of typical public opinion survey questions about the use of US military force. Due to differences in question wording, some of those questions framed the use of force as punishment, while others did not. As predicted, my analysis found a significant relationship between endorsement of revenge and support for military action only for the set of questions that included all three necessary elements of the punishment frame. Second, I reported the results of a survey experiment in which I manipulated the framing of a hypothetical conflict scenario while holding all other information about the situation constant. This analysis showed that vengeful individuals were more likely to support the use of force than non-vengeful individuals, but only in the treatment group that received the punishment frame. Finally, I compared two recent cases of conflict involving the United States: Iraq (2003) and Kosovo (1999). Based on an analysis of the rhetoric of Presidents George W. Bush and Bill Clinton, I argued that the Iraq War was clearly and consistently framed as a punishment, while intervention in Kosovo was not. I then showed, using contemporaneous public opinion polls, that endorsement of revenge (proxied by support for capital punishment) was a positive and significant predictor of support for military action in Iraq but not in Kosovo.

All in all, this evidence clearly points to the crucial role that framing plays in making revenge salient to individuals' attitudes toward the use of military force. Without all three elements of the punishment frame in place, there is no significant relationship between endorsement of revenge and support for war. However, when those elements combine, they form a narrative that casts the adversary in the role of an evildoer who deserves to be punished, which resonates strongly with individuals who hold revenge as a core value. Under these conditions, vengefulness emerges as an important predictor of support for the use of force. These findings represent a significant step forward in our understanding of the relationship between revenge and support for war. As I describe in greater detail in Chapter 2, the existing literature on this topic provides a diverse set of cases – historical, contemporary, and hypothetical – that clearly show that revenge *can* be an important driver of popular enthusiasm for war, but it does not tell us much about *when* and *how* this happens.

Furthermore, my empirical approach in this chapter also helps to rule out an important alternative explanation that prior studies have been unable to address satisfactorily. The concern is that what differentiates more vengeful people from less vengeful people is not their beliefs about the righteousness of giving wrongdoers their just deserts but rather a greater taste for violence in general, regardless of its moral justification. In other words, some individuals may simply like violence more than others, leading them both to express more vengeful beliefs and to favor the use of military force over other tools in international relations. The best way to rule out the possibility that a taste for violence is driving both endorsement of revenge and support for the use of military force is to identify cases or scenarios where we would expect to find greater support for force among individuals with a taste for violence but not among those who hold revenge as a core value. However, the existing literature does not (and cannot) provide such a test because it lacks a clear set of theoretical expectations about the conditions under which vengefulness should and should not translate into heightened enthusiasm for war.

In contrast, this chapter clearly shows that the relationship between revenge and support for the use of military force is conditional on whether or not that use of force is framed as a punishment. Crucially, as we saw in the invasion experiment, this is the case even when all the other details of the situation are held constant. This is strong evidence against the 'taste for violence' alternative explanation. Individuals who favor the use of military force because they have a general taste for violence should not be swayed by subtle changes in framing, especially when the substance of the situation remains unchanged. They should exhibit an unconditional preference for violent solutions to international problems. Instead, we see that while endorsement of revenge can be a powerful predictor of support for war in many different circumstances, its salience ultimately depends on the kind of narrative that political leaders choose to present to their citizens.

My findings align with the prevailing view on the role of core values in the formation of public opinion, which holds that while values are one of the basic wellsprings of political attitudes, ordinary people must rely on information conveyed by elite discourse to help translate their values – which are abstract and general – into specific issue positions (Zaller 1992; Hayes and Guardino 2013). For the average citizen, values serve as heuristics (or decision-making shortcuts) that allow them to generate coherent views about a wide range of complex issues about which they generally have little factual information. The costs of gathering and evaluating that information can be quite high, and value-based heuristics thus play a vital role in enabling ordinary people to form opinions about the world around them and to participate in the political debates of the day.

However, most political issues, including the use of military force, are multifaceted, touching on various (potentially contradictory) considerations. The crucial role that elite discourse plays in shaping which of those considerations ultimately becomes salient makes framing a powerful tool in leaders' arsenal of influence. By framing their preferred policies in ways that resonate with values that are widely shared among their constituents, leaders can set the terms of the debate and the premises on which the public evaluates their proposals in order to maximize popular support (Edwards 2009). When it comes to the use of military force, this chapter demonstrates that punishment framing can produce a substantial increase in support for war among those who hold revenge as a core value. In the next chapter, I show how this dynamic shapes the conflict behavior of democratic states.

5

Dangerous Democracies

Cross-National Variation in Revenge and Conflict Initiation

I now turn my attention from the individual-level micro-foundations of my theory to its international implications. In Chapter 2, I argued that due to divergent cultural legacies, there are persistent differences in the prevalence of revenge as a core value across national populations and that these differences can help to explain why some democracies are more belligerent than others. Leaders facing highly vengeful populations have a larger pool of latent support for the use of force available to be mobilized through the use of a punishment frame, and as a result, these leaders will (on average) be more successful at generating popular support for war than leaders with less vengeful populations. In turn, this superior ability to manage public opinion weakens the constraining effect of accountability, giving leaders with highly vengeful populations greater latitude to employ military force as a tool of foreign policy. Based on this argument, the *conflict initiation hypothesis* predicts that democracies with more vengeful populations will be more likely to initiate the use of military force than democracies with less vengeful populations.

In this chapter, I test the *conflict initiation hypothesis* using data on all militarized interstate disputes from 1945 to 2001. To begin, I examine survey data from fifty-nine countries to show that endorsement of revenge does indeed exhibit significant cross-national variation. Next, I introduce the variable that I use to measure this variation in my main analysis, which requires broader coverage both across countries and over time than the available survey data can provide. In brief, I use the legal status of capital punishment as a proxy for cross-national variation in vengefulness under the assumption that retentionist democracies (i.e., democracies that retain capital punishment for ordinary crimes) are more likely than abolitionist democracies to have populations that broadly endorse revenge. I support this assumption by showing that in the present day, democracies with more vengeful populations (as measured by public opinion surveys) are more likely to retain the death penalty. I then present the results of my main analysis, which finds a significant positive relationship between death penalty retention and the likelihood that a democracy will initiate a conflict with another state. Finally, I conclude the chapter with a discussion of how these results contribute to the existing literature on democratic conflict initiation, which has heretofore focused largely on institutional variation among democracies rather than cultural differences in core values.

CROSS-NATIONAL VARIATION IN VENGEFULNESS

As discussed in Chapter 2, numerous studies have documented cross-cultural differences in the frequency, intensity, and form of revenge behavior. In this section, I analyze survey data from fifty-nine countries to show that even in today's highly globalized world, the prevalence of revenge as a core value varies substantially across national populations. The data I use are from Gallup International's Voice of the People Millennium (VPM) Survey, which was conducted in the year 2000.[1]

As far as I am aware, the VPM survey is the only multi-country survey that asks about endorsement of revenge as a general principle. Specifically, survey respondents were asked what they thought the main aim of imprisonment should be. The response options were: (1) to reeducate the prisoner, (2) to protect other citizens, (3) to act as a deterrent to others, and (4) to make those who have done wrong pay for it. I coded respondents as vengeful if they chose the fourth option. These are individuals who clearly see imprisonment – which has become one of the most common forms of state-sponsored punishment around the world – first and foremost as a way to give offenders their just deserts, rather than a means to achieve some greater good for society by reducing crime or rehabilitating offenders

Figure 5.1 reports the percentage of vengeful people in each of the fifty-nine countries included in the survey, ranging from a low of 13% in Denmark to a high of 54% in South Korea. The United States falls right

---

[1] Gallup International Association, Voice of the People Millennium Survey, 2000 [computer file], ICPSR24661-v1 (Ann Arbor, MI: Inter-University Consortium for Political and Social Research [distributor], August 18, 2009).

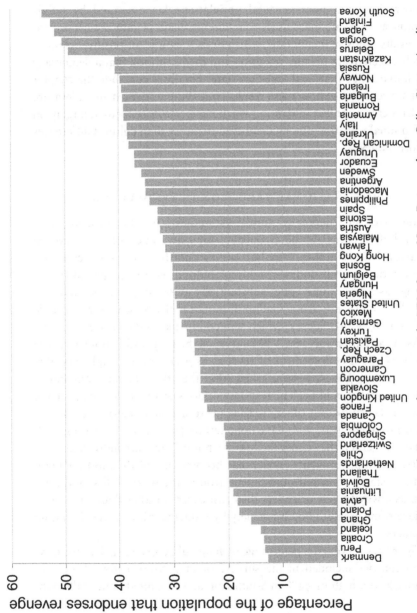

FIGURE 5.1 Variation in endorsement of revenge on the VPM Survey. Note: Data are from Gallup International's Voice of the People Millennium Survey (2000). Endorsement of revenge is measured by the percentage of respondents who said the main aim of imprisonment was "to make those who have done wrong pay for it."

at the average of 30%. This range is likely to be truncated given the underrepresentation of non-Western countries. A truly global sample would likely fill out the higher end of the range. However, even with this limitation, Figure 5.1 shows that cross-national variation in endorsement of revenge is real and meaningful. In countries like Peru, Iceland, and Poland, people who endorse revenge make up a small minority of the population, while in countries like Belarus, Japan, and South Korea, they are a majority or near majority.

Ideally, I would use a measure of endorsement of revenge based on public opinion surveys to test the *conflict initiation hypothesis*. Unfortunately, there is very little survey data on revenge, and even the VPM survey is not well suited for this purpose. The reason is that a rigorous test of this hypothesis requires a measure of cross-national variation in vengefulness that is widely available both across countries and over time. Using the VPM data would give us just fifty-nine country-year observations, and the countries included are not a random sample, which would raise questions about the generalizability of the results. Therefore, I use an alternative measurement strategy. Specifically, I use the legal status of capital punishment as an indicator for whether revenge is broadly endorsed by a country's population. Because it is based on policy rather than opinion, this measure can be coded consistently for all countries in the international system without any missing data or issues of cross-national or cross-temporal comparability.

I collected data on the legal status of capital punishment worldwide from 1945 to 2001 from Amnesty International. Based on this information, I created a dichotomous variable, *Death penalty retention*, which is equal to one in a given year if a country retains the death penalty for ordinary crimes.[2] In the case of the United States, which has the unique feature of making the legality of capital punishment a matter of both state and federal law, I base my coding on the latter. What matters for my theory is the average vengefulness of the US population as compared with other countries, and this is best indicated by national policy regarding capital punishment. Currently, capital punishment is legal under federal law, which reflects the fact that it is supported by a majority of Americans (60% according to a Gallup poll in October of 2016),[3] and that there is

---

[2] Ordinary crimes exclude crimes committed under military law and crimes committed in exceptional circumstances, such as treason or espionage.

[3] Jeffrey M. Jones, "U.S. Death Penalty Support at 60%," *Gallup.com*, October 25, 2016, www.gallup.com/poll/196676/death-penalty-support.aspx.

FIGURE 5.2 Number of retentionist democracies in the international system, 1945–2001. Note: A country is coded as a retentionist democracy in a given year if it has a Polity (IV) score greater than 16 and retains the death penalty for ordinary crimes.

therefore little appetite for abolition in the US Congress.[4] The fact that some states – a total of nineteen as of this writing – have abolished capital punishment tells us that people in some parts of the country are less vengeful than people in other parts. However, in the United States decisions about the use of military force are made by the president, who is accountable to the nation as a whole, and it is therefore aggregate opinion that I want to capture with my measure.

The *conflict initiation hypothesis* concerns democracies, and according to this measure, between 1945 and 2001, a total of sixty-six countries have been both democratic and retentionist in at least one year, and 41% of those had a duration of at least ten consecutive years. Figure 5.2 plots the number of retentionist democracies in each year from 1945 to 2001, showing that they have been a constant presence in the international system since 1945, although their number has fluctuated between ten

---

[4] For example, in 2013, a group of democratic lawmakers introduced a bill (H.R. 3471) in the House of Representatives that would have abolished the death penalty for federal offenses. The legislation never even came to the floor for a vote.

(in 1945) and thirty (in 1993 and 1994).[5] See the Appendix for a full list of all retentionist democracies during this period. In the present day, there are ten democracies that retain the death penalty: Botswana, Guatemala, India, Jamaica, Japan, Mongolia, South Korea, Taiwan, Trinidad, and Tobago, and the United States.[6]

Using *Death penalty retention* as a proxy for cross-national variation in vengefulness is a viable strategy for a number of reasons. First, numerous studies have linked cross-cultural disparities in beliefs and values to national-level policy differences among democracies across a variety of issue areas (e.g., Inglehart 1990; Cohen 1996; Kasser 2011), suggesting that policy often reveals information about values. Second, the global trend in the twentieth century has been toward the abolition of capital punishment, with an especially strong wave following World War II (Simmons 2009). As a result, governments that retain capital punishment in the post-1945 era do so as a deliberate choice and against the prevailing tide of international opinion.

In democracies, this decision rests on leaders' assessments of how their political fortunes will be affected by a move to abolish the death penalty. They are unlikely to take the risk if support for capital punishment is high and they expect a strong public backlash (Newburn and Jones 2005). Finally, as discussed in greater detail in Chapter 2, research on individual attitudes toward the death penalty has converged on the conclusion that, at the individual level, these attitudes are symbolic rather than instrumental (Tyler and Weber 1982; Ellsworth and Gross 1994) and that support is driven primarily by a desire for revenge, rather than by utilitarian concerns (Ellsworth and Ross 1983; Bohm 1992; Cotton 2000; Carlsmith et al. 2002).

All this suggests that retentionist democracies are places where revenge is particularly likely to enjoy more widespread endorsement.[7] To validate this relationship, I turn back to the data from the VPM survey. Of the

---

[5] The number of retentionist democracies spikes in the early 1990s because the breakup of the Soviet Union produced a number of newly democratic states that were "born" with the death penalty.

[6] This list is based on the Polity IV Project, which provides data on political regimes and regime transitions up through 2013. Individual country regime trends can be viewed online at www.systemicpeace.org/polity/polity4x.htm.

[7] I do not expect retention of the death penalty to be a reliable indicator of strong popular endorsement of revenge among autocracies. Overall, autocracies are more likely to retain the death penalty than democracies (Ruddell and Urbina 2004; Neumayer 2008; Kent 2010), and this likely has more to do with the utility of capital punishment as a tool of social control than it does with the values of ordinary people.

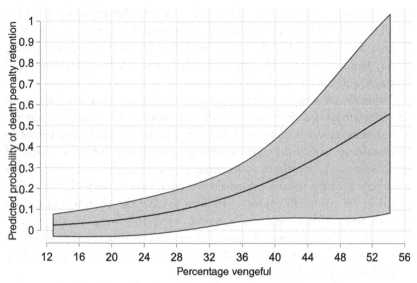

FIGURE 5.3 The effect of endorsement of revenge on death penalty retention in democracies. Note: Predicted probabilities are for death penalty retention in 2014. The shaded area represents the 95% confidence interval.

59 countries included in the survey, 43 were democracies. In a simple bivariate logit model, I regressed the present-day legal status of capital punishment (equal to one if the country retains the death penalty for ordinary crimes in 2014) on *Percent vengeful* (the percentage of people in each country who endorsed revenge as the main aim of imprisonment). Figure 5.3 illustrates the relationship between these two variables by plotting the predicted probability that a democracy will retain the death penalty as *Percent vengeful* varies over its range. We can see from Figure 5.3 that the probability that a democracy will retain the death penalty rises from 2.4% to 55.9% as *Percent vengeful* moves from its minimum to its maximum, a difference that is statistically significant ($\Delta = 53.5$, $p = 0.04$).

Using the same imprisonment question on the VPM survey, I also coded variables for the percentage of people who chose deterrence ("to act as a deterrent to others") as the main aim of imprisonment and the percentage who chose public safety ("to protect other citizens"). Both deterrence and public safety are commonly articulated justifications for capital punishment, but neither variable has a significant relationship with the likelihood that a democracy will retain the death penalty (see Appendix).[8]

---

[8] I also tried combining the deterrence and public safety options into a single variable, but this does not change the result.

The results of this analysis should increase our confidence that the legal status of the death penalty is a valid indicator of the prevalence of revenge in national populations.[9] It shows that retention of the death penalty is positively correlated with popular endorsement of revenge and that it is not correlated with cross-national variation in the prevalence of beliefs about the efficacy of punishment, thereby ameliorating the concern that the legal status of capital punishment might be proxying for the latter rather than the former. An additional concern has to do with other national attributes that may be correlated with both retention and the propensity to initiate conflict. I address this issue in the next section.

TESTING THE HYPOTHESIS ON MILITARIZED INTERSTATE DISPUTES

To test the *conflict initiation hypothesis*, I use the Correlates of War Project's data on militarized interstate disputes (MIDs), which are defined as threats, displays, or actual uses of military force that are both overt and government sanctioned (Ghosn et al. 2004). In this study, I examine MIDs that took place between 1945 and 2001. The unit of analysis is the directed dyad-year. Directed dyads are ordered pairs of states in which state A is the potential initiator and state B is the potential target. To eliminate dyads that have no opportunity for conflict, I restrict my analysis to "politically relevant" dyads (Lemke and Reed 2001), defined as pairs of states that are contiguous and/or include at least one major power. Out of more than one million total directed dyad-years between 1945 and 2001, this restriction leaves 116,174 observations.

Dependent Variable: MID Initiation

My dependent variable is the initiation of a militarized dispute. In the MIDs data, the initiator is defined as the state that made the first move by

---

[9] I use the legal status of the death penalty rather than its active use for both theoretical and empirical reasons. Some countries retain the death penalty for many years without carrying out an execution, suggesting that the demand for vengeance may be waning, and data on the year of last known execution are widely available. However, active use of the death penalty depends not only on public opinion but also on the type and frequency of crime in a society (Lofquist 2001) and on the accumulated decisions of a complex legal process that, in many democracies, is actively shielded from public pressure (Volcansek 2010). Thus, there will be significantly more noise in a measure of vengefulness based on last known execution. Empirically, *Percent vengeful* does not predict either the year of last known execution or the likelihood that a democracy will carry out an execution after the VPM survey was conducted in 2000 (see Appendix for details).

threatening, displaying, or using force. Initiation is a dichotomous variable equal to one if state A initiated a MID with state B in a given year. Between 1945 and 2001, there were 1,246 instances of initiation. In order to exclude relatively minor incidents that have little or no chance of ever coming to the attention of the mass public, I look only at high hostility level MIDs, which are those that involve an actual use of force or full-scale war. This leaves 710 instances of initiation in the data.

To identify democratic initiators, I use the combined Polity score from the Polity IV dataset, which ranges from zero (most strongly autocratic) to 20 (most strongly democratic). I code the initiating state as a democracy in a given year if its combined Polity score is greater than 16. In the analyses that follow, I subset the data on this variable in order to examine democratic and autocratic initiators separately. Overall, democracies with the death penalty make up 51.2% of all dyad-years with a democratic initiator.

During the period 1945–2001, retentionist democracies initiated 105 MIDs. The United States was responsible for the largest number (26 MIDs, or 24.8% of the total), followed by India (17 MIDs, or 16.2% of the total). Twenty-one other retentionist democracies also initiated at least one MID: Argentina, Armenia, Belgium, Botswana, France, Greece, Israel, Japan, Myanmar, Niger, Nigeria, Pakistan, Papua New Guinea, Russia, Somalia, South Korea, Sudan, Syria, Thailand, Turkey, and the United Kingdom.

Control Variables

I include two sets of control variables in my analysis. The first is a standard set of predictors based on existing studies of conflict initiation. I include these variables both to account for the influence of factors like proximity, shared interests, and military capabilities on the baseline risk of conflict and to compare the effect of *Death penalty retention* to the impact of these well-established predictors of initiation.

State power affects both the opportunity for conflict and the expected value of going to war, and I include a set of variables to capture both the absolute and relative power of the states in each dyad. These variables are: *Initiator capabilities score* (measures the initiator's material capabilities compared with all other states in the system), *Target capabilities score*[10] (measures the target's material capabilities compared with all

---

[10] Based on the CINC score from COW's National Material Capabilities Data (Singer 1987). Ranges from 0 to 1, with higher values indicating that a state has a larger share of the total resources of the international system.

other states in the system), *Balance of capabilities*[11] (measures how evenly matched the two states are in terms of their material capabilities), *Initiator share of capabilities*[12] (measures the strength of the initiator relative to the target), *Initiator major power* (an indicator of the initiator's major power status), and *Target major power*[13] (an indicator of the target's major power status).

To capture the effect of geographical proximity on opportunity for conflict (Gleditsch 1995), I include *Land contiguity*, which is a dichotomous variable equal to one if the states in a dyad share a land border. By contrast, states that are allied or that have similar strategic interests should have fewer opportunities for conflict (Gowa 2011). The former is measured by *Defensive pact* (a dichotomous variable equal to one if the states in the dyad have a formal agreement to aid one another militarily in the event of an attack), while the latter is measured by *Alliance portfolio similarity* (a measure of the extent to which states in a dyad are allied with similar countries).[14] In addition to these variables, I also include the regime type of the target state to capture any effect of the democratic peace. *Target democracy* is a dichotomous variable equal to one if target state's combined Polity score is greater than 16.

The second set of control variables addresses the problem of omitted variable bias. Having the death penalty is not itself a cause of conflict; rather, it is a proxy for widespread endorsement of revenge. Other factors will also influence retention, and thus we must carefully consider how retentionist democracies differ from abolitionist democracies and whether those differences are plausibly related to the likelihood of conflict initiation. There is a small literature on the determinants of cross-national death penalty retention, and these studies suggests a number of predictors of retention that are also cited as causes of conflict or that are correlated with conflict-generating processes.[15]

Ethnic fractionalization: Countries with greater ethnic fractionalization are more likely to retain the death penalty (Ruddell and Urbina 2004;

[11] Ranges from 0 to 1, higher values indicate a dyad with more similar capabilities.
[12] Ranges from 0 to 1, higher values indicate that the initiator is more powerful than the target.
[13] I also interact the two major power variables (*initiator MP * target MP*).
[14] The weighted global s-score, developed by Signorino and Ritter (1999). Ranges from −1 to 1, more similar portfolios produce higher values.
[15] Following King (2001), I use this theory-based approach instead of including fixed effects, which causes 96% of the observations to drop from the model because they never experience an initiation. In addition, a fixed effects model can only estimate the within-dyad effect of *Initiator death penalty*, whereas the analyses I present in the next section allow me to separate and compare the within- and between-dyad effects.

Simmons 2009). States that are more ethnically heterogeneous are also more likely to be home to a trans-border ethnic group, which may be a risk factor for interstate conflict (Woodwell 2004). I measure *Ethnic fractionalization* using data from Fearon and Laitin (2003). This variable ranges from 0 to 1 with higher values indicating a greater degree of fractionalization (i.e., the probability that two randomly selected individuals are from different ethnic groups).

Income inequality: Greater income inequality is positively correlated with retention (Jacobs and Carmichael 2002; Kent 2010). More unequal countries also tend to have stronger nationalism (Solt 2011), which is frequently cited as a cause of international conflict (Van Evera 1994). Unequal democracies also tend to build capital-intensive militaries, which lowers the cost of war for the median voter and decreases the political risk of initiation (Caverley 2014). I measure *Income inequality* as a Gini coefficient based on household market (pre-tax, pre-transfer) income, which ranges from 0 to 100. These data are available for 153 countries starting in 1960 (Solt 2009).

Civil war: Simmons (2009) finds that countries with a history of civil war are more likely to retain the death penalty, and civil wars can lead to conflicts between states through security spillovers or diversion (Gleditsch et al. 2008). These effects should be greatest during, and in the years immediately following, the civil conflict. I used Fearon and Laitin's (2003) data to code indicator variables for *Ongoing civil war*, *Five years post-civil war*, and *Ten years post-civil war*.

Executive ideology: Right-wing governments are less likely to abolish capital punishment (Neumayer 2008), and there is some evidence to indicate that they are more likely to initiate military conflicts (Arena and Palmer 2009). I used data from the World Bank's Database of Political Institutions (1975–2001) to create an indicator for *Right wing executive*, which is equal to one if the chief executive's party is coded as right wing (Beck et al. 2001).

Independence post-1990: Countries that gained independence after 1990 are more likely to have abolished capital punishment (Ruddell and Urbina 2004), and the frequency of international armed conflict has also declined since the collapse of the Soviet Union (Pinker 2011). Thus, states born after 1990 may have encountered fewer opportunities to initiate conflict due to this structural change. I therefore coded an indicator for *Independence post-1990*.

The literature on conflict initiation also suggests two more potential confounders. While these variables have not been tested as predictors of retention, there is a strong theoretical case for including them. First, states that routinely abuse their citizens' human rights appear more likely to engage in international conflict (Caprioli and Trumbore 2006; Sobek et al. 2006), and retention of the death penalty may reflect this lack of respect for human rights rather than popular attitudes toward revenge. To control for states' human rights records, I use the Political Terror Scale (PTS), which is available for the years 1976–2001 (Wood and Gibney 2010). The PTS is a five-point scale that measures the scope and severity of violations of physical or personal integrity rights carried out by a state.[16] I include *Initiator PTS score*, *Target PTS score*, and their inter-action in my analysis to control for the pacifying effect of joint respect for human rights found by Sobek et al. (2006).

Second, research has shown that the period following a transition to democracy can be particularly conflict prone (Mansfield and Snyder 2005), and capital punishment is also more commonly found in new democracies, which often inherit it from the previous autocratic regime. As a result, democratic age may be positively related to both abolition and increasingly pacific behavior. To account for this possibility in my analysis, I created the variable *Democratic duration*, which counts the number of consecutive years that a state has maintained a combined Polity score greater than 16.

Analysis and Results

The MIDs dataset is an example of clustered data, which are common-place in empirical studies of international relations. Clustered data consist of "repeated measurements on specific units of analysis, either over time in the form of panel or time-series cross-sectional data, or across space (e.g., multiple observations within a particular geographic area)" (Zorn 2001: 433). Specifically, the MIDs data have a time series cross-sectional structure with observations clustered on the directed dyad.

Clustered data present a challenge for statistical analysis because of a common yet underappreciated feature: independent variables that vary both within and between clusters. Consider the example of international trade. Trade flows vary between dyads (i.e., some dyads trade more, on average, than other dyads) as well as within dyads over time (i.e., trade flows between the same pair of states fluctuate from year to year). This

---

[16] Higher values on this scale indicate more severe violations. The PTS explicitly excludes state-sanctioned executions.

feature of clustered data creates the potential for what is known as "cluster confounding" (Zorn 2001; Ray 2003; Bartels 2015). The problem is that, as Ray (2003) puts it, "Causal relationships can operate over time, and across space. Furthermore, they may operate in different ways in both dimensions" (22). Consequently, some variables may have distinct within- and between-cluster effects. Zorn (2001) defines the between-cluster effect as the change in Y that corresponds to a one-unit difference in X across two units of analysis, while the within-cluster effect is the "average effect of a one-unit change in X on Y *within a particular unit of analysis*" (434). In spite of the potential for these two effects to vary in their size and direction, standard regression models, which estimate a single coefficient for each independent variable, assume that the within- and between-cluster effects are equal. As a result, they produce estimates that are "a weighted average of the between- and within-cluster effects for those variables that vary both within and across clusters" (Zorn 2001: 436). This, in turn, can lead to the incorrect interpretation of model coefficients and erroneous conclusions about the validity of hypotheses, especially in cases where the between- and within-cluster effects operate in different directions.

The case of trade once again furnishes an illustrative example. In his analysis of the relationship between trade and international conflict, Zorn (2001) finds that once cluster confounding is accounted for, trade has negative between-dyad effect but a positive within-dyad effect. In other words, dyads that trade more (on average) are less likely to enter into conflicts than dyads that trade less, but within a given dyad, an above-average level of trade is associated with an increased probability of conflict. This may help to explain why other studies (e.g., Beck et al. 1998) have found no relationship between trade and conflict: in a pooled model (one that estimates a single coefficient for each predictor), the negative between-dyad effect and the positive within-dyad effect wash each other out. Zorn's (2001) results also have important theoretical implications. They suggest that, at the "systematic, long-term level," liberal theorists are essentially correct: "higher average trade levels, and their associated greater levels of interdependence lower the incentives to engage in conflict in general" (440). At the same time, critics of liberal theory may be "closer to the truth in more individualized, short-term relations among nations," in that a higher-than-average level of trade between two nations may increase the potential for conflict due to increased contact, concerns over relative gains, or other factors (440). Thus, he recommends that testing for and correcting cluster confounding should become a standard step in the analysis of clustered data and that scholars of international relations would do well to pay more attention, both theoretically and empirically, to the "fundamental difference between static differences between states and dynamic changes occurring within those states" (441). Ray (2003) echoes this recommendation, noting that "over time and across space relationships between many 'standard' predictors and interstate conflict are consistently inconsistent," potentially calling into question the results of many previous studies that employ pooled models (27).

The potential for cluster confounding exists for any variable that varies both across dyads and within dyads over time. This is the case for *Initiator death penalty* and many of the control variables that I include in my analysis. To address the problem of cluster confounding, I use the method recommended by Bartels (2015) and based on prior work by Zorn (2001) and Skrondal and Rabe-Hesketh (2004). This involves transforming each time-varying independent variable into two separate components, one that captures the within-cluster variation and one that captures the between-cluster variation. The between-cluster transformation is calculated as the cluster-specific mean, while the within-cluster transformation is calculated as the deviation from the cluster-specific mean in any given year.[17] These two components are completely uncorrelated, making it possible to assess whether a unit change in a given variable predicts differences across and/or within clusters.

Thus, in the models presented below, I report two coefficients for each time-varying variable. For example, the between-dyad component of *Death penalty retention* is the proportion of dyad-years that the initiating state retained the death penalty (ranging from 0 to 1), while the within-dyad component subtracts this quantity from the observed value in a given year. In terms of the theory, we can interpret the former as the initiator's average level of vengefulness compared with other countries and the latter as longitudinal change in the initiator's level of vengefulness.

In Table 5.1, I present a series of logistic regression models for democratic initiators. Standard errors are clustered on the directed dyad, and cubic splines of the number of years since the last MID in the dyad are

---

[17] These transformations can be performed on any numerical variable. However, the substantive meaning of the cluster-specific mean and of deviations from that mean will depend on what is being measured and how the variable is being coded.

TABLE 5.1 Between-dyad and within-dyad effects of death penalty retention for democratic initiators

	Model 1		Model 2		Model 3		Model 4	
	Between-dyad	Within-dyad	Between-dyad	Within-dyad	Between-dyad	Within-dyad	Between-dyad	Within-dyad
Death penalty retention	1.29*** (0.40)	-0.18 (0.31)	0.87*** (0.31)	-0.53 (0.45)	1.40** (0.66)	-0.50 (0.54)	1.21* (0.70)	-0.48 (0.59)
Target democracy			-0.79*** (0.31)	-0.048 (0.31)	0.28 (0.56)	-0.72** (0.36)	0.20 (0.56)	-0.70** (0.35)
Initiator capabilities			2.99 (3.32)	-3.01 (4.68)	-28.19** (12.19)	-77.41*** (22.29)	-10.51 (27.71)	-76.56** (30.78)
Target capabilities			13.35 (8.31)	-7.34 (8.32)	30.20** (11.68)	19.41 (12.38)	29.13** (11.60)	19.13 (12.68)
Balance of capabilities			0.79* (0.46)	1.08 (1.24)	1.53** (0.71)	0.60 (1.48)	1.52** (0.75)	0.56 (1.49)
Initiator share of capabilities			0.91 (0.56)	4.49 (3.02)	2.66*** (0.86)	15.67*** (3.77)	2.47*** (0.89)	15.51*** (3.81)
Defensive pact			0.65* (0.35)	1.26** (0.54)	1.10** (0.53)	-0.13 (0.87)	1.13** (0.53)	-0.09 (0.87)
Alliance portfolio similarity			-0.61 (0.45)	-0.06 (0.76)	-0.59 (0.60)	0.75 (1.03)	-0.74 (0.64)	0.81 (0.99)
Initiator major power			-0.90** (0.44)	-1.03 (0.84)	-0.51 (0.77)	1.29 (0.85)	-0.71 (0.87)	1.30 (0.84)
Target major power			-2.28** (1.04)	2.55 (1.90)	-2.79* (1.45)	-2.65 (1.63)	-2.88** (1.42)	-2.88* (1.58)

InitMP * TargMP	0.86 (0.69)	1.13 (1.61)	—	—	—	—
Initiator PTS score			0.67 (0.48)	1.08* (0.56)	0.59 (0.48)	1.08* (0.56)
Target PTS score			0.60 (0.40)	1.46*** (0.32)	0.54 (0.40)	1.47*** (0.33)
InitPTS * TargPTS			-0.09 (0.13)	-0.36** (0.14)	-0.09 (0.13)	-0.37** (0.14)
Democratic duration			0.56 (0.34)	0.82** (0.35)	0.51 (0.36)	0.83** (0.36)
Ongoing civil war			-1.38* (0.80)	0.81 (0.58)	-1.72* (0.92)	0.86 (0.59)
Ten years post-civil war			0.73 (1.32)	-0.06 (0.39)	1.08 (1.34)	-0.06 (0.39)
Income inequality			0.21 (0.27)	-0.26 (0.19)	0.21 (0.32)	-0.26 (0.39)
Income inequality^2			-0.00 (0.00)	0.00 (0.00)	-0.00 (0.00)	0.00 (0.00)
Right-wing executive			-1.54* (0.90)	-0.26 (0.28)	-1.41 (1.04)	-0.25 (0.28)
Land contiguity	1.37*** (0.30)		0.93** (0.45)			0.87* (0.45)
Independence post-1990			-0.30 (0.83)			-0.33 (0.86)

(continued)

TABLE 5.1 (continued)

	Model 1		Model 2		Model 3		Model 4	
	Between-dyad	Within-dyad	Between-dyad	Within-dyad	Between-dyad	Within-dyad	Between-dyad	Within-dyad
Ethnic fractionalization					1.69*		1.68*	
					(0.90)		(0.99)	
Western Europe							−0.19	
							(0.46)	
United States							−2.99	
							(3.72)	
India							−0.13	
							(2.01)	
Constant	−6.55***		−3.81***		−14.51**		−13.96*	
	(0.31)		(0.58)		(6.90)		(8.19)	
N	46,505		40,967		19,600		19,600	

Note: All models are logistic regression models with standard errors clustered on the directed-dyad (reported in parentheses). For each model, the left column reports the between-dyad effect and the right column reports the within-dyad effect. A single coefficient is reported for *Land contiguity*, *Independence post-1990*, *Ethnic fractionalization*, *Western Europe*, *United States*, and *India* because these variables are not time-varying. The number of observations significantly decreases in Models 3 and 4 due to data availability (*Income inequality* starts in 1960, *Right-wing executive* starts in 1975, and PTS scores start in 1976). The *InitMP * TargMP* interaction was dropped in Models 3 and 4 because of perfect prediction. *Five years post-civil war* was also dropped because of perfect prediction (*Ten years post-civil war* is included instead). *Democratic duration* is logged. Cubic splines of time since the last MID are included in the model but not reported. Significance: * $p < 0.1$, ** $p < 0.05$, *** $p < 0.01$.

included to account for temporal dependence (Carter and Signorino 2010). Model 1 shows the bivariate relationship between *Death penalty retention* and the likelihood of initiation. Model 2 adds the standard predictors of MIDs, and Model 3 adds the omitted variable controls. Model 4 checks the robustness of the results to the inclusion of dummy variables for the United States, India, and Western Europe. The United States and India are both retentionist democracies that have initiated a disproportionate number of MIDs in the 1945–2001 period, while the nations of Western Europe have initiated disproportionately few MIDs while moving toward abolition more quickly and completely than any other region. It is therefore important to check that these outliers are not driving the results.

The results in Table 5.1 show that *Death penalty retention* is a positive and significant predictor of initiation across all model specifications.[18] They also show that *Death penalty retention* has distinct within-dyad and between-dyad effects. Change in the legal status of the death penalty within dyads over time appears to have no statistically significant effect on the likelihood that a democracy will initiate a militarized dispute. In contrast, the between-dyad variation in *Death penalty retention* has a significant positive effect on the likelihood of initiation. In other words, the greater the proportion of dyad-years that a democracy has retained the death penalty, the more likely it is to initiate a militarized dispute with another state, even when controlling for respect for human rights, the age of the democracy, ongoing and recent civil war experience, income inequality, executive ideology, independence post-1990, and ethnic fractionalization. Model 4 shows that this effect is not driven by the United States, India, or Western Europe. These variables are all statistically insignificant, and their inclusion does not substantially alter the size of coefficient on *Death penalty retention.*[19]

In Table 5.2, I compare the cluster corrected model with a pooled model (i.e., one that estimates a single coefficient for the time-varying predictors) for both democratic and autocratic initiators. The four model specifications are the same as those used in Table 5.1. Here, I report only

---

[18] See the Appendix for additional robustness checks.

[19] To address concern about ongoing conflicts getting counted as multiple initiations in the MIDs data, I excluded all directed-dyad years in which a conflict was ongoing, unless there was a new initiation in that year as well. I also cross-checked all the cases of initiation by retentionist democracies against Gibler et al. (2014) replication of the MIDs dataset. I found three cases that they identified as part of ongoing disputes. Dropping them does not substantively alter the results.

TABLE 5.2 *Comparing pooled and cluster-corrected models for democracies and autocracies*

	Democratic Initiators			Autocratic Initiators		
	Between-dyad	Within-dyad	Pooled	Between-dyad	Within-dyad	Pooled
Model 1	1.29***	−0.18	0.71***	0.22	−0.10	0.12
	(0.40)	(0.31)	(0.26)	(0.32)	(0.32)	(0.25)
Model 2	0.87***	−0.53	0.53**	0.45	−0.25	−0.03
	(0.31)	(0.45)	(0.24)	(0.28)	(0.33)	(0.25)
Model 3	1.40**	−0.50	0.43	0.07	−0.03	0.12
	(0.66)	(0.54)	(0.33)	(0.75)	(0.67)	(0.27)
Model 4	1.21*	−0.48	0.47	−	−	−
	(0.70)	(0.59)	(0.33)			

Note: This table reports only the coefficient and standard error (in parentheses) for *Death penalty retention*. For democratic initiators, the four model specifications are the same as those reported in Table 5.1. For autocratic initiators, the model specifications are the same with the following exceptions: *Democratic duration* is eliminated from Model 3, and Model 4 is not reported because the United States, India, and Western Europe do not contribute any observations to this group. All models are logistic regression models with standard errors clustered on the directed-dyad. Significance: * $p < 0.1$, ** $p < 0.05$, ** $p < 0.01$.

the coefficient and standard error on *Death penalty retention* (see the Appendix for full results). Results for democratic initiators are given in columns 1–3, with columns 1 and 2 reporting the between- and within-dyad effects of *Death penalty retention* from Table 5.1. In the pooled models for democracies, *Death penalty retention* has a smaller but statistically significant effect in Models 1 and 2, but not in the other specifications, which add the omitted variable controls (Model 3) and dummy variables for the United States, India, and Western Europe (Model 4).

This comparison shows that without accounting for cluster confounding, we would erroneously conclude that the effect of *Death penalty retention* is not robust to the inclusion of controls for omitted variables, when in fact the between-dyad effect remains large and statistically significant. Many of the control variables in my analysis also exhibit distinct between-dyad and within-dyad effects, which suggests that longitudinal changes in conflict behavior within dyads may not have the same causes as average differences in conflict behavior across dyads. As other scholars have noted, this is a phenomenon that deserves greater attention, both theoretically and empirically, in studies of interstate conflict (see also Zorn 2001 and Ray 2003).

I include results for autocracies in Table 5.2 because a significant coefficient on *Death penalty retention* among autocracies would indicate the presence of a problem, either with the theory (i.e., vengefulness affects conflict initiation through some mechanism common to democracies and autocracies) or with the measure (i.e., *Death penalty retention* is measuring something other than vengefulness that is common to democracies and autocracies). The absence of an effect does not guarantee the absence of such problems, but the presence of an effect would be informative. Results for autocratic initiators are given in columns 4–6, and as expected, I find no significant effect of *Death penalty retention* for autocracies in any specification, regardless of whether the model is pooled or cluster-corrected.

For democracies, *Death penalty retention* has a substantial impact on the likelihood of conflict initiation. My analysis shows that the most vengeful democracies (i.e., those that have retained the death penalty for all dyad-years) are more than twice as likely to initiate a militarized dispute compared with the least vengeful democracies (i.e., those that have abolished the death penalty for all dyad-years).[20] To make this effect more concrete, I calculated the predicted probability of initiation using the values of the control variables for four conflict-prone dyads with democratic initiators: United States–Iraq, India–Pakistan, Turkey–Cyprus, and Venezuela–Colombia. Specifically, for each dyad, I compare the predicted probability of initiation with *Death penalty retention* equal to one in all dyad-years with the predicted probability of initiation with *Death penalty retention* equal to zero in all dyad-years. This difference illustrates the effect of changing each initiator from fully abolitionist to fully retentionist while holding all other attributes of the dyad constant.

Figure 5.4 shows meaningful changes in the likelihood of initiation in all four dyads. Switching the United States from fully abolitionist to fully retentionist increases the predicted probability of initiation by 1.8%, which more than doubles the overall chances of initiation (3.2% vs. 1.4%). Similarly, initiation is more than twice as likely for a fully retentionist India (9.3% vs. 4.3%), Turkey (9.1% vs. 4.0%), and Venezuela (2.9% vs. 1.3%). This effect is similar in magnitude to the between-dyad effect of the target's major power status, which is significant and negative across all models indicating that initiation is less likely when the target is a long-lasting major power. Taking the values of the covariates for the

---

[20] Based on the between-dyad effect of *Initiator death penalty* in Model 2 in Table 5.2.

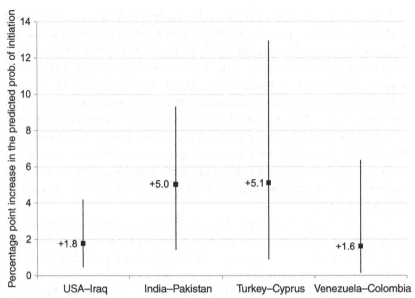

FIGURE 5.4 The marginal effects of a switch from full abolition to full retention
in four conflict-prone dyads. Note: Change in the predicted probability of
initiation was calculated using the between-dyad effect of *Initiator death penalty*
in Model 2 in Table 5.2, with all other variables set at their specific values for
each dyad. Error bars represent 95% confidence intervals.

United States–Iraq dyad, changing Iraq to a major power decreases
the predicted probability of initiation by 59%. In comparison,
changing the United States from fully retentionist to fully abolitionist
produces a 55% decrease in the likelihood of initiation.

The absence of a within-dyad effect for *Death penalty retention*
requires some explanation. If the population of a democracy becomes less
vengeful over time, we should observe a decrease in the likelihood of
initiation as it becomes more difficult for leaders to generate popular
support for war. However, generally speaking, this kind of societal-level
change is likely to be a gradual process. Studies suggest that core values
exhibit a great deal of stickiness and are often embedded in social structures and processes that inhibit rapid transformations (Nisbett and Cohen
1996; Voigtlander and Voth 2012; Alesina et al. 2013). The behavior of
leaders may also lag in responding to shifting values. Leaders cannot
directly observe the values of their citizens but must instead learn from
observation and experience which rhetorical strategies resonate and
which do not, and since militarized disputes are rare occurrences, such

learning opportunities will also be rare. As a result, a dichotomous measure such as *Death penalty retention* is likely too blunt to capture long-term, incremental change in attitudes toward revenge, making it difficult to detect any within-dyad effects that might be present.

Addressing the Issue of Reverse Causality

One issue that remains to be addressed is the question of reverse causality: is it possible that the frequent use of military force makes societies more vengeful and not the other way around? At the individual level, core values are generally considered to be stable personality characteristics (Rokeach 1973; Schwartz 1997; Jacoby 2013). However, there are circumstances under which they can and do evolve (Bardi et al. 2009), even to the extent of altering the average importance of a particular value in an entire population (Inglehart 1997). According to Bardi et al. (2009), one of the ways in which this kind of "mean-level change" in values can come about is through "a historical event that affects the personal lives of all people in society, such as war" (914).

That said, the literature on core value change remains sparse, and I know of no studies that have looked directly at the impact of war on core values in general or on revenge specifically. However, there is a small literature on the impact of wars on homicide rates and other violent crimes (Archer and Gartner 1976, 1987; Kleck 1987; Warner et al. 2007; Beckley 2013). In their pioneering work on this subject, Archer and Gartner (1976, 1987) compare homicide rates over time in eighty countries and find evidence of a post-war spike, especially in nations with large numbers of combat deaths. They consider a number of explanations for this pattern and conclude that it is most consistent with what they term the "legitimation of violence" model:

> What all wars have in common is the unmistakable moral lesson that homicide is an acceptable, even praiseworthy, means to certain ends. It seems likely that this lesson will not be lost on at least some of the citizens in a warring nation. Wars, therefore, contain in particularly potent form all the ingredients necessary to produce imitative violence: great numbers of violent homicides under official auspices and legitimation, with conspicuous praise and rewards for killing and the killers.
>
> (Archer and Gartner 1987: 66)

Archer and Gartner do not specify the mechanism through which sanctioned killing in wartime makes homicide seem more acceptable in the minds of ordinary people, but one possibility we should consider is that the experience of war leads to a shift in people's beliefs about revenge. If the government uses military force in a way that (at least some) people interpret as getting revenge on the adversary, this could make vengeance seem more legitimate in general, leading them to adopt it as a core value and to act on that value in their own lives.

However, there are good reasons to be skeptical about this proposed mechanism. First, the evidence for the legitimation of violence model is mixed at best. Archer and Gartner (1976) are transparent about the fact that their analysis does not provide a critical test of the legitimation of violence model and that "merely showing that rival explanations are disconfirmed or insufficient does not mean that the surviving theory is automatically the correct one" (958). Moreover, other more recent studies have not upheld their findings and provide little support for the idea that war legitimizes interpersonal violence (Kleck 1987; Warner et al. 2007; Beckley 2013). Second, even if the evidence for the legitimation of violence model were more compelling, a population-wide change in vengefulness seems unlikely to be the main mechanism. If war has the potential to change the vengefulness of an entire national population, there should be no better place to observe that change than in post–World War II Europe. Yet in the years since that cataclysmic conflict, the nations of Europe have moved decisively away from capital punishment and toward an overall approach to criminal justice founded on the principle of rehabilitation rather than just deserts (Tonry 1999; Mauer 2001; Whitman 2003).[21] This is the opposite of what we would expect if European populations had become more vengeful in the aftermath of the war, and it suggests that even if Archer and Gartner's original analysis is correct, something other than an increase in vengefulness is likely to be at work.

We can also look for evidence of a causal arrow running from war to vengefulness in the data on popular support for capital punishment in the United States. Since the 1930s, Gallup has regularly polled Americans about their attitudes toward the death penalty. If the use of military force has an impact on the average level of vengefulness in the US population, then we should see some signs of this effect in the death penalty time series, which spans a number of major wars, including World War II (1941–45), Korea (1950–53), Vietnam (1964–75), the Persian Gulf War

---

[21] Ram Subramanian and Alison Shames, "Sentencing and Prison Practices in Germany and the Netherlands," Vera Institute of Justice, 2013, www.vera.org/publications/sentencing-and-prison-practices-in-germany-and-the-netherlands-implications-for-the-united-states.

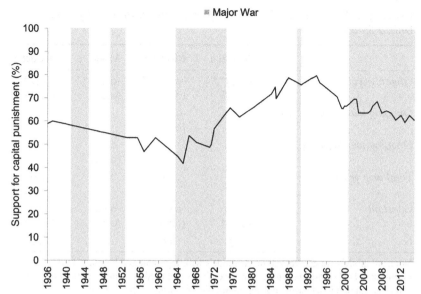

FIGURE 5.5 Major wars and support for the death penalty in the United States. Note: The solid line tracks support for the death penalty over time using data from Gallup (1936–2015). Shaded areas represent major wars (World War II, Korea, Vietnam, the Persian Gulf War, Afghanistan, and Iraq).

(1990–91), Afghanistan (2001–14), and Iraq (2003–10). Figure 5.5 shows the death penalty time series with periods of war indicated by the shaded areas.

If the use of military force does cause people to become more vengeful, how might that manifest itself in the death penalty time series? One possibility is that vengefulness, and therefore support for the death penalty, increases during wartime. It is also possible that the effect of war on vengefulness kicks in (or becomes detectable) only after the war is over, perhaps because core values take some time to shift in response to the wartime experience. If this is the case, support for the death penalty should be higher in the years following a conflict. Finally, perhaps the effect of war is cumulative such that vengefulness increases with the total number of years at war. In this case, we should observe a positive relationship between support for the death penalty at time t and the total number of war years prior to time t.

I test for all three possibilities by assembling the Gallup death penalty data into a longitudinal dataset with month and year as the unit of observation. Gallup has asked the death penalty question forty-five times in the period beginning in December of 1936 and ending in October of

TABLE 5.3 *War as a predictor of support for the death penalty in the United States*

	Model 1	Model 2	Model 3	Model 4
Ongoing war	−0.43***	−0.46***	−0.48***	−0.42***
	(0.09)	(0.09)	(0.09)	(0.09)
Ongoing war lagged 1 year		−0.14		
		(0.18)		
Ongoing war lagged 5 years			−0.12	
			(0.14)	
Total war years				−0.02
				(0.02)
Constant	0.00	0.02	0.04	0.02
	(0.23)	(0.22)	(0.21)	(0.22)
N	45	45	45	45

Note: All models are generalized linear models with logit link and binomial family. Robust standard errors are reported in parentheses. All models include controls for time and time squared (coefficients not reported). Significance: *** $p < 0.001$.

2015, with support ranging from 42% to 80%. I coded the variable *Ongoing war* as an indicator for whether or not the United States was involved in major combat operations abroad during a given month.[22] I also laged the *Ongoing war* variable by one year and by five years to test for post-war effects. Finally, for each month, I coded the variable *Total war years* as the number of years (beginning in 1936) that the United States has been at war prior to that month. Table 5.3 presents the results of a generalized linear model with the proportion of Americans who favor the death penalty as the dependent variable.[23]

This analysis shows that *Ongoing war* has a negative and significant effect on the level of support for the death penalty (Model 1), indicating that support is actually *lower* during wartime than during peacetime. In terms of post-war effects, neither of the lagged war variables is statistically significant, indicating that support for the death penalty does not increase in the first year (Model 2), or the first five years (Model 3), after a major war. Finally, the total number of war years has no significant effect on death penalty support (Model 4). Thus, while this is by no means a thorough analysis of the determinants of aggregate support for the death

[22] I code only the six major wars listed above.
[23] I also include controls for time (a count of the number of years since 1936) and time squared to account for time trends.

penalty in the United States, there is no evidence that the many major wars the United States has fought since 1936 have caused a significant increase in the overall vengefulness of the American populace.

In summary, this evaluation of the existing literature and evidence indicates that there is little reason to be concerned that the results of my analysis are the product of reverse causality. Overall, this chapter provides strong support for the *conflict initiation hypothesis*, and the separation of the within-dyad and between-dyad effects adds nuance to the interpretation. Although we cannot draw any conclusions from these data about the effect of longitudinal change in vengefulness, the significant within-dyad effect of *Death penalty retention* indicates that democracies with a higher average level of vengefulness are generally more likely to engage in belligerent behavior.

A NEW PERSPECTIVE ON DEMOCRATIC CONFLICT INITIATION

The findings of this chapter make an important new contribution to the existing literature on democratic conflict initiation. This literature has focused primarily on institutional variation to explain why some democracies are more warlike than others. The essence of the argument is that democratic institutions assume a diversity of forms that provide varying degrees of constraint on leaders' ability to take their nations to war. Studies in this vein have examined the relationship between initiation and the type of electoral system, the timing of elections, political competitiveness, the extent of political participation, and the strength of legislative constraints on the executive (Morgan and Campbell 1991; Auerswald 1999; Reiter and Tillman 2002; Leblang and Chan 2003; Clark and Nordstrom 2005; Boehmer 2008). However, taken together, this body of research has struggled to produce consistent theoretical or empirical insights.

Beyond their shared focus on institutions, there is little agreement among these studies about what the theoretically relevant dimensions of institutional variation are or how they should be measured, leading to a profusion of independent variables and empirical results that are often inconsistent across studies. For example, several studies have tested whether conflict initiation is more likely in presidential or parliamentary democracies. Auerswald (1999) finds that presidential democracies are more likely to use force, while Reiter and Tillman (2002) find that certain types of presidential systems are actually less likely to initiate conflicts, and both Leblang and Chan (2003) and Clark and Nordstrom (2005) find no difference between the two systems. Mixed results such as these are common in this literature and have made it difficult to draw any firm conclusions about the substantive effects of different institutional types or to adjudicate between alternative theoretical claims about the specific sources of constraint.

In contrast, a number of recent studies have found that institutional differences among autocracies have clear and substantial effects on various aspects of conflict behavior including dispute initiation (Peceny and Butler 2004; Lai and Slater 2006; Weeks 2012), audience costs and the ability to signal resolve in a crisis (Weeks 2008; Kinne and Marinov 2013), the use of force for diversionary purposes (Pickering and Kisangani 2010), and nuclear proliferation (Way and Weeks 2013). This raises an important question: why has the institutional approach been so productive for understanding the conflict behavior of autocracies but not democracies?

I argue that the answer lies in the fact that institutional differences among autocracies are far more profound than those that exist among democracies. This is particularly true when it comes to accountability, which scholars have long recognized as a key source of constraint on the behavior of leaders (Reiter and Tillman 2002). Institutions determine the size and composition of the group, or groups, whose support is necessary for leaders to take or retain power (Bueno de Mesquita et al. 2005), and there is wide variation among autocracies on these dimensions (Geddes 2003; Lai and Slater 2006; Weeks 2012). Non-personalist dictators, for example, can be held accountable by regime insiders, while personalist dictators face no such domestic audience that can restrict their policy choices (Weeks 2012).

In contrast, leaders in all types of democracies win and lose office through the mechanism of regular elections, making them accountable to the mass public. While some institutional features, such as the extent of political participation, may affect the strength of this accountability, they cannot tell the whole story. Regardless of the specific institutional context in which they operate, democratically elected leaders make their decisions in the shadow of the next election, knowing that if they lose the support of too many of their citizens, their ability to govern will be compromised and their hold on power will be jeopardized (Aldrich et al. 1989; Krosnick and Kinder 1990; Bueno de Mesquita and Siverson 1995; Sobel 2001; Baum 2004). Thus, to understand why some democracies are more belligerent than others, it is necessary to look beyond the institutions themselves and examine the attitudes and opinions of the people who are enfranchised by those institutions.

The degree to which democratic leaders are constrained by their accountability to the public will depend not only on their institutional milieu but also on whether their constituents favor or oppose war. When public opinion is averse to war, accountability will provide a check on the use of military force. The potential political cost of an unpopular war creates an incentive for leaders to choose non-military options. However, when the public supports going to war, the risk is reduced and initiation becomes a relatively more attractive option. Similar democratic institutions can thus produce very different patterns of conflict behavior depending on prevailing public attitudes toward war. As I have shown in this chapter, core values – which are a key ingredient in the formation of attitudes toward the use of military force – vary cross-nationally due to divergent cultural legacies. Consequently, these cultural differences play a key role in determining whether democratic institutions are a force for peace or for war.

While cross-cultural differences in values have been linked to differences in national policy in a variety of issue areas (Inglehart 1990; Lumsdaine 1993; Cohen 1996; Kasser 2011), they have been given scant attention in theories of war and peace. Here I have demonstrated the importance of cross-national variation in vengefulness for explaining why some democracies differ in their propensity to initiate military conflicts, but there are other core values that might impact the frequency and form of democratic conflict behavior through a similar mechanism. For instance, the core value of humanitarianism has been linked at the individual level with attitudes toward domestic policies such as welfare (Shen and Edwards 2005) and immigration (Pantoja 2006), and it is no stretch to surmise that it might also be related to support for humanitarian intervention abroad. If this is indeed the case, then perhaps cross-national variation in humanitarianism can help to explain why some democracies are more likely to engage in humanitarian intervention than others.

Considering how such culturally variable values strengthen or weaken the constraining effect of democratic institutions represents a productive new avenue of research on the differences in conflict behavior among democracies. Indeed, while it is beyond the scope of this book, it may be that the best answer to the question of why some democracies are more warlike than others lies in the interaction of institutions and values. In this case, we might find that the most constrained (and therefore most pacific) democracies are those with strong institutions of accountability and strong anti-war values, while the least constrained (and therefore most belligerent) democracies are those with relatively weaker institutions of accountability and strong pro-war values. However, in order to explore this possibility, we need more research at the individual level aimed at identifying which values can most easily be mobilized into support for war and which values can most easily be mobilized to promote peace.

CONCLUSION

To test the *conflict initiation hypothesis*, which predicts that democracies with more vengeful populations will be more likely to initiate the use of military force than democracies with less vengeful populations, this chapter first introduced a novel measure of cross-national variation in vengefulness: the legal status of the death penalty. At the individual level, the existing literature strongly indicates that support for capital punishment is a symbolic attitude driven by the desire for revenge rather than by instrumental concerns about improving public safety and reducing crime. At the national level, I presented evidence showing that in the present day, the higher the percentage of a country's population that endorses revenge as the main aim of imprisonment, the more likely that country is to retain the death penalty for ordinary crimes. Thus, although cross-national survey data on revenge is extremely limited in its availability and thus cannot be used for a rigorous test of my hypothesis, I argued that we can use death penalty retention as a reasonable proxy.

Using this measure, I found strong support for the *conflict initiation hypothesis* in an analysis of all militarized interstate disputes from 1945 to 2001. As predicted, the more years a democracy has retained the death penalty during this period, the greater its propensity to initiate disputes with other states, even when controlling for potential confounders including respect for human rights, the age of the democracy, ongoing and recent civil war experience, income inequality, executive ideology, independence post-1990, and ethnic fractionalization. This finding shows that the role of revenge as an individual-level source of support for war has important international implications in a world where there are significant cross-national differences in attitudes toward revenge, and it sheds new light on the conditions that make it easier for democratically elected leaders to traverse the path to war.

As I noted in Chapter 1, prior efforts to incorporate revenge into theories of international conflict have focused on either national leaders or states themselves as the locus of the desire for revenge, and both approaches have proved to be theoretically and empirically unsatisfying. My theory provides an alternative model for connecting revenge to state behavior that views the desire for revenge as an individual attribute, which national leaders can activate and direct toward support for certain types of policies, namely those that can be framed as delivering punishment to perpetrators of evil. Thus, revenge need not be conceptualized as a motive for war on the part of states or their leaders in order to shape state behavior on the international stage. Instead, its effect can arise out of the dynamic interaction between elected leaders, who behave strategically in order to secure support for their policies and maintain their position in power, and ordinary citizens, who rely on their core values to form their opinions about complex foreign policy questions.

6

Conclusion

This book began with a question: does revenge play a role in fomenting international conflict? The answer that I conclude with is yes, provided that we locate the desire for revenge in the proper place. The connection between war and revenge does not operate through leaders' desire for personal or national revenge, nor does it operate, as some constructivist scholars have posited, through the mechanism of state emotions (Harkavy 2000; Lowenheim and Heimann 2008). Rather, it operates through the mechanism of democratic politics, which links leaders' political fortunes to the attitudes and opinions of their citizens. Cross-national differences in vengefulness create systematic variation in the extent to which democratically elected leaders are constrained by their accountability to the public. In democracies where endorsement of revenge is widespread, leaders are less constrained in their use of military force because they can generate popular support for war more easily by employing rhetoric that frames the use of force as a punishment that the adversary deserves to suffer. Consequently, democracies with more vengeful citizens tend to behave more belligerently in their relations with other states than do democracies with less vengeful citizens.

Although this is ultimately a theory about the behavior of states, its micro-foundations lie in the beliefs and preferences of ordinary people. Thus, in Chapter 2, I began by defining revenge as a core value – a belief about what constitutes desirable behavior or outcomes that transcends specific situations and is used as an evaluative criterion for forming judgments and selecting actions (Schwartz and Bilsky 1987; Schwartz 1992). The essence of revenge, I argued, is the belief that wrongs deserve to be repaid, and in Chapter 3, I showed that individuals who endorse this belief are more likely to express approval of the use of violence to punish transgressors in a wide variety of scenarios. Vengeful individuals are more likely to support corporal punishment, vigilante killing, the death penalty, torturing terrorism suspects, and the use of deadly force to quell social unrest, and they are more likely to think that the courts are generally too easy on criminals and that the police ought to be given more power to enforce the law. Crucially, these results demonstrated that revenge is not restricted to the realm of the personal. It is a general principle that informs individuals' attitudes toward the use of punitive violence even when they themselves have suffered no direct harm.

Like other core values that have been studied by political scientists, individuals' beliefs about revenge serve as a heuristic or decision-making shortcut that allows them to form coherent opinions across a range of issues that would otherwise require a depth and breadth of information that most people do not possess. Conceptualizing revenge as a core value runs counter to the pejorative view of revenge that has long dominated Western philosophical and legal thinking. This "anti-vengeance discourse" is rooted in normative judgments about the primitive or uncivilized nature of revenge, rather than in empirical evidence about how ordinary people actually think about revenge (Miller 1998). This book, along with the growing body of multidisciplinary research on revenge that I reviewed in Chapter 2, advances a new understanding of revenge, not as an immoral, irrational, or pathological impulse but as a widely shared belief that in a just world, those who inflict suffering on others will be made to suffer in return.

This understanding of revenge also provides an important new insight into when and how revenge becomes salient to individuals' attitudes toward the use of military force. A number of previous studies have found a strong relationship between endorsement of revenge and support for the use of force, but on the whole, this literature has not clearly identified the conditions necessary for this relationship to obtain (Liberman 2006, 2013, 2014; Gollwitzer 2014; Washburn and Skitka 2015). To fill in this gap, I turned to well-established theories of public opinion formation that highlight the critical role of political elites. Core values, as abstract and general principles, do not usually translate directly into opinions on specific issues, which are often complex and multifaceted. Generally speaking, elite communication, and particularly the way in which that communication frames the issue at hand, provides citizens with the contextual information that they need to connect their values to specific issue positions (Zaller 1992). By emphasizing certain pieces of information and minimizing others, framing influences how people understand what the essence of an issue is, and different frames therefore make different values foremost in their minds as they formulate their opinions (Entman 1993; Gamson and Modigliani 1994; Nelson and Kinder 1996; Chong and Druckman 2007).

In Chapter 2, I argued that in order for revenge to be salient, the use of force must be framed as a punishment. As I defined it, a punishment frame consists of three essential elements: a clear act of wrongdoing, a clear perpetrator, and a proposed military response that will cause harm to the perpetrator in return. When these elements are combined, they create a narrative that renders a complex international crisis into a simple and familiar story – a bad guy who deserves to be punished. For individuals who hold revenge as a core value, this framing transforms the use of military force into a righteous act, worthy of approbation regardless of the cost or future consequences. On the basis of this argument, I hypothesized that vengeful individuals will be more supportive of the use of force than non-vengeful individuals when (and only when) that use of force is framed as a punishment.

In Chapter 4, I tested this hypothesis using three different empirical approaches. As an initial test, I exploited differences in question wording on public opinion surveys to show that across a variety of standard survey questions about the use of military force, revenge predicted support for force only on those questions that clearly established all three elements of the punishment frame. Next, to isolate the effect of framing, I presented the results of a survey experiment in which I showed that the relationship between endorsement of revenge and support for the use of force is conditional on how the conflict is framed, even when holding all other information about the situation constant. Finally, to demonstrate the external validity of these results, I examined two recent cases of conflict involving the United States: Kosovo (1999) and Iraq (2003). A close examination of the pre-war rhetoric in each case revealed that the conflict with Iraq was clearly and consistently framed as a punishment, while intervention in Kosovo was not, and as my theory would predict, endorsement of revenge (proxied by support for capital punishment) was a positive predictor of support for the use of force in the case of Iraq but not in the case of Kosovo. All in all, the evidence presented in this chapter provided strong support for the framing hypothesis. Revenge can be a powerful source of support for war, but its salience to a particular conflict depends on how leaders choose to frame the situation.

Several other key insights also came out of the analyses in Chapter 4. First, we saw that the use of a punishment frame is not limited to cases in which the nation's homeland or its citizens have suffered a direct attack. An act of wrongdoing, the first crucial element of a punishment frame, can also be established by highlighting the adversary's transgressions against a third state or by focusing on its record of crimes against its own people. Indeed, my theory may help to explain why the "rhetoric of atrocities" – detailed, personalized stories of human rights abuses, such as rape, torture, and the victimization of children – has become such an important part of leaders' wartime rhetoric, even in cases where the use of force is clearly not humanitarian in character (Ben-Porath 2007). This kind of language can help boost support for war by helping to establish, in the eyes of vengeful individuals, that the adversary deserves to be punished and that the use of military force is therefore a just and necessary response. Second, the evidence presented in Chapter 4 showed that revenge is not synonymous with a general taste for violence or preference for military solutions to international problems. If this were the case, we would expect endorsement of revenge to have a positive effect on support for the use of military force regardless of how the conflict is framed. Instead, the evidence shows that revenge is a principled belief about the right way to deal with transgressors. Vengeful individuals believe strongly that wrongs deserve to be repaid, and they therefore require to know the nature of the crime and the identity of the perpetrator before they endorse the punishment. Where this information is lacking, vengeful individuals are no more bloodthirsty or militaristic than non-vengeful individuals.

Having established that leaders can use a punishment framing strategy to help generate popular support for war under a wide variety of circumstances, I turned to testing the international implications of this relationship. In a world where the extent of popular endorsement of revenge varies cross-nationally, leaders with more vengeful populations have a larger source of latent support for war at their disposal and will therefore be less constrained by the potential political consequences of an unpopular war. Therefore, I hypothesized that democracies with more vengeful populations will be more likely to initiate the use of military force than democracies with less vengeful populations.

To test this hypothesis, I developed a novel proxy measure of cross-national variation in vengefulness – the legal status of capital punishment – and showed that democracies that retain the death penalty for longer periods of time are more likely to initiate militarized disputes with other states, even when controlling for potential confounders, including respect for human rights, the age of the democracy, ongoing and recent civil war experience, income inequality, executive ideology, independence post-1990, and ethnic fractionalization. This effect is substantial: a democracy that retained the death penalty for the entire period from 1945 to 2001 was more than twice as likely to initiate a dispute compared to a democracy that remained fully abolitionist during that time. In other words, democracies with more vengeful citizens have a greater propensity to behave belligerently in their relations with other states.

Thus, my theory can help us to identify which democracies are more likely to behave this way *on average*. For instance, a number of former Soviet states are characterized by relatively high levels of vengefulness according to the survey data reported in Chapter 5 (e.g., Russia, Kazakhstan, Ukraine, Georgia), suggesting that successful democratization is no guarantee of peaceful relations in this region. In fact, the combination of widespread endorsement of revenge with long-standing historical grievances and unresolved conflicts of interest between these states and their neighbors may prove to be a particularly combustible combination, providing leaders with both ample opportunities to use force to pursue their states' interests and the fodder to construct a compelling case for avenging the wrongs of the past. In these places, democratic accountability is unlikely to be a strong constraint on elected leaders' willingness to initiate disputes.

IMPLICATIONS FOR THEORIES OF DEMOCRACY AND WAR

Beyond Democracy versus Autocracy: Recognizing the Diversity of Democracies

This book makes an important contribution to the existing literature on democracy and war by demonstrating that persistent cultural differences in the values that shape popular support for war can have a powerful influence on democratic conflict behavior. Previous studies of conflict initiation by democracies have attributed variation in the propensity to use force to heterogeneous institutional rules, such as the type of electoral system (Morgan and Campbell 1991; Auerswald 1999; Reiter and Tillman 2002; Leblang and Chan 2003; Clark and Nordstrom 2005; Boehmer 2008). However, when it comes to understanding variation in conflict behavior among democracies, it is not just the institutions of accountability that matter, but the views and values of the ordinary people who are enfranchised by those institutions.

The idea that domestic culture and values shape the behavior of states in the international system is certainly not a new one. This is the core claim of the normative strand of the democratic peace literature (Maoz and Russett 1993), and it has also been advanced by several studies that examine the relationship between domestic repression or inequality and international conflict (Caprioli and Trumbore 2006; Hudson et al. 2009). However, both these literatures have largely failed to articulate a clear mechanism through which domestic values are externalized, and neither has addressed differences among democracies specifically.[1] In the democratic peace literature, domestic norms of peaceful conflict resolution are considered to be the defining feature of democracies, not something that distinguishes democracies from one another. In the literature on domestic repression and inequality, regime type is used as a control variable in order to identify the independent effect of domestic values rather than considering how those values interact with the political institutions of the state. Here, I have offered an explicit theory of that interaction by drawing on the rich literatures on core values, framing, and opinion formation.

In doing so, this book has also challenged two key assumptions that undergird what Caverley (2014) calls the "democratic exceptionalism" thesis, which posits that accountability to the public is the wellspring of a number of normatively desirable aspects of democratic conflict behavior, including the tendency of democratic states to win their wars more often, more quickly, and at lower cost than autocratic states (Siverson 1995; Bennett and Stam 1996; Bueno de Mesquita et al. 1999; Reiter and Stam 2002; Filson and Werner 2004; Slantchev 2004; Valentino et al. 2010).

First, instead of assuming that democratic publics are generally averse to war, I argued that there is variation in the public's latent willingness to support the use of military force due to cultural differences in core values. Second, rather than assuming that leaders cannot manufacture support for war, I argued that they can do so by employing the power of the bully pulpit and the resulting ability to shape how the use of military force is framed. However, this is not an unlimited power. Public opinion is not clay to be molded into any shape that a leader desires. If this were the case, then democracy would have very little meaning indeed. Rather, the degree to which leaders can successfully manage public opinion depends both on their willingness and ability to craft rhetoric that resonates with

---

[1] An important exception is Busby (2010), who shows how advocacy campaigns around issues such as climate change and AIDS mobilize moral values to successfully alter US foreign policy.

their citizens' core values and on how widespread those values are in the population as a whole. Consequently, the persistence of cross-national differences in the prevalence of core values like revenge creates systematic variation *among democracies* in the degree to which leaders are constrained by their accountability to the public and, in turn, the degree to which their behavior conforms to the expectations of democratic exceptionalism.

This book has addressed one aspect of democratic conflict behavior – the initiation of militarized disputes – but there is a pressing need for more scholarship that sheds light on what drives differences among democracies, rather than continuing to fixate on the traditional democracy/autocracy dichotomy. The crucial question that remains to be answered is why similar democratic institutions can nonetheless produce very different patterns of conflict behavior. I do not claim that my theory provides a complete answer to this question, but it does point to values as an important factor that interacts with democratic institutions to produce the differences we observe in how democracies use their military power.

There is much work still to be done on tracing out the consequences of this interaction. For instance, some research indicates that not only does revenge increase support for the use of punitive violence; it also reduces the impact of concerns about costs and procedural justice (Skitka and Mullen 2002). As such, vengeful individuals may be more likely to tolerate high cost conflicts and to disregard the standards of international law in order to give evildoers their just deserts. Future research could investigate whether democracies with more vengeful populations are more likely to go to war without international authorization, fight long and bloody conflicts, and violate the laws of war in pursuit of their aims. Furthermore, there are other core values that vary across cultures (Schwartz 1994) and that may influence the conflict behavior of democracies through the same mechanism that I have outlined here. To give just one example, cross-national variation in humanitarianism has been linked to differences among developed countries in both domestic welfare spending and foreign aid (Lumsdaine 1993). Could it also help to explain which democracies are more likely to engage in humanitarian intervention? As I hope these examples illustrate, the large literature on values and policy attitudes represents a rich and largely untapped source of new research questions and new theory for IR scholars who study the domestic politics of international conflict.

As democracy continues to spread around the globe, the need for such research is becoming more urgent, for both scholars and policy makers.

For scholars, the spread of democracy means that understanding variation in democratic conflict behavior is becoming increasingly important for understanding the patterns of war and peace in the international system as a whole. For policy makers, it means a need for caution when making optimistic predictions with respect to the effects of democratization on international peace and security. Previous research has encouraged such optimism by highlighting the ways in which democracy makes wars less frequent, shorter, and less deadly. However, until quite recently, the group of states defined as democracies was dominated by Western countries with a great deal of shared cultural heritage. It remains to be seen whether the same patterns of behavior that characterized this group will hold as democracy continues to spread to new places.

Indeed, by calling attention to the impact that cross-national variation in values can have on the behavior of democratic states, this book suggests that there is some reason to doubt the persistence of the most important empirical regularity in international politics: the democratic peace, i.e., the absence of major wars between mature democracies over the past two centuries. Tomz and Weeks (2013) argue that public opinion is one of the mechanisms upholding the democratic peace. The key to their argument is the idea that accountability to the public represents a constraint on democratic leaders. Thus, if the public disapproves of going to war against another democracy, leaders will be reluctant to do so. Consistent with this argument, they find strong evidence that in both the United States and the United Kingdom, people are much less likely to support using military force against a democratic adversary. Furthermore, they find that this effect is due in large part to the belief that going to war against a fellow democracy is morally wrong:

The foreign and domestic policies of democracies reflect the will of the people. Knowing this, people in democracies will feel morally reluctant to overturn policies that the citizens of other democracies have chosen freely. Coercively interfering with another democracy would, by this argument, count as an illegitimate assault on the freedom and self-determination of individuals.

(Tomz and Weeks 2013: 852)

The idea that it would be morally wrong to violate the self-determination of other people regardless of their nationality appears to have its roots in a particular notion of morality, one that defines moral and immoral behavior according to whether or not the action in question causes harm (broadly construed to include not only physical harm but also psychological harm, injustice, and violations of rights). Harm-based morality is dominant in Western societies, but cultural psychologists have long recognized that the "domain of morality" is not the same in all cultures (Haidt et al. 1993). In other words, morality has different foundations in different places (Shweder et al. 1987; Haidt et al. 1993; Henrich et al. 2010). In particular, one prominent theory distinguishes between the "individualizing foundations" of harm and fairness and the "binding foundations" of loyalty, authority, and purity (Haidt and Joseph 2004; Graham et al. 2009). If aversion to using military force against another democracy is based on the individualizing foundations, then it should be stronger in places where those values predominate, and weaker (or perhaps entirely absent) in places where the binding foundations are more prevalent.

This suggests that Tomz and Weeks's (2013) findings may not be globally generalizable and, more importantly, that in the past the democratic peace may have been partly undergirded by a shared set of moral foundations that prevail in the West but are less dominant in other non-Western societies. In turn, this raises the question of whether the public opinion mechanism will continue to support the democratic peace as the institutions of democracy spread to more and more places where morality has meaning beyond just playing fair and avoiding harm. Since major interstate wars are relatively rare events, it remains to be seen whether there is any truth to this speculation. However, in the meantime, further research on the micro-foundations of the democratic peace would do well to incorporate, both theoretically and empirically, cross-cultural variation in morality.

The Behavioral Revolution in International Relations and the Problem of Aggregation

There is a behavioral revolution taking place in International Relations today. According to Hafner-Burton et al. (2017), the defining feature of this revolution is "the use of empirical research on preferences, beliefs, and decision-making to modify choice- and game-theoretic models" (S2). Within this broad umbrella, one of the most prominent streams of research has focused on mass attitudes toward war, not least because those attitudes play a crucial role in a number of important theories of democracy and war (e.g., Bueno de Mesquita and Siverson 1995; Reiter and Stam 2002; Valentino et al. 2010). Indeed, it is common for studies of public opinion and war to cite these theories in order to motivate their focus on individuals rather than states (Gartner and Segura 1998; Chapman and Reiter 2004; Gartner 2008; Horowitz and Levendusky 2011).

Some of this work is explicit about testing the micro-foundations of established theories of conflict (see Kertzer 2017 for a review), but on the whole this literature has neither challenged existing theory in a meaningful way nor led to the development of new theory.

The problem, Powell (2017) argues, is one of aggregation. The actors in most IR theories are not individuals but aggregates, such as states or rebel groups that are typically treated as unitary actors. Thus, incorporating the individual-level findings of the behavioral revolution into these theories poses a significant challenge. In his view, there are two broad approaches to this challenge. The first is for scholars to continue to treat groups as unitary actors that "deviate from the standard rational-actor assumptions in the same ways that behavioral research has shown individuals deviate" (S266). The second, and more direct, approach is to try to build bottom-up theories that make individuals the key actors, and attempt to link their beliefs, preferences, and decision-making processes to international outcomes. The result would be, in Powell's view, a true first-image theory of international relations.

The theory that I develop in this book tackles the problem of aggregation directly, taking Powell's second approach. Individual beliefs and preferences are the cornerstone of my theory, particularly the role that core values (a specific type of belief) play in shaping preferences about the use of military force. This reliance on core values as a heuristic is a general phenomenon, but individuals vary in terms of the importance that they place on particular values. The link between these behavioral insights and international outcomes lies in the relationship between democratic leaders and their citizens. Rather than assuming that public opinion influences leaders, but not the other way around, I conceive of this relationship as an interaction. Because values are abstract and general and international crises are often remote and complex, ordinary people rely on communication from political elites, and particularly national leaders, in order to translate their values into specific policy preferences. At the same time, leaders recognize that unpopular wars carry domestic political costs, and they therefore have a powerful incentive to use the tools of their office to influence public opinion by appealing to their citizens' values.

Thus, leaders face a landscape of opportunity for generating popular support for war whose topography is shaped by the distribution of values among their constituents. Individual heterogeneity in values determines who will respond to a particular value-based appeal, and the prevalence of the value being invoked in the population as a whole determines how much support a leader can hope to gain from his or her appeal. Because certain core values (like revenge) can be channeled into support for war more easily than others, and because the prevalence of those values varies cross-nationally, there exist systematic differences in the degree of constraint that accountability to the public places on leaders' ability to use force as a tool of statecraft.

By relaxing the common assumption that democratic leaders cannot manufacture support for war, and by recognizing that their ability to do so is conditioned by heterogeneity in values both among individuals and across cultures, my theory provides the kind of fleshed-out account of aggregation that has largely been missing from the literature on public support for war. Not only is this an important contribution in its own right, but it also provides a model for dealing with the aggregation issue in future research. It is not just values that vary cross-culturally but other facets of human psychology as well (Henrich et al. 2010; Nisbett 2010), and these differences carry the potential to alter how tightly the constraint of accountability binds. Realizing this potential will require more engagement with the literature on cross-cultural psychology, a greater commitment by scholars engaged in behavioral research in IR to testing their theories in culturally diverse contexts, and a more sophisticated understanding of how democratic politics works than the simplistic model of constraint that lies at the heart of so many prominent theories of democracy and war.

OTHER PATHWAYS FROM REVENGE TO WAR

In this book, I have explored how the political incentives of democratic leaders create a link between individual vengefulness and state violence. However, there may be other pathways that lead from revenge to war. In this section, I suggest two possibilities that could be explored in future research.

Revenge and the Development of Enduring Rivalries

Enduring international rivalries are "long term hate-affair[s] between nations" or, more technically, "repeated militarized interstate disputes between the same set of states over time" (Maoz and Mor 1996: 141). Understanding these rivalries is critically important because although they themselves are relatively rare, they account for about 40% of all militarized disputes and half of all wars in the international system (Goertz and Diehl 1992). Moreover, disputes that occur within a rivalry rather than in isolation are more than twice as likely to escalate to war, and particularly contentious issues, such as territorial changes, are three times more likely to be violent within the context of a rivalry than outside of one (Maoz and Mor 1996).

In their groundbreaking work on the development of enduring rivalries, Stinnett and Diehl (2001) suggest that the severity of the initial conflict may be one of the factors that determines whether a dispute between states develops into an enduring rivalry. However, they note that this variable can have two disparate effects. On the one hand, a large-scale initial conflict, such as a major war, could create a "war weariness" effect, making subsequent confrontations less likely and decreasing the chances that an enduring rivalry will develop. On the other hand, for the losing side, a severe defeat may exacerbate hatred and hostility between the two sides, creating conditions that are ripe for revenge, and making it more likely that an enduring rivalry will develop. Thus, Stinnett and Diehl (2001) remain theoretically agnostic about the direction of the effect of initial conflict severity, and empirically they find no relationship between this variable and the likelihood that a rivalry will develop.

My theory suggests that this null result may be concealing a heterogeneous effect among democracies depending on the vengefulness of their populations. It may be that in low vengefulness democracies, it is the war weariness effect that prevails, while in high vengefulness democracies, leaders are able to counteract that effect by appealing to their citizens' desire to avenge the initial defeat. As a result, high vengefulness democracies may be more likely than low vengefulness democracies to develop the kind of protracted rivalries that are the cause of so much of the violence that we observe in the international system. Indeed, out of the list of enduring rivalries compiled by Diehl and Goertz (2001), approximately 56% of rivalries that began after 1945 involved a state that was a democracy in the year the rivalry started, and of those, more than 84% involved a high vengefulness democracy.[2] This pattern alone should not be taken as

---

[2] As in Chapter 5, I define a vengeful democracy as a democracy that retains the death penalty for ordinary crimes. I look only at rivalries that began after 1945 because my data on death penalty retention begin in that year. According to Goertz and Diehl (2001), there were 34 enduring rivalries that began post-1945. Their list goes up through 1992, so any rivalries that may have begun after that year are not included. Those rivalries that involved at least one vengeful democracy at their start year are US–Cuba, US–Ecuador, US–Peru, US–USSR, US–China, US–North Korea, UK–Iraq, Cyprus–Turkey, Uganda–Kenya, Somalia–Ethiopia, Ethiopia–Sudan, Egypt–Israel, Syria–Israel, Jordan–Israel, China–India, and South Korea–Japan.

evidence that revenge contributes to the development of enduring rivalries, but it does suggest that the possibility is worth investigating.

Revenge, Nationalism, and War

Nationalism is frequently cited as a contributing factor to both the frequency and intensity of interstate wars (Posen 1993; Van Evera 1994; Saideman and Ayres 2012). Political elites often play an important role in fostering nationalist sentiments (Solt 2011), and an early episode from American history suggests that revenge can be a powerful tool for forging a diverse and divided people into a cohesive nation.

In July of 1777, the American Revolution was approaching a turning point. In September and October would come the Saratoga campaign and a victory for the rebels that would bring them the foreign assistance they so desperately needed. As the forces of British General John Burgoyne moved into New York that summer, skirmishes with the rebels became more common as did collateral damage. One of the victims was a woman named Jenny McCrea, who was killed by Indians allied to the British during a skirmish near Fort Edward. The first report of her death accorded it no special importance, merely noting that she was one of several people who had been killed in the encounter (Engels and Goodale 2009).

However, as the historians Jeremy Engels and Greg Goodale (2009) note, the bare facts of McCrea's death were soon embellished into a much more compelling narrative with McCrea as a virginal bride, "murdered in her wedding gown" by Indians entrusted to escort her safely across the battlefield to be reunited with her Tory fiancé, David Jones, who was an officer in Burgoyne's army (93). In this version of the tale, McCrea is not only killed but also raped and scalped, and her "long golden tresses" are presented to her fiancé for payment, in accordance with British policy of paying for American scalps. In this altered form, the story spread rapidly through the press and was later memorialized in poetry, theater, and art, making Jenny McCrea one of the "first cultural icons in the United States" (95). According to Engels and Goodale, this was no mere coincidence. Rather, McCrea's death offered up the raw materials necessary for a truly inspiring piece of propaganda that would unite the politically divided colonists into a nation of Americans by stirring in them a shared desire for revenge: a beautiful and virginal victim, a menacing and barbarous killer, and behind him, the unscrupulous British master, eager to pay money for a young girl's scalp simply because she was an American.

Scouring the historical record, Engels and Goodale find no answer to the question of why McCrea was killed other than the fact that collateral damage from the fighting was a regular occurrence, but this did not stop the proponents of independence from framing McCrea's death as an act of violence against all Americans. The call to avenge her death was intended to unify the colonists against the British, galvanize support for the war effort, and inspire a wave of enlistment. Many contemporary observers and historians concluded that in these respects it was a resounding success and that the killing of Jenny McCrea was instrumental in the victory at Saratoga. "The blood of this unfortunate girl ... was not shed in vain. Armies sprang up from it," wrote Washington Irving (100).

The story of Jenny McCrea, the perfidy of her Indian killers and their British masters, and the need to avenge her death remained an integral part of what it meant to be an American throughout the Republic's first century. Once the war for independence was won and the nascent country turned its eye to the west, the killing of Jenny McCrea was once again used to unite Americans behind a shared vision of their national destiny and to lend an aura of righteousness to westward expansion and the consequent devastation of the continent's native population. This strategy is epitomized by Philip Freneau's 1778 poem "America Independent," in which he uses McCrea's death to justify revenge against the Indians, the British, and anyone else who might stand in the way of the making of a great American empire. "Americans! Revenge your country's wrongs," Freneau exhorts, "to you the honor of this deed belongs" (quoted in Engels and Goodale 2009: 100).

In this way, the proponents of westward expansion built upon and compounded what Engels and Goodale call a "national narrative of revenge as an act of loyalty, patriotism and submission," in which "we become patriots when willing to revenge wrongs against our nation" (109). Jenny McCrea remained a household name up until the Civil War, but as the press for westward expansion eased, her story lost its political utility and largely disappeared from public memory.[3] However, Engels and Goodale suggest that revenge still lies at the heart of many people's understanding of what it means to be an American.

This example suggests that places where revenge is broadly endorsed may be particularly fertile ground for the cultivation of strong national

---

[3] After 9/11, there was a local resurgence of interest in Jenny McCrea in the town of Fort Edward where she originally perished, and she received a new gravestone accompanied by a deeply patriotic dedication ceremony (Engels and Goodale 2009).

attachments that can, in turn, pave the way for aggressive policies toward out-groups that are perceived to have committed wrongs against the nation. Indeed, in the current era, we may be seeing this process play out in the growth of Chinese nationalism. Among observers of China, there is a mounting concern that Chinese nationalism is increasingly being fueled by anti-Japanese sentiment and the desire to avenge the wrongs inflicted on China during it's "century of humiliation" (Gries 2005; He 2007).[4]

The narrative of China's humiliation at the hands of Japan is one that has been promoted by the regime for its own domestic political ends, but it has also unleashed a rising tide of anger and bellicosity toward Japan that may prove difficult to control. Although China is by no means a democracy, the growing consensus among China scholars is that the regime is attentive to public opinion, and having made nationalism the foundation of its legitimacy, it is particularly sensitive where matters of national pride are engaged (Lagerkvist 2005; He 2007; Reilly 2013). Nor can the regime simply use its repressive apparatus to reign in the more extreme nationalists because to do so would "contradict the government's own claims to be the foremost defender of national interest and pride" (He 2007: 18). Consequently, as time goes on, the regime may find that when it comes to Japan, its hands are increasingly tied by the popular anti-Japanese nationalist sentiment that its own propaganda has helped to create:

Having been exposed to the history of Japanese atrocities presented in minute detail, stark acerbity and frequent exaggeration, the general public has developed enormous grievances as well as a strong sense of entitlement with regards to Japan. Whenever there is a conflict of interest with Japan, the Chinese people always expect Japan to make concessions because it owed China so much

---

[4] Although surveys that directly measure attitudes toward revenge in China are lacking, research on Chinese attitudes toward the death penalty can give us some idea of the prevalence of these views in Chinese society. For instance, Wu et al. (2011) compared the attitudes of Chinese and American college students. When presented with a revenge-based justification for capital punishment ("people who take a life or bring severe harm to society deserve it"), 77.3% of the Chinese students said they either agreed or strongly agreed. By contrast, 42.9% of the American students endorsed the revenge-based justification. Of course, a sample of college students is not representative of either national population, but to the extent that education tends to move people toward non-revenge-based justifications of punishment (Kohlberg and Elfenbein 1975), we would expect endorsement of revenge to be lower among college students than in the general population. Thus, these data suggest that endorsement of revenge is quite widespread in China, and substantially more so than in the contemporary United States.

throughout history ... If the Chinese government wants to compromise, then public rage will quickly turn against the "traitorous" government. In order to placate public anger and deflect anti-establishment challenges, the government has to maintain a hard-line policy towards Japan.

(He 2007, 10)

Given the myriad of ongoing issues that have the potential to ignite Sino-Japanese conflict – including the problem of Taiwan, territorial disputes over offshore islands, and competition over maritime resources – the upsurge of anti-Japanese nationalism in China may make it more difficult to avert a great power war in East Asia.

IMPLICATIONS FOR AMERICAN FOREIGN POLICY

While the main aim of this book has been to develop a general theory of how revenge contributes to the occurrence of interstate war, it also offers some important insights into US foreign policy. Today, the United States holds a unique position in the international system. For good or for ill, American foreign policy has the power to shape the fates of both men and nations far beyond its own borders. America's tenure as sole superpower has been marked by a succession of conflicts and interventions around the world. Indeed, since the end of the Cold War, the United States has spent more years at war than it has at peace, and this pattern shows no sign of abating. A college freshman in 2018 has already lived through two of America's longest wars in Iraq and Afghanistan, and looming on the horizon are questions about what, if anything, the United States is going to do about the ongoing sectarian conflict in the Middle East, Russian military intervention in Ukraine, and flaring tensions in East Asia.

In contemporary political debates, the title of "world's policeman" is often used both to laud and to criticize US interventions abroad. This term first entered the American lexicon during the Vietnam War, and when US interventionism increased after the end of the Cold War, so too did the use of the term.[5] To be sure, not all of America's post–Cold War interventions have been popular with the public, but many have garnered majority support (Eichenberg 2005). Subject to certain conditions (multilateral burden sharing, for example), the American people want their country to play a leading role in world affairs, and time and again they have

---

[5] Based on data from Google's Ngram Viewer, which tracks the frequency of key phrases in the corpus of published English language books.

proved willing to support military intervention, even when no core US interests are at stake.

During this same time period, as the United States increasingly took on the role of policing the world's trouble zones, it was also building the world's largest system of incarceration at home. Beginning in the mid-1960s, the United States was hit by a wave of violent crime that peaked in the early 1990s and then off dropped precipitously to hit a hundred-year low in 2013.[6] In response, incarceration rates began to rise dramatically in the 1970s, reaching a peak rate of 751 per 100,000 people in 2008, making the United States the world's leader in incarceration. With the exception of Russia, with an incarceration rate of 627, no other major industrialized nation even comes close to the United States. For comparison, in that same year, England's rate was 151, Germany's was 88, and Japan's was just 63.[7] With more than 2.4 million[8] people incarcerated in a vast array of state prisons, federal prisons, juvenile correctional facilities, military prisons, immigration detention facilities, and civil commitment centers, the United States houses almost a quarter of the world's total prisoners even though it represents just 5% of the world's population.[9]

I suggest that it is no coincidence that the world's policeman is also the world's leader in mass imprisonment. Both phenomena reflect the nature of American values and the ways in which political elites use those values in pursuit of their political goals. The growth of mass incarceration in the United States owes at least as much to politics as it does to either rising crime rates or racial prejudice (Young and Brown 1993; Tonry 1994, 1999; Blumsten and Beck 1999; Mauer 2001). In addition to being a time of social unrest, the 1960s were a time of partisan realignment. The civil rights movement and the passage of the Civil Rights Act in 1964 divided the Democratic Party first in the South and then in the country as a whole. This created an opportunity for the Republican Party to attract social and racial conservatives who had previously identified as Democrats. Republican strategists seized this opportunity by "defining sharp differences between the parties on three wedge issues: crime control, welfare, and

[6] Kevin Drum, "The US Murder Rate Is on Track to Be Lowest in a Century," *Mother Jones*, May 17, 2013.

[7] Adam Liptak, "U.S. Prison Population Dwarfs That of Other Nations," *New York Times*, April 23, 2008.

[8] Pete Wagner and Leah Sakala, "Mass Incarceration: The Whole Pie," *Prison Policy Initiative*, March 12, 2014, www.prisonpolicy.org/reports/pie.html.

[9] Liptak, "U.S. Prison Population Dwarfs That of Other Nations."

affirmative action" (Tonry 1999). Focusing on these issues allowed Republicans to communicate their conservative stance on issues of race without having to express overtly racist sentiments (Mendelberg 2001). The success of this electoral strategy was so impressive that many Democrats concluded the only way for them to compete was to stake out even tougher law-and-order positions (Friedman 1993; Walker 1998).

As a result of this competition to appear tough on crime, sentencing policies in the United States have become more and more determinate, meaning that the length of sentences for particular crimes is set through legislation rather than allowing judges to decide the appropriate sentence based on the particulars of each case.[10] Consequently, it has become increasingly likely that an individual arrested for a felony offense in the United States will be sentenced to prison and that he or she will receive a lengthy term (Blumstein and Beck 1999). In this way, the tough on crime movement has had a ratchet effect on the severity of sentencing policy in the United States, with few politicians willing to take the risk of appearing soft on crime in order to advocate for reform (Tonry 1999).

It is important to note that this is not a simple story of policy makers responding to public demand for harsher penalties in the face of rising crime. Rather, widespread concern about the menace of crime was initially sparked and then maintained over time by the political discourse around crime and the way crime has been covered by the mainstream media (Tonry 1999; Lowry et al. 2003). Violent crime in the United States has been dropping rapidly since the early 1990s, yet public opinion polls show that fear of becoming a victim of crime has held steady over that period and a majority of Americans report that they believe crime is actually getting worse, and there has been little movement to moderate the policies produced by the tough on crime movement.[11]

If American politicians have sought, won, and maintained political power by "persistently bank[ing] the fires of public fear of crime, and then offer[ing] harsh policies to dampen those fires," it is because many ordinary Americans find these policies appealing (Tonry 1999). Getting

---

[10] For example, many US states have implemented mandatory minimum sentences for certain classes of crime (namely, drug possession), three strikes laws that impose harsh penalties on offenders who have been convicted of two "serious" prior offenses, and truth in sentencing provisions that require offenders to serve a substantial portion of their official sentence, thereby limiting the discretion of parole boards to grant early release for good behavior or other mitigating factors.

[11] Lydia Saad, "Most Americans Believe Crime in U.S. Is Worsening," *Gallup.com*, October 31, 2011, www.gallup.com/poll/150464/Americans-Believe-Crime-Worsening.aspx.

tough on crime is not the only available response to an increase in lawlessness (Mauer 2001). Many European countries saw their crime rates rise during the same period as the United States, but their prison populations did not expand nearly as dramatically as those in the United States. In some cases, the incarceration rate actually decreased as violent crime rose due to deliberate policy choices that expanded the use of alternatives to imprisonment, "based on the belief that increased incarceration is neither an appropriate nor an effective response to rising crime rates" (Tonry 1999). The difference is that in the United States, harsh criminal penalties were very popular and remain so today. This is what made getting tough on crime a winning electoral strategy rather than focusing on rehabilitation or addressing the root causes of crime through social programs.

The popularity of harsh criminal penalties in the United States is due in no small part to the widespread endorsement of revenge among ordinary Americans.[12] Indeed, there is little evidence that public support for harsh penalties is driven by personal experience of crime, fear of victimization, or the belief that such punishments provide an effective deterrent (Taylor et al. 1979; Lotz and Regoli 1980; Ellsworth and Ross 1983; Cullen et al. 1985; Bohm 1987; Ellsworth and Gross 1994; Gross 1997; Tyler and Boeckman 1997). Instead, the biggest driver of support for severe punishments is the desire for revenge (Darley et al. 2000; Carlsmith et al. 2002; Alter et al. 2007; Carlsmith et al. 2007; Carlsmith 2008; Carlsmith and Darley 2008; Aharoni and Fridlund 2012). Many Americans support these penalties, in spite of the obvious destructive consequences for their fellow citizens[13] and the damage to their country's international reputation,[14] because their sense of justice demands it. They believe that wrongs must be repaid and that the suffering the American criminal justice system currently inflicts on offenders is nothing more or less than what they deserve.

The United States has grown into the world's largest "carceral state" because for many years, American politicians have played to their citizens'

---

[12] Revenge is the most commonly articulated rationale among supporters of capital punishment. See the Appendix for more details.

[13] The US prison system is rife with abuses, and for those who survive these conditions and secure their release from prison, the ordeal often continues through various forms of post-prison supervision and disenfranchisement.

[14] In many other countries, the American criminal justice system is viewed as barbaric, and its scope and severity are regularly criticized by human rights groups (Mauer 2003).

values in order to advance their political fortunes. At the same time, presidents have taken advantage of those same values to inspire popular support for American interventionism abroad. The nation "acts abroad much as it does at home" because in both domains, widespread popular endorsement of revenge enables and encourages elected leaders to use force to address social problems (Sherry 2005: 246). And while we may never observe the counterfactual, my theory suggests that if a less vengeful democracy held the title of world's sole superpower, its method of international governance might not rely as heavily on military intervention as the United States has done during its reign.

Looking to the future of US foreign policy, one might wonder whether the public's appetite for military intervention has been undermined by the experience of the messy, protracted, and largely unsuccessful wars in Iraq and Afghanistan. While President Obama attempted to "pivot to Asia" during his administration, events in the Middle East, including the Arab spring uprisings, the continuing sectarian violence in Iraq, and the rise of the Islamic State, have ensured that the region will remain the prime target of US intervention, at least in the near future. Since the end of the Iraq War, there has been support for some limited kinds of intervention in the Middle East, such as establishing a no-fly zone in Libya in 2011 (70%) and conducting air strikes against the Islamic State (75%).[15] However, support for sending US troops to the region is substantially weaker. Just 28% of Americans supported sending troops to Libya in 2011, while a mere 13% did so for Syria in 2013.[16] Even in the case of the Islamic State, less than half (47%) of Americans support sending ground troops into combat operations against the group in either Iraq or Syria.[17]

However, we should not necessarily conclude from these polls that the American people have developed a deep-seated aversion to the boots on the ground type of intervention. President Obama consistently proved himself to be extremely cautious about escalating US military involvement

---

[15] The data on Libya are from a poll conducted by CNN/Opinion Research Corporation (March 18–20, 2011; N = 1,012 adults nationwide; margin of error ±3). The data on the Islamic State are from a poll by CBS News (November 19–22, 2015; N = 1,205 adults nationwide; margin of error ±3).

[16] The data on Libya are from a poll conducted by CNN/Opinion Research Corporation (March 18–20, 2011; N = 1,012 adults nationwide; margin of error ±3). The data on Syria are from a poll conducted by McClatchy-Marist (September 7–8, 2013; N = 963 adults nationwide; margin of error ±3.2).

[17] The data on the Islamic State are from a poll conducted by CNN/Opinion Research Corporation (August 13–16, 2015; N = 1,001 adults nationwide; margin of error ±3).

in the Middle East, and during his presidency, he neither proposed a major return of US troops to the region nor made any concerted effort to garner support for such a policy from the American people. Similarly, no such effort has (yet) been made during Donald Trump's presidency. However, my theory suggests that if events inspire President Trump to pursue a more aggressive military strategy in the trouble zones of the Middle East, he could substantially improve on the current poll numbers by clearly and consistently framing the use of force as a punishment. In particular, the Islamic State, with its string of successful terrorist attacks in the West and its myriad of barbaric practices – torture, beheadings, immolations, mass rape – represents just the kind of "useful enemy" around which it would be particularly easy to build a compelling punishment narrative.

Indeed, it is telling that while most of Trump's major policy proposals have thus far proved to be widely unpopular, his decision to launch a cruise missile strike on Syria in response to President Bashar al-Assad's use of chemical weapons in Khan Sheikhoun is a notable exception. Trump's remarks on the strike clearly framed it as a punishment for Assad's use of nerve gas to "[choke] out the lives of helpless men, women, and children," and more than 60% of Americans supported his decision to retaliate with military force.[18] Whether or not this kind of rhetoric is powerful enough to produce a majority in favor of another major war in the Middle East must await the unfolding of events both in the United States and abroad. However, given the complex and combustible conditions in much of the region, combined with Trump's veneration of military strength and his apparent personal affinity for revenge – he has stated, for example, that his favorite bible verse is "an eye for an eye"[19] – it seems frighteningly likely that we will get the chance to find out.

THE FUTURE OF RESEARCH ON REVENGE IN POLITICAL SCIENCE

I began this book by noting that the field of International Relations has paid surprisingly little attention to the topic of revenge. However, the

---

[18] NBC News/Wall Street Journal Poll conducted by Hart Research Associates (D) and Public Opinion Strategies (R) (April 17–20, 2017; *N* = 900 adults nationwide; margin of error ±3.3).

[19] Nolan D. McCaskill, "Trump's Favorite Bible Verse: 'Eye for an Eye,'" *POLITICO*, April 14, 2016, http://politi.co/1qVydmu.

same could be said of political science as a whole. Interstate war is but one of the many forms of political violence that shape our modern world, and in this final section, I review some of the emerging interdisciplinary research on the role that revenge plays in both terrorism and civil war and on the problems that it creates for establishing lasting peace in post-conflict societies. This research shows both the promise of taking revenge seriously as a subject of scholarly inquiry, rather than dismissing it as an unsavory and archaic aberration, and how very far we have to go in understanding the myriad ways in which revenge contributes to the production of political violence.

Terrorism, Civil War, and Genocide

"If there is a single common emotion that drives the individual to become a terrorist," writes Martha Crenshaw (1981), "it is vengeance on behalf of comrades or even the constituency the terrorist aspires to represent" (394). The importance of revenge as a motive for terrorism has been observed in many different times and places, including anarchist terrorism in France in the 1890s (Crenshaw 1981), anti-Turkish Armenian terrorism in the 1920s (Derogy 1990), present-day Chechen suicide terrorism in Russia (Speckhard and Ahkmedova 2006), Palestinian suicide terrorism in Israel (Moghadam 2003), and high-profile domestic terror attacks in the United States, such as the Unabomber and the Oklahoma City bombing (Gallimore 2004). State repression and other atrocities often serve as the catalyst for terrorist campaigns by creating martyrs to be avenged. According to Crenshaw (1981), "during the Algerian war, the French execution of the FLN prisoners; in Northern Ireland, British troops firing on civil rights demonstrators; in West Germany, the death of a demonstrator at the hands of the police – all served to precipitate terrorism as militants sought to avenge their comrades" (394).

In some cases, revenge appears to be the explicit goal of the terrorist organization itself. For instance, Derogy (1990) argues that in the aftermath of the Ottoman genocide of the Armenians during World War I, the Armenian Revolutionary Federation planned and carried out a string of revenge assassinations against those whom they deemed responsible for the genocide. However, most terrorist organizations are not solely dedicated to revenge. Rather, they have political goals, such as extracting concessions from the target state (Pape 2005). Yet even for these groups, revenge can play an important role in the recruitment process. In writing about Palestinian suicide terrorism, Moghadam (2003) observes that terrorism involves two sets of motives: those of the organization and those of the individuals who must carry out its operations. These two sets of motives meet one another at the recruitment stage, "when organizations identify and mobilize individuals who have professed a willingness to die" (68–69). He goes on to observe that in the case of Palestine,

Due to the tiny size of the area ravaged by decades of conflict, an extremely high population density, and high casualty and injury rates especially during the Second Intifada, scarcely any Palestinian has remained untouched by the violence, and many Palestinians ... personally know someone who has been injured or killed during the conflict. As a result, calls for revenge have been extremely common.

(Moghadam 2003: 73)

According to Nasra Hassan, a leader of the Al-Qassam Brigades, the military arm of Hamas, "it is easy for us to sweep the streets for boys who want to do a martyrdom operation" (Moghadam 2003: 71). Thus, Moghadam (2005) argues, the suffering imposed on the Palestinians and the consequent desire for revenge experienced by many of those people has created a ready supply of potential suicide bombers that groups like Hamas can use to achieve their political ends.

Speckhard and Ahkmedova (2006) observe a similar pattern in Chechnya, where brutal Russian military operations have traumatized large swaths of the civilian population. Since 2000, Chechen separatist groups have carried out dozens of suicide attacks against Russian targets, including several mass hostage-taking operations. According to Speckhard and Ahkmedova's (2006) research into the lives and motivations of the individuals who carried out these attacks, "a lethal mix occurs when individuals in Chechnya are vulnerable to self-recruitment into suicide terrorism due to traumatic experiences and feeling a duty to revenge and this vulnerability is combined with exposure to groups that recruit and equip suicide terrorists with both an ideology and the means to explode themselves" (429). Here again, the organizations that sponsor Chechen suicide terrorism do so in pursuit of specific political goals, but their ability to recruit depends on exploiting the desire for revenge among those who have personally suffered at the hands of Russian forces.

Chechnya is a particularly interesting case because, in contrast to the Palestinian case, the general population "publicly decries acts of terrorism and in particular deplores suicide terrorism," and the parents of suicide bombers do not take pride in their martyrdom (441).[20] At the same time,

---

[20] Speckhard and Ahkmedova (2006) note that "this trend could change over time as it did for the Palestinians between the first and second Intifada" (441).

Chechen culture has a strong norm of revenge: individuals (typically men) have a duty to avenge the deaths of family members. This duty to avenge is usually governed by strict rules, including that revenge should be taken only against the murderer and not his family members or associates. However, Speckhard and Ahkmedova (2006) report that among individuals who experienced severe personal trauma, such as witnessing the death of close family members or experiencing torture themselves, these cultural rules often break down and are replaced by a generalized desire for revenge against all Russians. Thus, in spite of widespread popular revulsion against the tactic of suicide terrorism, Chechen separatist groups have no trouble in recruiting foot soldiers who are willing to lay down their lives.

Looking toward the future of the conflict in Chechnya, Speckhard and Ahkmedova (2006) conclude that, "the more Russian military and police actions wreak trauma on the population of Chechnya, the more likely the civilian population of Russia can expect acts of retribution from those who no longer feel they must find the guilty party – any member(s) of the ethnic group can stand in his place" (467). More broadly, their research suggests that places with strong norms of revenge may be particularly fertile ground for terrorist groups to take root because those norms can facilitate recruitment even in the face of a generally hostile local population.

Revenge can also function as a mobilizing tool or mechanism in civil conflicts (Petersen 2011).[21] For insurgent groups, mobilizing supporters to engage in violent and risky activities represents a serious challenge. Civilian casualties caused by counterinsurgent forces have been argued to spur mobilization through a variety of different mechanisms, including the desire to seek revenge for harm done to family, friends, or neighbors. In their study of the recent counterinsurgency campaigns in Iraq and Afghanistan, Condra et al. (2010) find strong evidence that in Afghanistan, this "revenge effect" has led to a significant increase in insurgent violence over the long run. Moreover, they find that these effects are driven almost entirely by behavior in areas dominated by the Pashtun ethnic group, lending credence to the idea that the strong norm of revenge

---

[21] Ferguson (1992) makes a similar argument about the role of revenge in tribal warfare: "Two belief systems frequently work together to galvanize support for war, the ideologies of revenge and witchcraft. Both are invoked frequently in the deliberations which precede a raid, as are whatever other societal values that may be applicable to the situation. It may be a cultural universal that those seeking to create a consensus for war, and to justify the profoundly anti-social behavior which is demanded by war, will couch their appeal in terms of the highest applicable moral principle" (73).

that is part of the Pashtun social code (Pashtunwali) has played an important role in supporting the insurgency in Afghanistan (Johnson and Mason 2008).[22] As in Chechnya, it appears that the combination of a strong cultural norm of revenge with traumatic wartime experiences is a particularly combustible mixture. Interestingly, Condra et al. find no revenge effect in Iraq, and it remains to be seen why, as Fielding and Shortland (2010) observe, similar counterinsurgency strategies appear to reduce conflict intensity in some places by disrupting the organization of insurgent groups and acting as a deterrent to future violence, while in others they seem to escalate the conflict as more civilians take up arms in the name of revenge.

Furthermore, revenge may play a role in the targeting of civilians during civil wars. For instance, Balcells (2010) argues that in conventional civil wars – i.e., those that have clear front lines and major battles that determine the winners and losers – the killing of civilians behind the front lines can be motivated by revenge as well as by political incentives. Specifically, when territory changes hands during a conventional civil war, the group that has seized control has the opportunity to seek revenge against the local supporters of its adversary. In turn, this motivation to seek revenge will be shaped by the extent to which the group's own supporters were victimized by the adversary in the previous period. In the case of the Spanish civil war, Balcells (2010) finds strong evidence of this pattern in the spatial distribution of violence against civilians in Catalonia: the more executions the leftist forces carried out in a particular territory, the greater the number of executions carried out by the rightist forces after they gained control. Given that more than half of all civil wars since 1945 have been conventional in nature (Balcells 2010), this revenge dynamic may be an important part of understanding why civil conflicts have taken such an awful toll on civilian populations (Valentino et al. 2004).

In addition to Balcells's (2010) study, there is also some evidence from journalistic accounts of the ongoing sectarian violence in Iraq – an asymmetric conflict that features guerrilla-style fighting rather than conventional armies – that revenge attacks are contributing to the civilian death toll. Reporting in the *New York Times* in 2010, Healey and Al-Jawoshy describe how the family members of insurgents have been driven from their homes and killed in a "vicious cycle of killing and revenge," which is

---

[22] The Taliban and other extremist groups in the Afghanistan–Pakistan border region are primarily Pashtun (Condra et al. 2010).

rooted in "tribal cultures that permit – even demand – a harsh accounting, in which blood is paid with blood."[23] This phenomenon of civilians being swept up in cycles of revenge has also been observed in Afghanistan. For instance, in 2012, Rubin and Rahimi reported on an incident in Uruzgan Province in which a Pashtun village was attacked, killing at least nine civilians.[24] Officials said that the raid, led by a Hazara commander, was an act of revenge for the killing of two fellow Hazaras by Taliban militants, most of whom are ethnic Pashtuns. In response, a large group of Pashtuns gathered at the center of the district to demand that the Hazara commander be punished, leading a member of the provincial council to express concern that this incident would "lead to a campaign of revenge against the Hazaras." It remains to be seen whether these incidents reflect a broader pattern of behavior in Iraq and Afghanistan (and beyond). However, these stories suggest that cycles of revenge can lead to increased violence against civilians in irregular civil wars as well as conventional ones, and that intra-ethnic or intra-sectarian revenge-motivated killings may represent a serious obstacle to contemporary counterinsurgency strategy, which relies on winning the "hearts and minds" of the civilian population by providing stability and security.

Post-Conflict Processes

After a conflict ends, revenge can still complicate the transition from war to peace in a variety of ways. First, revenge can contribute to new outbreaks of violence that threaten to disrupt a tentative and fragile peace (Hartwell 2005; Boyle 2010). In some cases, individuals may take the initiative to seek revenge for what they have suffered during the conflict or for what they perceive as unfair treatment after the conflict has ended. On their own, such actions are unlikely to lead to widespread violence, but in post-conflict situations where tension and distrust between the formerly warring parties remains high, isolated incidents carry a much higher risk of causing a spiral of retaliation and counterretaliation that leads back to large-scale conflict. In other cases, groups or factions who have a strategic interest in renewed armed struggle can take advantage of individuals'

---

[23] Jack Healy and Omar Al-Jawoshy, "Kin of Insurgents Are Targets of Blood Revenge in Iraq," *New York Times*, June 4, 2011.

[24] Alissa J. Rubin and Sangar Rahimi, "9 Afghans Killed in Latest Ethnic Violence," *New York Times*, August 3, 2012.

desire for revenge to recruit new members, thereby increasing their capacity to "spoil" the peace. Finally, armed groups can use individual acts of revenge as cover for their own strategic attacks.

Amidst dozens of real revenge attacks, armed groups can use violence to clear territory of unwanted groups, to change their electoral fortunes in contested areas, or to claim important economic resources. What allows these illicit goals to be achieved with relatively little notice is that they occur amidst waves of violence . . . that provide them with political cover.

(Boyle 2010: 196–97)

In the wake of a traumatic conflict, and particularly in places with strong norms of revenge, violence that appears to be enacted in the name of vengeance is more likely to be seen as justified and less likely to meet with widespread disapprobation than violence that is obviously strategic in nature. Thus, individual acts of revenge can provide a smoke-screen for armed groups' politically motivated violence, reducing the chances that those groups will meet with vigorous opposition to their activities (Hartwell 2005).

Second, even if renewed violence can be avoided, revenge can still pose a challenge to important aspects of the process of reconciliation in post-conflict societies, including integrating former combatants, developing a strong sense of the rule of law and government legitimacy, and encouraging citizens to participate in government institutions. According to Petersen and Zukerman (2009), "communities and societies filled with individuals saturated with anger and the desire for revenge" will find it difficult to achieve these aims (43). In their view, overcoming these emotions requires a process that includes not just truth and reparations, but punishment as well. However, the dominant model of post-conflict reconciliation, based on South Africa's Truth and Reconciliation Commission (TRC), is explicitly non-punitive and treats revenge as the antithesis of forgiveness and reconciliation (Hartwell 2005). Yet for many people, revenge is seen as a legitimate form of justice, and harboring a desire for revenge against those held responsible for one's suffering is a common experience in post-conflict societies (Field and Chhim 2008). By ignoring or disparaging the desire for revenge, the TRC model can create a disconnect between official policy and popular attitudes, leaving many people dissatisfied and unreconciled (Hamber and Wilson 2002; Hartwell 2005; Mendeloff 2009). There is peril, Wilson (2001) warns, in ignoring local conceptualizations of justice in the pursuit of an idealized image of reconciliation as truth-telling and forgiveness.

Similarly, there is peril for political scientists in continuing to neglect revenge as a serious subject of study. Though much of the discussion in this section was highly speculative, what little evidence we have hints at the potential for research on revenge to provide novel answers to some of the most important questions in our discipline. What motivates individuals to participate in political violence? Why are some conflicts so intractable? How can we build stable and lasting peace in societies that have been wracked by violence? If vengeful citizens can make for violent states, it is time to reject the tempting fiction that revenge is no more than a quickly vanishing vestige of an earlier, less civilized time.

Appendix

Wording of Punitive Violence Questions

In Chapter 3, I analyzed the relationship between endorsement of revenge and the use of punitive violence in six scenarios. The precise wording of these items is as follows:

- *Punch stranger*: If a man slapped his own wife in public, would you approve or disapprove if a stranger responded by punching the man? (Disapprove strongly / Disapprove somewhat / Neither approve nor disapprove / Approve somewhat / Approve strongly)
- *Kill rapist*: If a man raped someone else's child, would you approve or disapprove if the child's parent responded by killing the rapist? (Disapprove strongly / Disapprove somewhat / Neither approve nor disapprove / Approve somewhat / Approve strongly)
- *Parental punishment*: Do you approve or disapprove of parents using physical punishment to discipline their own children? (Disapprove strongly / Disapprove somewhat / Neither approve nor disapprove / Approve somewhat / Approve strongly)
- *School punishment*: Do you favor or oppose the use of physical punishment by grade-school teachers to discipline their students? (Disapprove strongly / Disapprove somewhat / Neither approve nor disapprove / Approve somewhat / Approve strongly)
- *Death penalty*: Do you favor or oppose the death penalty for persons convicted of murder? (Disapprove strongly / Disapprove somewhat /

Neither approve nor disapprove / Approve somewhat / Approve strongly)

- *Torture*: Do you favor or oppose the use of torture to get information from people suspected of involvement in terrorism? (Disapprove strongly / Disapprove somewhat / Neither approve nor disapprove / Approve somewhat / Approve strongly)

CHAPTER 4

Classification of Punitive and Non-Punitive Scenarios

In Chapter 4, I compared the effect of endorsement of revenge on support for the use of military force in punitive and non-punitive scenarios. Below I describe how I classified these scenarios based on the three necessary elements of a punishment frame: (1) a clear act of wrongdoing, (2) a clear perpetrator, and (3) a proposed military action that will cause some harm to the perpetrator.

Punitive Scenarios
Do you approve or disapprove of the US military action that killed Osama bin Laden?

- Is there a clear perpetrator? Yes. Osama bin Laden is mentioned by name.
- Is there an act of wrongdoing? Yes. I assume that most people know that Osama bin Laden was the mastermind of the 9/11 terrorist attacks.
- Does the proposed action harm the perpetrator? Yes. Osama bin Laden was killed by the military action.

A foreign terrorist group has attacked the United States, killing dozens of people. Would you favor or oppose using US military forces to attack the foreign terrorist group?

- Is there a clear perpetrator? Yes. The foreign terrorist group is the perpetrator.
- Is there an act of wrongdoing? Yes. The terrorist group carried out an attack that killed dozens of people.
- Does the proposed action harm the perpetrator? Yes. The proposed action is an attack on the foreign terrorist group.

A foreign country has attacked one of its neighbors using nuclear weapons. Would you favor or oppose using US nuclear weapons to attack the foreign country?

- Is there a clear perpetrator? Yes. The foreign country is the perpetrator.
- Is there an act of wrongdoing? Yes. The foreign country attacked its neighbor using nuclear weapons.
- Does the proposed action harm the perpetrator? Yes. The proposed action is an attack on the foreign country using US nuclear weapons.

Non-Punitive Scenarios

Would you approve of the use of US military troops in order to ensure the supply of oil?

- Is there a clear perpetrator? No. The question does not mention any specific country, group, or individual.
- Is there an act of wrongdoing? No. The question does not specify whether the need to ensure the supply of oil arises from some wrongful action on the part of another actor.
- Does the proposed action harm the perpetrator? No. There is no perpetrator identified, and in any case, the verb "to ensure" does not necessarily imply any harmful action.

Would you approve of the use of US military troops in order to destroy a terrorist camp?

- Is there a clear perpetrator? Unclear. The question establishes the existence of a terrorist camp, but we do not know if it is associated with any particular group or individual.
- Is there an act of wrongdoing? Unclear. Even if we assume that the camp is associated with a particular group, the question does not establish that the group is responsible for any act of wrongdoing.
- Does the proposed action harm the perpetrator? Unclear. Even if we assume that the camp is associated with a terrorist group that has carried out an attack, we do not know the purpose of the camp and so there is no certainty that destroying it will cause harm to the perpetrators of that attack.

Would you approve or disapprove of the use of US troops to intervene in a region where there is a genocide or a civil war?

- Is there a clear perpetrator? No. Nothing in the question identifies the actor that is responsible for starting the civil war or carrying out the genocide.

- Is there an act of wrongdoing? Unclear. Genocide is unambiguously an act of wrongdoing, but civil war may or may not be considered as such depending on the circumstances.
- Does the proposed action harm the perpetrator? Unclear. Intervention does not necessarily involve any actions that would harm the perpetrator (assuming that there is one). Intervention could take the form of a peacekeeping mission, for example.

Would you approve or disapprove of the use of US troops to assist the spread of democracy?

- Is there a clear perpetrator? No.
- Is there an act of wrongdoing? No.
- Does the proposed action harm the perpetrator? No.

Would you approve or disapprove of the use of US troops to protect American allies under attack by foreign nations?

- Is there a clear perpetrator? Yes. The foreign nations are the perpetrators.
- Is there an act of wrongdoing? Yes. Attacking US allies is an act of wrongdoing.
- Does the proposed action harm the perpetrator? Unclear. The verb "to protect" could encompass any number of actions by the United States. It is not clear from the question that such protection will take the form of an action that will cause harm to the foreign nations that have attacked US allies.

Would you approve or disapprove of the use of US troops to help the United Nations uphold international law?

- Is there a clear perpetrator? No.
- Is there an act of wrongdoing? No.
- Does the proposed action harm the perpetrator? No.

Documents Used to Analyze the Rhetoric of Iraq And Kosovo

Also in Chapter 4, I analyzed and compared the rhetoric of President George W. Bush prior to the 2003 Iraq War with the rhetoric of President Bill Clinton prior to the 1999 NATO air campaign in Kosovo. Tables A4.1 and A4.2 list the specific documents used in this analysis, along with the codes used to refer to them in the main text. All documents are available online courtesy of Gerhard Peters and John T. Woolley of The American Presidency Project (www.presidency.ucsb.edu).

TABLE A4.1 *President Bush's statements on Iraq (September 12, 2002, to March 19, 2003)*

Code	Details
B091802	"Remarks Following a Meeting with Congressional Leaders and an Exchange with Reporters." September 18, 2002.
B091902	"Remarks Following a Visit with Homeland Security Employees and an Exchange with Reporters." September 19, 2002.
B091902	"Remarks Following a Meeting with Secretary of State Colin L. Powell and an Exchange with Reporters." September 19, 2002.
B092302a	"Remarks to the Community in Trenton, New Jersey." September 23, 2002.
B092302b	"Remarks at a Luncheon for Senatorial Candidate Doug Forrester in Trenton." September 23, 2002.
B092402a	"Remarks Following a Cabinet Meeting and an Exchange with Reporters." September 24, 2002.
B092402b	"Remarks at a Reception for Senatorial Candidate John R. Thune." September 24, 2002.
B092502a	"Remarks Prior to Discussions with President Alvaro Uribe of Colombia and an Exchange with Reporters." September 25, 2002.
B092502b	"Remarks at the National Republican Senatorial Committee Dinner." September 25, 2002.
B092602a	"Remarks Following a Meeting with Congressional Leaders." September 26, 2002.
B092602b	"Remarks at a Reception for Senatorial Candidate John Cornyn in Houston, Texas." September 26, 2002.
B092702a	"Remarks at a Luncheon for Congressional Candidate Bob Beauprez in Denver, Colorado." September 27, 2002.
B092702b	"Remarks at a Dinner for Gubernatorial Candidate Matt Salmon in Phoenix, Arizona." September 27, 2002.
B092702c	"Remarks at a Rally for Congressional Candidate Rick Renzi in Flagstaff, Arizona." September 27, 2002.
B092802	"The President's Radio Address." September 28, 2002.
B100102	"Remarks Following a Meeting with Congressional Leaders and an Exchange with Reporters." October 1, 2002.
B100202a	"Remarks Announcing Bipartisan Agreement on a Joint Resolution to Authorize the Use of United States Armed Forces against Iraq." October 2, 2002.
B100202b	"Remarks at a Reception for Gubernatorial Candidate Robert L. Ehrlich, Jr., in Baltimore, Maryland." October 2, 2002.
B100302a	"Remarks to Hispanic Leaders." October 3, 2002.
B100302b	"Remarks Calling for Congressional Action on Terrorism Insurance Legislation." October 3, 2002.

(continued)

TABLE A4.1 *(continued)*

Code	Details
B100402	"Remarks at a Reception for Gubernatorial Candidate Mitt Romney in Boston, Massachusetts." October 4, 2002.
B100502a	"Remarks at a Reception for Senatorial Candidate John Sununu in Manchester." October 5, 2002.
B100502b	"Remarks to the Community in Manchester, New Hampshire." October 5, 2002.
B100502c	"The President's Radio Address." October 5, 2002.
B100720	"Address to the Nation on Iraq from Cincinnati, Ohio." October 7, 2002.
B100802a	"Remarks in Alcoa, Tennessee." October 8, 2002.
B100802b	"Remarks at a Luncheon for Gubernatorial Candidate Van Hilleary in Knoxville, Tennessee." October 8, 2002.
B101402a	"Remarks on the Terrorist Attack in Indonesia and an Exchange with Reporters." October 14, 2002.
B101402b	"Remarks at a Dinner for Congressional Candidate Thaddeus McCotter in Dearborn, Michigan." October 14, 2002.
B101402c	"Remarks in Waterford, Michigan." October 14, 2002.
B101602a	"Remarks Following Discussions with Prime Minister Ariel Sharon of Israel and an Exchange with Reporters." October 16, 2002.
B101602b	"Statement on Signing the Authorization for Use of Military Force against Iraq Resolution of 2002." October 16, 2002.
B101602c	"Remarks on Signing the Authorization for Use of Military Force against Iraq Resolution of 2002." October 16, 2002.
B101802	"Remarks at Rochester Community and Technical College in Rochester, Minnesota." October 18, 2002.
B102102	"Remarks Following Discussions with Secretary General Lord Robertson of the North Atlantic Treaty Organization and an Exchange with Reporters." October 21, 2002.
B102202a	"Remarks in Downingtown, Pennsylvania." October 22, 2002.
B102202b	"Remarks in Bangor, Maine." October 22, 2002.
B102402a	"Remarks in Charlotte, North Carolina." October 24, 2002.
B102402b	"Remarks in Auburn, Alabama." October 24, 2002.
B102402c	"Remarks in Columbia, South Carolina." October 24, 2002.
B102502	"The President's News Conference with President Jiang Zemin of China in Crawford, Texas." October 25, 2002.
B102702	"Remarks in Phoenix, Arizona." October 27, 2002.
B102802a	"Remarks in Denver, Colorado." October 28, 2002.
B102802b	"Remarks in Alamogordo, New Mexico." October 28, 2002.
B103102a	"Remarks in South Bend, Indiana." October 31, 2002.

Code	Details
B103102b	"Remarks in Aberdeen, South Dakota." October 31, 2002.
B103102c	"Remarks in Charleston, West Virginia." October 31, 2002.
B110102a	"Remarks in Harrisburg, Pennsylvania." November 1, 2002.
B110102b	"Remarks in Louisville, Kentucky." November 1, 2002.
B110102c	"Remarks in Portsmouth, New Hampshire." November 1, 2002.
B110202a	"Remarks in Atlanta, Georgia." November 2, 2002.
B110202b	"Remarks in Tampa, Florida." November 2, 2002.
B110202c	"Remarks in Savannah, Georgia." November 2, 2002.
B110202d	"Remarks in Blountville, Tennessee." November 2, 2002.
B110302a	"Remarks in Sioux Falls, South Dakota." November 3, 2002.
B110302b	"Remarks in Springfield, Illinois." November 3, 2002.
B110302c	"Remarks in St. Paul, Minnesota." November 3, 2002.
B110402a	"Remarks in Bentonville, Arkansas." November 4, 2002.
B110402b	"Remarks in Cedar Rapids, Iowa." November 4, 2002.
B110402c	"Remarks in St. Louis, Missouri." November 4, 2002.
B110402d	"Remarks in Dallas, Texas." November 4, 2002.
B110702	"The President's News Conference." November 7, 2002.
B110802	"Remarks on the Passage of a United Nations Security Council Resolution on Iraq." November 8, 2002.
B110902	"The President's Radio Address." November 9, 2002.
B111102	"Remarks at a White House Reception for Veterans." November 11, 2002.
B111302	"Remarks Following a Cabinet Meeting and an Exchange with Reporters." November 13, 2002.
B111602	"The President's Radio Address." November 16, 2002.
B111802a	"Interview with Radio Free Europe/Radio Liberty." November 18, 2002.
B111802b	"Interview with Czech Television." November 18, 2002.
B111802c	"Interview with European Journalists." November 18, 2002.
B111802d	"Interview with Russia's NTV." November 18, 2002.
B112002a	"The President's News Conference with President Vaclav Havel of the Czech Republic in Prague, Czech Republic." November 20, 2002.
B112002b	"Remarks to the Prague Atlantic Student Summit in Prague." November 20, 2002.
B112102	"Remarks Prior to Discussions with Prime Minister Tony Blair of the United Kingdom and an Exchange with Reporters in Prague, Czech Republic." November 21, 2002.

(continued)

TABLE A4.1 *(continued)*

Code	Details
B112302	"Remarks to the People of Romania in Bucharest." November 23, 2002.
B120202	"Remarks on Signing the Bob Stump National Defense Authorization Act for Fiscal Year 2003 in Arlington, Virginia." December 2, 2002.
B120302a	"Remarks at a Luncheon for Senatorial Candidate Suzanne Haik Terrell in New Orleans, Louisiana." December 3, 2002.
B120302b	"Remarks in Shreveport, Louisiana." December 3, 2002.
B120402	"Remarks on Signing the Dot Kids Implementation and Efficiency Act of 2002 and an Exchange with Reporters." December 4, 2002.
B120502	"Remarks Prior to Discussions with President Daniel T. arap Moi of Kenya and Prime Minister Meles Zenawi of Ethiopia and an Exchange with Reporters." December 5, 2002.
B120702	"The President's Radio Address." December 7, 2002.
B122002	"Remarks Following Discussions with the Quartet Principals and an Exchange with Reporters." December 20, 2002.
B122802	"The President's Radio Address." December 28, 2002.
B123102	"Exchange with Reporters in Crawford, Texas." December 31, 2002.
B010203	"Exchange with Reporters in Crawford." January 2, 2003.
B010303	"Remarks to the Troops at Fort Hood, Texas." January 3, 2003.
B010603	"Remarks Following a Cabinet Meeting and an Exchange with Reporters." January 6, 2003.
B010703	"Remarks to the Economic Club of Chicago in Chicago, Illinois." January 7, 2003.
B011403	"Remarks Prior to Discussions with President Aleksander Kwasniewski of Poland and an Exchange with Reporters." January 14, 2003.
B011603	"Remarks at the University of Scranton in Scranton, Pennsylvania." January 16, 2003.
B012103	"Remarks Following a Meeting with Economists and an Exchange with Reporters." January 21, 2003.
B012203	"Remarks on the National Economy in St. Louis, Missouri." January 22, 2003.
B012803	"Address before a Joint Session of the Congress on the State of the Union." January 28, 2003.
B012903	"Remarks in Grand Rapids, Michigan." January 29, 2003.

Code	Details
B013003	"Remarks Prior to Discussions with Prime Minister Silvio Berlusconi of Italy and an Exchange with Reporters." January 30, 2003.
B013103	"The President's News Conference with Prime Minister Tony Blair of the United Kingdom." January 31, 2003.
B020603	"Remarks on the Iraqi Regime's Noncompliance with United Nations Resolutions." February 6, 2003.
B020703	"Remarks Prior to the Swearing-In Ceremony for John Snow as Secretary of the Treasury and an Exchange with Reporters." February 7, 2003.
B020803	"The President's Radio Address." February 8, 2003.
B020903	"Remarks at the 'Congress of Tomorrow' Republican Retreat Reception in White Sulphur Springs, West Virginia." February 9, 2003.
B021003a	"Remarks at the National Religious Broadcasters Convention in Nashville, Tennessee." February 10, 2003.
B021003b	"Remarks Following Discussions with Prime Minister John Howard of Australia and an Exchange with Reporters." February 10, 2003.
B021303	"Remarks at Naval Station Mayport in Jacksonville." February 13, 2003.
B021403	"Remarks on Improving Counterterrorism Intelligence." February 14, 2003.
B021803	"Remarks at the Swearing-In Ceremony for William Donaldson as Chairman of the Securities and Exchange Commission and an Exchange with Reporters." February 18, 2003.
B022003	"Remarks in Kennesaw, Georgia." February 20, 2003.
B022203	"The President's News Conference with President Jose Maria Aznar of Spain in Crawford, Texas." February 22, 2003.
B022403	"Remarks to the National Governors Association Conference." February 24, 2003.
B022503	"Remarks Following a Meeting with the National Economic Council and an Exchange with Reporters." February 25, 2003.
B022603a	"Remarks at the American Enterprise Institute Dinner." February 26, 2003.
B022603b	"Remarks to the Latino Coalition." February 26, 2003.
B022703	"Remarks Following Discussions with President Hamid Karzai of Afghanistan and an Exchange with Reporters." February 27, 2003.
B030103	"The President's Radio Address." March 1, 2003.

(*continued*)

TABLE A4.1 *(continued)*

Code	Details
B030403	"Remarks to the American Medical Association National Conference." March 4, 2003.
B030603	"The President's News Conference." March 6, 2003.
B030803	"The President's Radio Address." March 8, 2003.
B031503	"The President's Radio Address." March 15, 2003.
B031603a	"The President's News Conference with Prime Minister Jose Manuel Durao Barroso of Portugal, President Jose Maria Aznar of Spain, and Prime Minister Tony Blair of the United Kingdom in the Azores, Portugal." March 16, 2003.
B031603b	"Statement of the Atlantic Summit: A Vision for Iraq and the Iraqi People." March 16, 2003.
B031703	"Address to the Nation on Iraq." March 17, 2003.
B031903	"Address to the Nation on Iraq." March 19, 2003.

TABLE A4.2 *President Clinton's statements on Kosovo (March 31, 1998, to March 31, 1999)*

Code	Details
C050698	"The President's News Conference with Prime Minister Romano Prodi of Italy." May 6, 1998.
C051398	"Statement on the Situation in Kosovo." May 13, 1998.
C060298	"Remarks in a Roundtable Discussion on the 2000 Census in Houston, Texas." June 2, 1998.
C060998	"The President's News Conference with President Kim of South Korea." June 9, 1998.
C070398	"The President's News Conference in Hong Kong Special Administrative Region." July 3, 1998.
C071898	"Remarks to the Arkansas State Democratic Committee in Little Rock, Arkansas." July 18, 1998.
C090298	"Joint Statement on the Situation in Kosovo." September 2, 1998.
C091698	"The President's News Conference with President Václav Havel of the Czech Republic." September 16, 1998.
C092398	"Statement on the United Nations Security Council Resolution on Kosovo." September 23, 1998.
C100298	"Remarks on Initiatives for the International Economy and an Exchange with Reporters." October 2, 1998.
C100698	"Remarks at the International Monetary Fund/World Bank Annual Meeting." October 6, 1998.

Code	Details
C100798	"Remarks at a Democratic National Committee Dinner." October 7, 1998.
C100898	"Remarks on the Decision of Certain Health Maintenance Organizations to Opt Out of Some Medicare Markets." October 8, 1998.
C101298	"Remarks in New York City on the Situation in Kosovo." October 12, 1998.
C011699	"Statement on the Situation in Kosovo." January 16, 1999.
C011999	"Address before a Joint Session of the Congress on the State of the Union." January 19, 1999.
C012999	"Remarks to the United States Conference of Mayors." January 29, 1999.
C020499	"Remarks on Presenting the Malcolm Baldrige National Quality Awards." February 4, 1999.
C021399	"The President's Radio Address." February 13, 1999.
C021999	"The President's News Conference with President Jacques Chirac of France." February 19, 1999.
C022399	"Remarks Prior to a Meeting with Congressional Leaders and an Exchange with Reporters." February 23, 1999.
C022499	"The President's News Conference with President Jerry John Rawlings of Ghana." February 24, 1999.
C022599	"Interview with Janet Langhart Cohen of the Armed Forces Television Network." February 25, 1999.
C022699	"Remarks on United States Foreign Policy in San Francisco." February 26, 1999.
C030599	"The President's News Conference with Prime Minister Massimo D'Alema of Italy." March 5, 1999.
C031199	"Closing Remarks at the Central America Summit in Antigua and an Exchange with Reporters." March 11, 1999.
C031599	"Remarks Prior to Discussions with NATO Secretary General Javier Solana and an Exchange with Reporters." March 15, 1999.
C031999	"The President's News Conference." March 19, 1999.
C032299	"Remarks on the Situation in Kosovo." March 22, 1999.
C032399	"Remarks at the Legislative Convention of the American Federation of State, County, and Municipal Employees." March 23, 1999.
C032499	"Address to the Nation on Airstrikes against Serbian Targets in the Federal Republic of Yugoslavia (Serbia and Montenegro)." March 24, 1999.
C032799	"The President's Radio Address." March 27, 1999.
C033199	"Interview with Dan Rather of CBS News." March 31, 1999.

CHAPTER 5

List of All Retentionist Democracies, 1945–2001

In Chapter 5, I defined a country as a retentionist democracy if in a given year it (1) has a combined Policy score of >16, and (2) it retains the death penalty for ordinary crimes. Table A5.1 shows a list of all retentionist democracies in the system from 1945 to 2001.

TABLE A5.1 *Retentionist democracies, 1945–2001*

Country	Number of dyad-years	Total dyad-years (%)	Duration
Argentina*	20	0.08	1983–84
Armenia*	42	0.18	1991–94
Australia	269	1.13	1945–84
Bangladesh	14	0.06	1972–73
Belarus	44	0.18	1991–94
Belgium*	480	2.01	1945–96
Bolivia	174	0.73	1982–97
Botswana*	286	1.2	1969–2001
Brazil	12	0.05	1946
Bulgaria	111	0.47	1990–98
Canada	181	0.76	1945–76
Chile	125	0.52	1989–2001
Cyprus	205	0.86	1960–62, 1968–83
Czechoslovakia	25	0.1	1945–46, 1990
Dominican Rep.	11	0.05	1962
Fiji	50	0.21	1970–79
Finland	35	0.15	1945–49
France*	2,794	11.72	1946–57, 1969–81
Gambia	178	0.75	1965–93
Greece*	303	1.27	1945–48, 1975–93
Guatemala	76	0.32	1996–2001
Hungary	9	0.04	1990
India*	699	2.93	1950–2001
Ireland	227	0.95	1945–90
Israel*	55	0.23	1948–54
Italy	9	0.04	1947
Jamaica	490	2.06	1962–2001
Japan*	2,294	9.63	1952–2001
Laos	18	0.08	1958–59
Latvia	123	0.52	1991–99

Country	Number of dyad-years	Total dyad-years (%)	Duration
Lesotho	64	0.27	1966–69, 1993–97
Lithuania	103	0.43	1991–98
Madagascar	100	0.42	1992–2001
Malaysia	127	0.53	1957–68
Mali	69	0.29	1992–96
Mauritius	170	0.71	1968–95
Mexico	22	0.09	2000–2001
Moldova	26	0.11	1993–95
Mongolia	69	0.29	1992–2001
Myanmar*	128	0.54	1948–61
New Zealand	76	0.32	1945–61
Niger*	59	0.25	1992–95
Nigeria*	153	0.64	1960–65, 1979–83
Pakistan*	160	0.67	1956–57, 1973–76, 1988–98
Papua New Guinea*	242	1.02	1975–2001
Paraguay	10	0.04	1992
Philippines	99	0.42	1987
Poland	115	0.48	1991–97
Russia*	373	1.57	2000–2001
Senegal	26	0.11	2000–2001
Somalia*	78	0.33	1960–68
South Africa	39	0.16	1993–95
South Korea*	32	0.13	1960, 1998–2001
Spain	11	0.05	1978
Sri Lanka	178	0.75	1948–77
Sudan*	127	0.53	1956–57, 1965–68, 1986–88
Syria*	36	0.15	1954–57
Taiwan*	73	0.31	1992–2001
Thailand*	132	0.55	1992–2001
Trinidad & Tobago	444	1.86	1962–2001
Turkey*	716	3	1946–53, 1960–70, 1973–79, 1983–2001
Uganda	37	0.16	1962–65
Ukraine	94	0.39	1994–99
United Kingdom*	2,847	11.95	1945–73
United States*	7,410	31.09	1945–2001
Yugoslavia	27	0.11	2000–2001

Note: Countries marked with an asterisk (*) initiated at least one militarized interstate dispute (MID) in the period 1945–2001.

TABLE A5.2 *The effect of revenge, deterrence, and public safety on death penalty retention*

	Coeff.	Std. Error	P	Pseudo R^2
% Endorsing revenge	0.10	0.05	0.039	0.142
% Endorsing deterrence	0.05	0.04	0.142	0.061
% Endorsing public safety	−0.03	0.05	0.523	0.012
% Endorsing utilitarianism (deterrence + public safety)	0.02	0.03	0.460	0.016

Note: Each row reports the results of a bivariate logistic regression model with current death penalty retention as the dependent variable (N = 43).

Revenge, Deterrence, and Public Safety as Predictors of Current Death Penalty Retention

To validate using death penalty retention as a proxy for the vengefulness of a country's population, I analyzed the relationship between endorsement of different punishment goals as measured by a question about the main aim of imprisonment from Gallup International's Voice of the People Millennium (VPM) Survey (2000). The question asked respondents what the main aim of imprisonment should be: revenge ("to make those who have done wrong pay for it"), deterrence ("to act as a deterrent to others"), or public safety ("to protect other citizens"). For each of the forty-three democracies included in the VPM survey, I calculated the percentage of the population that selected each punishment goal. Since both deterrence and public safety are common utilitarian rationales for imprisonment, I also tried combining them into a single variable. The models reported in Table A5.2 are bivariate logistic regression models with current death penalty retention as the dependent variable (N = 43).

Revenge as a Predictor of Active Executions

As I noted in Chapter 5, I use the legal status of the death penalty rather than its active use as my proxy for vengefulness. Some countries retain the death penalty for many years without carrying out an execution, suggesting that the demand for vengeance may be waning, and data on the year of last known execution are widely available. However, active use of the death penalty depends not only on public opinion but also on the type and frequency of crime in a society (Lofquist 2001) and on the accumulated decisions of a complex legal process that, in many democracies, is actively

TABLE A5.3 *The effect of revenge on executions*

	Model 1 Year of last execution	Model 2 Recent executions
% Endorsing revenge	0.07 (0.07)	0.05 (0.04)
R^2	0.03	0.03
N	42	42

Note: All models are logistic regression models with standard errors in parentheses. Significance: * $p < 0.05$, ** $p < 0.01$, *** $p < 0.001$.

shielded from public pressure (Volcansek 2010). Thus, there will be significantly more noise in a measure of vengefulness based on last known execution. Using the measure of *Percent vengeful* derived from the VPM survey ($N = 43$ democracies), I find that there is no relationship between the vengefulness of a democracy's population and either the year of last execution (see Model 1 in Table A5.3) or the likelihood that the country carried out an execution after the survey was conducted in 2000 (see Model 2 in Table A5.3).

Testing Alternative Measures of Cross-National Variation in Vengefulness

I also replicated my main models of conflict initiation with two alternative measures of the main independent variable based on the last known execution in every country (see Tables A5.4 and A5.5). As expected, neither measure has a significant effect on the likelihood of conflict initiation.

Active Executions
- An indicator variable equal to 1 up to and including the year of last known execution and 0 in all years thereafter.

Death Penalty Intensity
- Equal to 2 in the years up to and including the year of last known execution.
- Equal to 1 in the years between last known execution and abolition of the death penalty for ordinary crimes.
- Equal to 0 in all years after abolition.

Note that in the models reported below, I treat *Death penalty intensity* as a continuous variable. Transforming this variable into its between-dyad and within-dyad components produces two continuous variables (the former ranges from 0 to 2, and the latter ranges from −1.89 to 1.89).

TABLE A5.4 *Cluster-corrected models with death penalty intensity*

	Model 1		Model 2	
	Between-dyad	*Within-dyad*	*Between-dyad*	*Within-dyad*
Death penalty intensity	0.61***	−0.18	0.35	−0.42
	(0.18)	(0.17)	(0.33)	(0.40)
Target democracy			0.22	−0.70*
			(0.58)	(0.37)
Initiator capability score			−19.55	−68.91***
			(12.72)	(22.71)
Target capabilities score			30.64**	18.49
			(12.32)	(12.56)
Balance of capabilities			1.52*	0.24
			(0.78)	(1.56)
Initiator share of capability			2.61***	15.17***
			(0.90)	(4.08)
Defensive pact			0.98*	−0.09
			(0.59)	(0.91)
Alliance portfolio similarity			−0.46	0.76
			(0.65)	(1.01)
Initiator major power			−0.79	1.32
			(0.75)	(0.82)
Target major power			−2.80*	−2.70
			(1.51)	(1.65)
InitiatorMP * TargetMP			–	–
Initiator PTS score			0.46	1.02*
			(0.48)	(0.57)
Target PTS score			0.56	1.40***
			(0.40)	(0.32)
InitiatorPTS * TargetPTS			−0.08	−0.34**
			(0.13)	(0.14)

	Model 1		Model 2	
	Between-dyad	*Within-dyad*	*Between-dyad*	*Within-dyad*
Democratic duration			0.35 (0.32)	0.73** (0.35)
Ongoing civil war			0.75 (0.63)	−0.81 (0.74)
Ten years post–civil war			1.24 (1.41)	−0.13 (0.44)
Income inequality			0.23 (0.32)	−0.25 (0.20)
Income inequality²			−0.00 (0.00)	0.00 (0.00)
Right-wing executive			−1.14 (0.84)	−0.26 (0.28)
Land contiguity			0.92** (0.45)	
Independence post-1990			−0.19 (0.87)	
Ethnic fractionalization			1.65 (1.04)	
Constant	−6.43*** (0.27)		−13.53* (7.57)	
N	46,342		19,496	

Note: All models are logistic regression models with standard errors clustered on the directed-dyad (reported in parentheses). For each model, the left column reports the between-dyad effect and the right column reports the within dyad effect. A single coefficient is reported for *Land contiguity, Independence post-1990, Ethnic fractionalization, Western Europe, United States,* and *India* because these variables are not time-varying. The number of observations significantly decreases in Model 2 due to data availability (*Income inequality* starts in 1960, *Right-wing executive* starts in 1975, and PTS scores start in 1976). The *Initiator MP * Target MP* interaction was dropped in Model 2 because of perfect prediction. *Five years post–civil war* was also dropped because of perfect prediction (*Ten years post–civil war* is included instead). *Democratic duration* is logged. Cubic splines of time since last MID are included in the model but not reported. Significance: * $p < 0.1$, ** $p < 0.05$, *** $p < 0.01$.

TABLE A5.5 *Cluster-corrected models with active executions*

	Model 1		Model 2	
	Between-dyad	*Within-dyad*	*Between-dyad*	*Within-dyad*
Active executions	0.98***	−0.29	−0.25	−0.48
	(0.33)	(0.34)	(0.56)	(0.73)
Target democracy			0.22	−0.63*
			(0.59)	(0.37)
Init. cap. score			−8.99	−57.30***
			(12.34)	(21.13)
Targ. cap. score			33.17	17.91
			(13.56)	(12.56)
Balance of capabilities			1.64**	−0.18
			(0.80)	(1.57)
Init. share of cap.			2.83***	14.67***
			(0.91)	(4.03)
Defensive pact			0.71	−0.19
			(0.64)	(0.92)
Alliance portfolio sim.			−0.19	0.89
			(0.72)	(0.98)
Initiator major power			−0.85	1.29
			(0.78)	(0.80)
Target major power			−2.81*	−2.71
			(1.69)	(1.80)
InitMP * TargMP			–	–
Initiator PTS score			0.28	0.99
			(0.49)	(0.57)
Target PTS score			0.55	1.41***
			(0.39)	(0.32)
InitPTS * TargPTS			−0.07	−0.35**
			(0.13)	(0.14)
Democratic duration			0.15	0.81**
			(0.28)	(0.36)
Ongoing civil war			1.00	−0.35
			(0.66)	(0.66)
Ten yrs. post–civil war			1.47	−0.06
			(1.39)	(0.44)
Income inequality			0.17	−0.26
			(0.30)	(0.20)

	Model 1		Model 2	
	Between-dyad	*Within-dyad*	*Between-dyad*	*Within-dyad*
Income inequality^2			−0.00	0.00
			(0.00)	(0.00)
Right-wing executive			−0.80	−0.25
			(0.75)	(0.28)
Land contiguity			1.01	
			(0.46)**	
Indep. post-1990			−0.37	
			(0.83)	
Ethnic fract.			1.74	
			(1.08)	
Constant	−6.23***		−11.80	
	(0.23)		(7.15)	
N	46,404		19,548	

Note: All models are logistic regression models with standard errors clustered on the directed-dyad (reported in parentheses). For each model, the left column reports the between-dyad effect and the right column reports the within-dyad effect. A single coefficient is reported for *Land contiguity, Independence post-1990, Ethnic fractionalization, Western Europe, United States,* and *India* because these variables are not time-varying. The number of observations significantly decreases in Model 2 due to data availability (*Income inequality* starts in 1960, *Right-wing executive* starts in 1975, and PTS scores start in 1976). The *Initiator MP * Target MP* interaction was dropped in Model 2 because of perfect prediction. *Five years post–civil war* was also dropped because of perfect prediction (*Ten years post–civil war* is included instead). *Democratic duration* is logged. Cubic splines of time since last MID are included in the model but not reported. Significance: * $p < 0.1$, ** $p < 0.05$, *** $p < 0.01$.

Additional Robustness Checks for Table 5.1

All models presented in Table A5.6 are cluster-corrected models that include the full set of militarized interstate dispute (MID) control variables. I report only the between-dyad effects since I find no within-dyad effect of *Death penalty retention* in any model specification. I do not report the effects of the MID controls to save space and highlight the relevant comparisons.

• **Model A** is the same as Model 2 from Table 5.1 for purposes of comparison.
• **Model B** replicates the specification of Model 2 from Table 5.1 using the reduced sample from Model 4.

TABLE A5.6 *Results of additional robustness checks for Table 5.1*

	Model A	Model B	Model C	Model D	Model E	Model F
Death penalty retention	0.87***	0.73*	0.15	1.39**	1.38**	1.21*
	(0.31)	(0.40)	(0.41)	(0.66)	(0.66)	(0.70)
Democratic duration			−0.08	0.55	0.56*	0.51
			(0.16)	(0.34)	(0.34)	(0.36)
Indep. post-1990			0.41**	−0.31		−0.33
			(0.21)	(0.85)		(0.86)
Western Europe			−0.25	−0.05	−0.02	−0.19
			(0.49)	(0.46)	(0.46)	(0.46)
United States			−2.01			−2.99
			(1.43)			(3.72)
India			−0.11			−0.13
			(0.78)			(2.01)
Ongoing civil war			−0.59	−1.35*	−1.34*	−1.72*
			(0.37)	(0.78)	(0.77)	(0.92)
Ten years post–civil war			−0.06	0.72	0.75	1.08
			(1.17)	(1.33)	(1.29)	(1.34)
Ethnic fractionalization			2.15	1.67*	1.70*	1.68
			(0.76)	(0.86)	(0.90)	(0.99)
Initiator PTS score				0.65	0.65	0.59
				(0.48)	(0.48)	(0.48)
Target PTS score				0.60	0.59	0.54
				(0.40)	(0.40)	(0.40)
InitPTS * TargPTS				−0.09	−0.09	−0.09
				(0.13)	(0.13)	(0.13)
Right-wing executive				−1.54*	−1.49	−1.41
				(0.89)	(0.92)	(1.04)
Income inequality				0.22	0.22	0.22
				(0.28)	(0.28)	(0.32)
Income inequality^2				−0.00	0.00	−0.00
				(0.00)	(0.00)	(0.00)
Constant	−3.81***	−3.86***	−4.00***	−14.49**	−14.75**	−13.96*
	(0.58)	(0.84)	(0.88)	(6.86)	(6.90)	−(8.19)
N	40,967	19,600	37,778	19,600	19,600	19,600

Notes: This table reports only between-dyad effects (there are no significant within-dyad effects of *Death penalty retention* in any model specification). All models are logistic regression models with standard errors clustered on the directed-dyad (reported in parentheses). Variables that are included but not reported are *Target democracy*, *Initiator capabilities score*, *Target capabilities score*, *Defensive pact*, *Alliance portfolio similarity*, *Initiator major power*, *Target major power*, *InitiatorMP * TargetMP*, and *Land contiguity*. Cubic splines of years since last MID are included in the model but not reported. Significance: * $p < 0.1$, ** $p < 0.05$, *** $p < 0.01$.

- **Model C** excludes control variables with significant missing data (*Initiator PTS, Target PTS, InitiatorPTS *T argetPTS, Right-wing executive, Income inequality,* and *Income inequality²*).
- **Model D** includes all controls except the dummy variables for *United States* and *Europe*.
- **Model E** includes all control variables except *Independence post-1990*, and the dummy variables for *United States* and *Europe*.

Model B illustrates the effect of the reduced sample size in Model 4 of Table 5.1 compared with Model 2 (reported here as Model A). Model 4 has a significantly reduced sample size as a result of missing data for a number of control variables (N = 19,600 vs. N = 40,967 for Model 2). Most notably, the PTS scores are available only starting in 1976, executive ideology is available only starting in 1975, and income inequality is available only starting in 1960. Thus, Model B includes only observations that have complete data for all of the control variables (N = 19,600). Compared with Model A, the coefficient on *Death penalty retention* is reduced slightly and the standard error is increased slightly as one would expect with a sample size reduced by more than 50%. However, the conclusion remains basically the same: *Death penalty retention* has a substantively large and statistically significant effect on the likelihood of initiation.

Model C includes only those control variables that have complete or mostly complete data (*Democratic duration, Independence post-1990, Ongoing civil war, Ten years post–civil war, Ethnic fractionalization,* and the dummy variables for *Western Europe, United States,* and *India*). Here, the size of the coefficient on *Death penalty retention* is substantially reduced and is no longer statistically significant. However, there is good reason to believe that this is an undesirable specification of the model. It excludes a set of variables (*Initiator PTS, Target PTS, InitiatorPTS * TargetPTS, Right-wing executive, Income inequality,* and *Income inequality²*) that are correlated both with *Death penalty retention* and with other covariates in the model. As a result, we may be getting biased estimates of the effect of both *Death penalty retention* and the control variables in Model C. When the excluded control variables are added back into the model (see Model F), the effect of *Death penalty retention* becomes substantively large and statistically significant, and the size, significance, and sign of several of the other predictors change as well.

Models D and E show the effect of excluding control variables that may be extraneous. To make this determination, I added each control variable individually to a baseline model (Model 2 from Table 5.1). The dummy variables for the *United States* and *India* had no effect on the size of the coefficient on *Initiator death penalty*, and *Independence post-1990* caused only a minor reduction, suggesting that these variables can be excluded from the model without increased omitted variable bias. The results from Model D (excluding *United States* and *India*) and Model E (excluding *United States, India*, and *Independence post-1990*) do not alter my conclusions; if anything, the effect of *Death penalty retention* become slightly stronger.

Full Results for Table 5.2

In this section, Table A5.7 reports the full results of the pooled models for democratic imitators in Table 5.2 (column 4). Table A5.8 reports the full results of the pooled models for autocratic initiators in Table 5.2 (column 7). Table A5.9 reports the full results of the cluster-corrected models for autocratic initiators in Table 5.2 (columns 5 and 6).

TABLE A5.7 *Pooled models for democratic initiators*

	Model 1	Model 2	Model 3	Model 4
Death penalty retention	0.71***	0.52**	0.45	0.34
	(0.26)	(0.24)	(0.34)	(0.39)
Target democracy		−0.77***	−1.05*	0.05
		(0.24)	(0.56)	(0.35)
Initiator capabilities score		2.61	−2.74	−45.90**
		(1.67)	(6.10)	(22.48)
Target capabilities score		3.04	16.32*	22.39**
		(3.61)	(8.78)	(10.66)
Balance of capabilities		0.62	0.38	1.29**
		(0.39)	(0.47)	(0.50)
Initiator share of capability		1.27**	1.99***	2.92***
		(0.55)	(0.73)	(0.90)
Defensive pact		0.48	0.76*	−0.10
		(0.31)	(0.40)	(0.41)
Alliance portfolio similarity		−0.23	−0.52	0.06
		(0.35)	(0.61)	(0.67)
Initiator major power		−1.10***	−1.20**	−0.56
		(0.36)	(0.57)	(0.86)
Target major power		−0.68	−1.43	−1.12
		(0.50)	(0.98)	(1.13)
InitiatorMP * TargetMP		1.70***	−	−
		(0.60)		

	Model 1	Model 2	Model 3	Model 4
Land contiguity		1.67***	1.48***	2.20***
		(0.27)	(0.40)	(0.47)
Initiator PTS score			0.87***	0.91**
			(0.30)	(0.40)
Target PTS score			1.12***	1.16**
			(0.21)	(0.27)
*InitiatorPTS * TargetPTS*			−0.29***	−0.27**
			(0.08)	(0.10)
Democratic duration			0.13	0.14
			(0.15)	(0.17)
Ongoing civil war			−0.12	0.08
			(0.39)	(0.50)
Ten years post–civil war			−0.43	−0.08
			(0.47)	(0.53)
Income inequality			−0.02	−0.01
			(0.16)	(0.17)
Income inequality²			0.00	0.00
			(0.00)	(0.00)
Right-wing executive			−0.08	0.01
			(0.26)	(0.26)
Independence post-1990			−0.31	0.04
			(0.74)	(0.80)
Ethnic fractionalization			1.18	−0.03
			(0.83)	(1.18)
United States				5.51**
				(2.60)
India				2.18
				(1.62)
Western Europe				−0.53
				(0.46)
Constant	−6.13	−5.12***	−8.77**	−11.36***
	(0.21)	(0.53)	(3.87)	(4.10)
N	46,505	40,967	19,705	19,705

Notes: All models are logistic regression models with standard errors clustered on the directed-dyad (reported in parentheses). These models are not corrected for cluster confounding and therefore only one coefficient is reported for the time-varying variables. The number of observations significantly decreases in Models 3 and 4 due to data availability (*Income inequality* is available starting in 1960, *Right-wing executive* is available starting in 1975, and PTS scores are available starting in 1976). The *Initiator MP * Target MP* interaction was dropped from Models 3 and 4 because of perfect prediction. *Five years post–civil war* was also dropped because of perfect prediction (*Ten years post–civil war* is included instead). *Democratic duration* is logged. Cubic splines of time since last MID are included in the model but not reported. Significance: * $p < 0.1$, ** $p < 0.05$, *** $p < 0.01$.

TABLE A5.8 *Pooled models for autocratic initiators*

	Model 1	Model 2	Model 3
Death penalty retention	0.12	−0.00	0.12
	(0.25)	(0.28)	(0.42)
Target democracy		0.55***	0.46
		(0.19)	(0.29)
Initiator capabilities score		2.56	−5.92
		(3.70)	(9.47)
Target capabilities score		8.63***	8.47
		(1.59)	(6.66)
Balance of capabilities		0.35	0.31
		(0.28)	(0.54)
Initiator share of capabilities		1.06***	1.03
		(0.31)	(0.72)
Defensive pact		−0.72***	−1.24***
		(0.17)	(0.31)
Alliance portfolio similarity		−0.28	1.54**
		(0.28)	(0.72)
Initiator major power		−1.45***	−1.10
		(0.51)	(0.97)
Target major power		−1.68***	−1.18
		(0.44)	(0.91)
*InitiatorMP * TargetMP*		2.66***	2.67**
		(0.55)	(1.13)
Land contiguity		1.88***	1.30***
		(0.22)	(0.43)
Initiator PTS score			1.38***
			(0.33)
Target PTS score			0.95***
			(0.33)
*InitiatorPTS * TargetPTS*			−0.20**
			(0.09)
Ongoing civil war			0.25
			(0.27)
Ten years post–civil war			−0.02
			(0.10)
Income inequality			0.01
			(0.10)
Income inequality^2			0.00
			(0.00)

	Model 1	Model 2	Model 3
Right-wing executive			0.54
			(0.34)
Independence post-1990			−0.18
			(0.49)
Ethnic fractionalization			−0.12
			(0.62)
Constant	−4.84***	−5.82***	−12.50***
	(0.25)	(0.47)	(2.80)
N	62,653	59,131	14,979

Notes: All models are logistic regression models with standard errors clustered on the directed-dyad (reported in parentheses). These models are not corrected for cluster confounding and therefore only one coefficient is reported for the time-varying variables. The number of observations significantly decreases in Model 3 due to data availability (*Income inequality* is available starting in 1960, *Right-wing executive* is available starting in 1975, and PTS scores are available starting in 1976). Variables equal to 0 for all autocracies are excluded: *Democratic duration*, *United States*, *India*, and *Western Europe*. Cubic splines of years since last MID are included in the model but not reported. Significance: * $p < 0.1$, ** $p < 0.05$, *** $p < 0.01$.

TABLE A5.9 *Cluster-corrected models for autocracies*

	Model 1		Model 2		Model 3	
	Between-dyad effects	Within-dyad effects	Between-dyad effects	Within-dyad effects	Between-dyad effects	Within-dyad effects
Death pen. retention	0.22	−0.10	0.45	−0.25	0.07	−0.03
	(0.32)	(0.32)	(0.28)	(0.33)	(0.75)	(0.67)
Target democracy			0.38*	−0.01	0.14	−0.00
			(0.21)	(0.26)	(0.44)	(0.55)
Init. cap. score			−0.06	1.68	9.51	14.86
			(5.81)	(5.77)	(12.75)	(14.21)
Targ. cap. score			9.50***	3.19	7.45	7.08
			(2.47)	(3.19)	(5.61)	(10.49)
Balance of cap.			0.40	0.95	−0.46	2.45
			(0.28)	(0.70)	(0.68)	(1.72)
Init. share of cap.			1.32***	1.23	0.07	0.90
			(0.27)	(1.38)	(0.67)	(3.18)
Defensive pact			0.08	0.27	0.09	0.27
			(0.18)	(0.24)	(0.51)	(0.69)
Alliance portfolio sim.			−0.60*	0.34	0.92	3.48**
			(0.33)	(0.53)	(1.04)	(1.55)

(*continued*)

TABLE A5.9 *(continued)*

	Model 1		Model 2		Model 3	
	Between-dyad effects	Within-dyad effects	Between-dyad effects	Within-dyad effects	Between-dyad effects	Within-dyad effects
Init. major power			−0.99 (0.68)	0.92 (1.63)	−2.12** (1.03)	−10.25 (18.08)
Target major power			−1.10** (0.42)	−2.42 (0.72)***	−1.17 (0.88)	−3.37 (3.50)
InitMP * TargMP			0.42 (0.48)	1.79 (1.18)	0.30 (1.30)	4.31 (3.78)
Initiator PTS score					2.01*** (0.57)	1.18*** (0.39)
Target PTS score					0.03 (0.54)	1.00** (0.40)
InitPTS * TargPTS					0.01 (0.14)	−0.20* (0.11)
Ongoing civil war					0.01 (0.40)	−1.92** (0.74)
Ten yrs. post-civil war					−1.60* (0.92)	−0.59 (0.48)
Income inequality					−0.01 (0.18)	−0.05 (0.14)
Income inequality^2					0.00 (0.00)	0.001 (0.001)
Right wing exec.					0.51 (0.49)	−0.49 (0.64)
Land contiguity				1.11*** (0.17)		1.03*** (0.36)
Indep. post-1990						−0.64 (0.62)
Ethnic frac.						0.16 (0.63)
Constant			−4.93*** (0.30)	−2.98*** (0.45)		−8.52** (4.15)
N			62,653	59,131		14,979

Notes: All models are logistic regression models with standard errors clustered on the directed-dyad (reported in parentheses). The number of observations significantly decreases in Model 3 due to data availability (*Income inequality* is available starting in 1960, *Right-wing executive* is available starting in 1975, and PTS scores are available starting in 1976). Variables equal to 0 for all autocracies are excluded: *Democratic duration, United States, India,* and *Western Europe*. Cubic splines of years since last MID are included in the model but not reported. Significance: * $p < 0.1$, ** $p < 0.05$, *** $p < 0.01$.

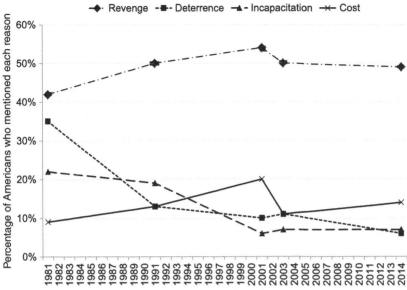

FIGURE A6.1 Americans' reasons for supporting the death penalty, 1981–2014.

CHAPTER 6

In Chapter 6, I noted that in the United States, revenge is the most commonly articulated rationale among supporters of the death penalty, as shown in Figure A6.1. The data for this figure are drawn from Gallup polls that asked proponents of capital punishment, "Why do you favor the death penalty for persons convicted of murder?" Open-ended responses were coded as revenge (an eye for an eye / they took a life / fits the crime / they deserve it), deterrence (deterrent for potential crimes / set an example), incapacitation (they will repeat crime / keep them from repeating it), and cost (save taxpayers money / cost associated with prison). The total in any given year may add up to more than 100% because respondents could mention more than one reason.

Works Cited

Achen, Christopher H. 1975. "Mass Political Attitudes and the Survey Response." *The American Political Science Review* 69 (4): 1218–31.

Aharoni, Eyal, and Alan J. Fridlund. 2012. "Punishment without Reason: Isolating Retribution in Lay Punishment of Criminal Offenders." *Psychology, Public Policy, and Law* 18 (4): 599–625.

Aldrich, John H., Christopher Gelpi, Peter Feaver, Jason Reifler, and Kristin Thompson Sharp. 2006. "Foreign Policy and the Electoral Connection." *Annual Review of Political Science* 9 (1): 477–502.

Aldrich, John H., John L. Sullivan, and Eugene Borgida. 1989. "Foreign Affairs and Issue Voting: Do Presidential Candidates 'Waltz before a Blind Audience?'" *The American Political Science Review* 83 (1): 123–41.

Alesina, Alberto, Paola Giuliano, and Nathan Nunn. 2013. "On the Origins of Gender Roles: Women and the Plough." *The Quarterly Journal of Economics* 128 (2): 469–530.

Alexandrov, Stanimir A. 1996. *Self-Defense against the Use of Force in International Law.* The Hague: Kluwer Law International.

Algan, Yann, and Pierre Cahuc. 2010. "Inherited Trust and Growth." *The American Economic Review* 100 (5): 2060–92.

Almond, Gabriel Abraham. 1950. *The American People and Foreign Policy.* New York: Harcourt, Brace.

Alter, Adam L., Julia Kernochan, and John M. Darley. 2007. "Transgression Wrongfulness Outweighs Its Harmfulness as a Determinant of Sentence Severity." *Law and Human Behavior* 31 (4): 319.

Altschuler, Bruce E. 1990. *LBJ and the Polls.* Gainesville: University Press of Florida.

Alvarez, R. Michael, and John Brehm. 2002. *Hard Choices, Easy Answers: Values, Information, and American Public Opinion.* Princeton, NJ: Princeton University Press.

Aquino, Karl, Thomas M. Tripp, and Robert J. Bies. 2001. "How Employees Respond to Personal Offense: The Effects of Blame Attribution, Victim

Status, and Offender Status on Revenge and Reconciliation in the Workplace." *Journal of Applied Psychology* 86 (1): 52.

Archer, Dane, and Rosemary Gartner. 1976. "Violent Acts and Violent Times: A Comparative Approach to Postwar Homicide Rates." *American Sociological Review* 41 (6): 937–63.

———. 1987. *Violence and Crime in Cross-National Perspective*. New Haven, CT: Yale University Press.

Arena, Philip, and Glenn Palmer. 2009. "Politics or the Economy? Domestic Correlates of Dispute Involvement in Developed Democracies." *International Studies Quarterly* 53 (4): 955–75.

Arian, Asher, Michal Shamir, and Raphael Ventura. 1992. "Public Opinion and Political Change: Israel and the Intifada." *Comparative Politics* 24 (3): 317–34.

Auerswald, David P. 1999. "Inward Bound: Domestic Institutions and Military Conflicts." *International Organization* 53 (3): 469–504.

Ayers, Edward L. 1984. *Vengeance and Justice: Crime and Punishment in the 19th Century American South*. New York: Oxford University Press.

Baker, David N., Eric G. Lambert, and Morris Jenkins. 2005. "Racial Differences in Death Penalty Support and Opposition: A Preliminary Study of White and Black College Students." *Journal of Black Studies* 35 (4): 201–24.

Balcells, Laia. 2010. "Rivalry and Revenge: Violence against Civilians in Conventional Civil Wars." *International Studies Quarterly* 54 (2): 291–313.

Bardi, Anat, Julie Anne Lee, Nadi Hofmann-Towfigh, and Geoffrey Soutar. 2009. "The Structure of Intraindividual Value Change." *Journal of Personality and Social Psychology* 97 (5): 913–29.

Barnoux, Magali, and Theresa A. Gannon. 2014. "A New Conceptual Framework for Revenge Firesetting." *Psychology, Crime & Law* 20 (5): 497–513.

Barreca, Regina. 1995. *Sweet Revenge: The Wicked Delights of Getting Even*. New York: Harmony Books.

Bartels, Brandon. 2015. "Beyond 'Fixed versus Random Effects': A Framework for Improving Substantive and Statistical Analysis of Panel, TSCS, and Multilevel Data." In *Quantitative Research in Political Science*, edited by Robert J. Franzese. Thousand Oaks, CA: Sage.

Baum, Matthew A. 2004. "How Public Opinion Constrains the Use of Force: The Case of Operation Restore Hope." *Presidential Studies Quarterly* 34 (2): 187–226.

Baum, Matthew A., and Tim J. Groeling. 2009. *War Stories: The Causes and Consequences of Public Views of War*. Princeton, NJ: Princeton University Press.

———. 2010. "Reality Asserts Itself: Public Opinion on Iraq and the Elasticity of Reality." *International Organization* 64 (3): 443–79.

Baum, Matthew A., and Philip B. K. Potter. 2008. "The Relationships between Mass Media, Public Opinion, and Foreign Policy: Toward a Theoretical Synthesis." *Annual Review of Political Science* 11: 39–65.

———. 2015. *War and Democratic Constraint: How the Public Influences Foreign Policy*. Princeton, NJ: Princeton University Press.

Bayram, A. Burcu. 2015. "What Drives Modern Diogenes? Individual Values and Cosmopolitan Allegiance." *European Journal of International Relations* 21 (2): 451–79.

Beck, Nathaniel, Jonathan N. Katz, and Richard Tucker. 1998. "Taking Time Seriously: Time-Series-Cross-Section Analysis with a Binary Dependent Variable." *American Journal of Political Science* 42(4): 1260–88.

Beck, Thorsten, George Clarke, Alberto Groff, Philip Keefer, and Patrick Walsh. 2001. "New Tools in Comparative Political Economy: The Database of Political Institutions." *The World Bank Economic Review* 15 (1): 165–76.

Beckerman, Stephen, Pamela I. Erickson, James Yost, Jhanira Regalado, Lilia Jaramillo, Corey Sparks, Moises Iromenga, and Kathryn Long. 2009. "Life Histories, Blood Revenge, and Reproductive Success among the Waorani of Ecuador." *Proceedings of the National Academy of Sciences* 106 (20): 8134–39.

Beckley, Amber L. 2013. "Correlates of War? Towards an Understanding of Nativity-Based Variation in Immigrant Offending." *European Journal of Criminology* 10 (4): 408–23.

Bennett, W. Lance, Regina G. Lawrence, and Steven Livingston. 2006. "None Dare Call It Torture: Indexing and the Limits of Press Independence in the Abu Ghraib Scandal." *Journal of Communication* 56 (3): 467–85.

Bennett, D. Scott, and Allan C. Stam III. 1996. "The Duration of Interstate Wars, 1816–1985." *The American Political Science Review* 90 (2): 239–57.

Ben-Porath, Eran N. 2007. "Rhetoric of Atrocities: The Place of Horrific Human Rights Abuses in Presidential Persuasion Efforts." *Presidential Studies Quarterly* 37 (2): 181–202.

Berinsky, Adam J. 2007. "Assuming the Costs of War: Events, Elites, and American Public Support for Military Conflict." *Journal of Politics* 69 (4): 975–97.
    2009. *In Time of War: Understanding American Public Opinion from World War II to Iraq.* Chicago: University of Chicago Press.

Berinsky, Adam J., and Donald R. Kinder. 2006. "Making Sense of Issues through Media Frames: Understanding the Kosovo Crisis." *Journal of Politics* 68 (3): 640–56.

Bies, Robert J., and Thomas M. Tripp. 2001. "A Passion for Justice: The Rationality and Morality of Revenge." In *Justice in the Workplace: From Theory to Practice*, edited by Russell Cropanzano. Hillsdale, NJ: L. Erlbaum Associates.

Black, Donald. 1983. "Crime as Social Control." *American Sociological Review* 48 (1): 34–45.

Black-Michaud, Jacob. 1975. *Feuding Societies.* Oxford: Blackwell.

Bleiker, Roland, and Emma Hutchison. 2008. "Fear No More: Emotions and World Politics." *Review of International Studies* 34 (Supplement S1): 115–35.

Blick, Jeffrey P. 1988. "Genocidal Warfare in Tribal Societies as a Result of European-Induced Culture Conflict." *Man* 23 (4): 654–70.

Blumstein, Alfred, and Allen J. Beck. 1999. "Population Growth in U.S. Prisons, 1980–1996." *Crime and Justice: A Review of Research* 26: 17.

Boehm, Christopher. 1984. *Blood Revenge: The Enactment and Management of Conflict in Montenegro and Other Tribal Societies.* Lawrence: University Press of Kansas.

Boehmer, Charles R. 2008. "A Reassessment of Democratic Pacifism at the Monadic Level of Analysis." *Conflict Management and Peace Science* 25 (1): 81–94.

Bohm, Robert M. 1987. "American Death Penalty Attitudes: A Critical Examination of Recent Evidence." *Criminal Justice and Behavior* 14 (3): 380–96.

——— 1992. "Retribution and Capital Punishment: Toward a Better Understanding of Death Penalty Opinion." *Journal of Criminal Justice* 20 (3): 227–36.

Boon, Susan D., Vicki L. Deveau, and Alishia M. Alibhai. 2009. "Payback: The Parameters of Revenge in Romantic Relationships." *Journal of Social and Personal Relationships* 26 (6–7): 747–68.

Borrelli, Stephen A., and Brad Lockerbie. 2008. "Framing Effects on Public Opinion during Prewar and Major Combat Phases of the US Wars with Iraq." *Social Science Quarterly* 89 (2): 502–22.

Boyle, Michael J. 2010. "Revenge and Reprisal Violence in Kosovo." *Conflict, Security & Development* 10 (2): 189–216.

Bradfield, Murray, and Karl Aquino. 1999. "The Effects of Blame Attributions and Offender Likableness on Forgiveness and Revenge in the Workplace." *Journal of Management* 25 (5): 607–31.

Brewer, Paul R. 2001. "Value Words and Lizard Brains: Do Citizens Deliberate about Appeals to Their Core Values?" *Political Psychology* 22(1): 45–64.

Brewer, Paul R., and Kimberly Gross. 2005. "Values, Framing, and Citizens' Thoughts about Policy Issues: Effects on Content and Quantity." *Political Psychology* 26 (6): 929–48.

Brewer, Paul R., Kimberly Gross, Sean Aday, and Lars Willnat. 2004. "International Trust and Public Opinion about World Affairs." *American Journal of Political Science* 48 (1): 93–109.

Brooks, Deborah Jordan, and Benjamin A. Valentino. 2011. "A War of One's Own: Understanding the Gender Gap in Support for War." *Public Opinion Quarterly* 75 (2): 270–86.

Bruce, Dickinson D. Jr. 1979. *Violence and Culture in the Antebellum South.* Austin: University of Texas Press.

Buckholtz, Joshua W., Christopher L. Asplund, Paul E. Dux, David H. Zald, John C. Gore, Owen D. Jones, and René Marois. 2008. "The Neural Correlates of Third-Party Punishment." *Neuron* 60 (5): 930–40.

Bueno de Mesquita, Bruce, and Randolph M. Siverson. 1995. "War and the Survival of Political Leaders: A Comparative Study of Regime Types and Political Accountability." *American Political Science Review* 89 (4): 841–55.

Bueno de Mesquita, Bruce, James D. Morrow, Randolph M. Siverson, and Alastair Smith. 1999. "An Institutional Explanation of the Democratic Peace." *American Political Science Review* 93 (4): 791–807.

Bueno de Mesquita, Bruce, Alastair Smith, Randolph M. Siverson, and James D. Morrow. 2005. *The Logic of Political Survival.* Cambridge, MA: MIT Press.

Burk, James. 1999. "Public Support for Peacekeeping in Lebanon and Somalia: Assessing the Casualties Hypothesis." *Political Science Quarterly* 114 (1): 53–78.

Burris, Val. 2008. "From Vietnam to Iraq: Continuity and Change in Between-Group Differences in Support for Military Action." *Social Problems* 55 (4): 443–79.

Busby, Joshua W. 2010. *Moral Movements and Foreign Policy.* New York: Cambridge University Press.

Campbell, Angus, Philip E. Converse, Warren E. Miller, and Donald E. Stokes. 1960. *The American Voter*. New York: John Wiley.

Canes-Wrone, Brandice. 2010. *Who Leads Whom?: Presidents, Policy, and the Public: Presidents, Policy, and the Public*. Chicago: University of Chicago Press.

Caprioli, Mary, and Peter F. Trumbore. 2006. "Human Rights Rogues in Interstate Disputes, 1980–2001." *Journal of Peace Research* 43 (2): 131–48.

Cardozo, Barbara Lopes, Alfredo Vergara, Ferid Agani, and Carol A. Gotway. 2000. "Mental Health, Social Functioning, and Attitudes of Kosovar Albanians Following the War in Kosovo." *JAMA* 284 (5): 569–77.

Carlsmith, Kevin M. 2008. "On Justifying Punishment: The Discrepancy between Words and Actions." *Social Justice Research* 21 (2): 119–37.

Carlsmith, Kevin M., and John M. Darley. 2008. "Psychological Aspects of Retributive Justice." *Advances in Experimental Social Psychology* 40: 193–236.

Carlsmith, Kevin M., and Avani Mehta Sood. 2009. "The Fine Line between Interrogation and Retribution." *Journal of Experimental Social Psychology* 45 (1): 191–96.

Carlsmith, Kevin M., John M. Darley, and Paul H. Robinson. 2002. "Why Do We Punish?: Deterrence and Just Deserts as Motives for Punishment." *Journal of Personality and Social Psychology* 83 (2): 284.

Carlsmith, Kevin M., John Monahan, and Alison Evans. 2007. "The Function of Punishment in the 'Civil' Commitment of Sexually Violent Predators." *Behavioral Sciences & the Law* 25 (4): 437–48.

Carr, Edward H. 1939. *Twenty Years' Crisis, 1919–1939*. London: Macmillan.

Casey, Steven. 2001. *Cautious Crusade: Franklin D. Roosevelt, American Public Opinion, and the War against Nazi Germany*. New York: Oxford University Press.

Cash, W. J. 1941. *The Mind of the South*. New York: Alfred A. Knopf.

Caverley, Jonathan D. 2014. *Democratic Militarism: Voting, Wealth, and War*. New York: Cambridge University Press.

Chagnon, Napoleon A. 1988. "Life Histories, Blood Revenge, and Warfare in a Tribal Population." *Science* 239 (4843): 985–92.

Chapman, Terrence L. 2012. *Securing Approval: Domestic Politics and Multilateral Authorization for War*. Chicago: University of Chicago Press.

Chapman, Terrence L., and Dan Reiter. 2004. "The United Nations Security Council and the Rally 'Round the Flag Effect." *Journal of Conflict Resolution* 48 (6): 886–909.

Chernoff, Fred. 2004. "The Study of Democratic Peace and Progress in International Relations." *International Studies Review* 6 (1): 49–78.

Chong, Dennis, and James N. Druckman. 2007. "Framing Theory." *Annual Review of Political Science* 10 (1): 103–26.

Clark, David H., and Timothy Nordstrom. 2005. "Democratic Variants and Democratic Variance: How Domestic Constraints Shape Interstate Conflict." *The Journal of Politics* 67 (1): 250–70.

Cohen, Bernard Cecil. 1995. *Democracies and Foreign Policy: Public Participation in the United States and the Netherlands*. Madison: University of Wisconsin Press.

Cohen, Dov. 1996. "Law, Social Policy, and Violence: The Impact of Regional Cultures." *Journal of Personality and Social Psychology* 70 (5): 961–78.

Cohen, Dov, and Richard E. Nisbett. 1997. "Field Experiments Examining the Culture of Honor: The Role of Institutions in Perpetuating Norms about Violence." *Personality and Social Psychology Bulletin* 23(11): 1188–99.

Cohen, Dov, Richard E. Nisbett, Brian F. Bowdle, and Norbert Schwartz. 1996. "Insult, Aggression, and the Southern Culture of Honor: An 'Experimental Ethnography.'" *Journal of Personality and Social Psychology* 70 (5): 945–60.

Colaresi, Michael. 2012. "A Boom with Review: How Retrospective Oversight Increases the Foreign Policy Ability of Democracies." *American Journal of Political Science* 56 (3): 671–89.

Colgan, Jeff D. 2013. "Fueling the Fire: Pathways from Oil to War." *International Security* 38 (2): 147–80.

Concannon, Diana M. 2013. *Kidnapping: An Investigator's Guide*. London: Elsevier.

Condra, Luke N., Joseph H. Felter, Radha K. Iyengar, and Jacob N. Shapiro. 2010. "The Effect of Civilian Casualties in Afghanistan and Iraq." Working Paper 16152. National Bureau of Economic Research. www.nber.org/papers/w16152.

Conover, Pamela Johnston, and Virginia Sapiro. 1993. "Gender, Feminist Consciousness, and War." *American Journal of Political Science* 37 (4): 1079–99.

Converse, Philip E. 1964. "The Nature and Origin of Belief Systems in Mass Publics." In *Ideology and Discontent*, edited by D. Apterl, 188–215. New York: Free Press.

Cota-McKinley, Amy L., William Douglas Woody, and Paul A. Bell. 2001. "Vengeance: Effects of Gender, Age, and Religious Background." *Aggressive Behavior* 27 (5): 343–50.

Cotton, Michele. 2000. "Back with a Vengeance: The Resilience of Retribution as an Articulated Purpose of Criminal Punishment." *The American Criminal Law Review* 37 (4): 1313–62.

Crawford, Neta C. 2000. "The Passion of World Politics: Propositions on Emotion and Emotional Relationships." *International Security* 24 (4): 116–56.

Crenshaw, Martha. 1981. "The Causes of Terrorism." *Comparative Politics* 13 (4): 379–99.

Croco, Sarah E. 2015. *Peace at What Price?: Leader Culpability and the Domestic Politics of War Termination*. New York: Cambridge University Press.

Crombag, Hans, Eric Rassin, and Robert Horselenberg. 2003. "On Vengeance." *Psychology, Crime & Law* 9 (4): 333–44.

Cullen, Francis T., Gregory A. Clark, John B. Cullen, and Richard A. Mathers. 1985. "Attribution, Salience, and Attitudes toward Criminal Sanctioning." *Criminal Justice and Behavior* 12 (3): 305–31.

Dafoe, Allan, and Devin Caughey. 2016. "Honor and War: Southern US Presidents and the Effects of Concern for Reputation." *World Politics* 68(2): 341–81.

Dafoe, Allan, John R. Oneal, and Bruce Russett. 2013. "The Democratic Peace: Weighing the Evidence and Cautious Inference." *International Studies Quarterly* 57 (1): 201–14.

Daly, Martin, and Margo Wilson. 1988. *Homicide*. Hawthorne, NY: Aldine de Gruyter.

Darley, John M., Kevin M. Carlsmith, and Paul H. Robinson. 2000. "Incapacitation and Just Deserts as Motives for Punishment." *Law and Human Behavior* 24 (6): 659.

Delli Carpini, Michael X., and Scott Keeter. 1997. *What Americans Know about Politics and Why It Matters*. New Haven, CT: Yale University Press.

Derogy, Jacques. 1990. *Resistance and Revenge: The Armenian Assassination of the Turkish Leaders Responsible for the 1915 Massacres and Deportations*. New Brunswick, NJ: Transaction Publishers.

Diamond, Stephen R. 1977. "The Effect of Fear on the Aggressive Responses of Anger Aroused and Revenge Motivated Subjects." *The Journal of Psychology* 95(2): 185–88.

Diehl, Paul F., and Gary Goertz. 2001. *War and Peace in International Rivalry*. Ann Arbor: University of Michigan Press.

Diehl, Paul F., Daniel Druckman, and James Wall. 1998. "International Peacekeeping and Conflict Resolution: A Taxonomic Analysis with Implications." *Journal of Conflict Resolution* 42(1): 33–55.

Doepke, Matthias, and Fabrizio Zilibotti. 2008. "Occupational Choice and the Spirit of Capitalism." *The Quarterly Journal of Economics* 123 (2): 747–93.

Doty, Richard M., David G. Winter, Bill E. Peterson, and Markus Kemmelmeier. 1997. "Authoritarianism and American Students' Attitudes about the Gulf War, 1990–1996." *Personality and Social Psychology Bulletin* 23 (11): 1133–43.

Edelman, Murray. 1993. "Contestable Categories and Public Opinion." *Political Communication* 10 (3): 231–42.

Edwards, George C. 1976. "Presidential Influence in the House: Presidential Prestige as a Source of Presidential Power." *American Political Science Review* 70 (1): 101–13.

2009. *The Strategic President: Persuasion and Opportunity in Presidential Leadership*. Princeton, NJ: Princeton University Press.

Eichenberg, Richard C. 2005. "Victory Has Many Friends: U.S. Public Opinion and the Use of Military Force, 1981–2005." *International Security* 30 (1): 140–77.

Ellison, Christopher G., John P. Bartkowski, and Michelle L. Segal. 1996. "Conservative Protestantism and the Parental Use of Corporal Punishment." *Social Forces* 74 (3): 1003–28.

Ellison, Christopher G., Jeffrey A. Burr, and Patricia L. McCall. 2003. "The Enduring Puzzle of Southern Homicide: Is Regional Religious Culture the Missing Piece?" *Homicide Studies* 7(4): 326–52.

Ellsworth, Phoebe C., and Samuel R. Gross. 1994. "Hardening of the Attitudes: Americans' Views on the Death Penalty." *Journal of Social Issues* 50 (2): 19–52.

Ellsworth, Phoebe C., and Lee Ross. 1983. "Public Opinion and Capital Punishment: A Close Examination of the Views of Abolitionists and Retentionists." *Crime & Delinquency* 29 (1): 116–69.

Elster, Jon. 1990. "Norms of Revenge." *Ethics* 100 (4): 862–85.

Engels, Jeremy, and Greg Goodale. 2009. "'Our Battle Cry Will Be: Remember Jenny McCrea!': A Précis on the Rhetoric of Revenge." *American Quarterly* 61 (1): 93–112.

Entman, Robert M. 1993. "Framing: Towards Clarification of a Fractured Paradigm." *Journal of Communication* 43 (4): 51–58.

———. 2003. *Projections of Power: Framing News, Public Opinion, and U.S. Foreign Policy*. Chicago: University of Chicago Press.

Ericksen, Karen Paige, and Heather Horton. 1992. "'Blood Feuds': Cross-Cultural Variations in Kin Group Vengeance." *Cross-Cultural Research* 26 (1–4): 57–85.

Farber, Henry S., and Joanne Gowa. 1995. "Polities and Peace." *International Security* 20 (2): 123–46.

Fearon, James D. 1995. "Rationalist Explanations for War." *International Organization* 49: 379–414.

Fearon, James D., and David D. Laitin. 2003. "Ethnicity, Insurgency, and Civil War." *American Political Science Review* 97 (1): 75–90.

Fehr, Ernst, and Urs Fischbacher. 2004. "Third-Party Punishment and Social Norms." *Evolution and Human Behavior* 25 (2): 63–87.

Feldman, Stanley. 1988. "Structure and Consistency in Public Opinion: The Role of Core Beliefs and Values." *American Journal of Political Science* 32 (2): 416–40.

———. 2003. "Values, Ideology, and the Structure of Political Attitudes." In *Oxford Handbook of Political Psychology*, edited by David O. Sears, Leonie Huddy, and Robert Jervis, 477–508. New York: Oxford University Press.

Ferguson, R. Brian. 1992. "The General Consequences of War: An Amazonian Perspective." In *Effects of War on Society*, edited by G. Ausenda, 59–86. Rochester, NY: Boydell & Brewer.

Fernández, Raquel, and Alessandra Fogli. 2009. "Culture: An Empirical Investigation of Beliefs, Work, and Fertility." *American Economic Journal: Macroeconomics* 1 (1): 146–77.

Ferrari, Joseph R., and Robert A. Emmons. 1994. "Procrastination as Revenge: Do People Report Using Delays as a Strategy for Vengeance?" *Personality and Individual Differences* 17 (4): 539–44.

Field, Nigel P., and Sotheara Chhim. 2008. "Desire for Revenge and Attitudes Toward the Khmer Rouge Tribunal among Cambodians." *Journal of Loss and Trauma* 13 (4): 352–72.

Fielding, David, and Anja Shortland. 2010. "'An Eye for an Eye, a Tooth for a Tooth': Political Violence and Counter-Insurgency in Egypt." *Journal of Peace Research* 47 (4): 433–47.

Figueredo, Aurelio José, Ilanit Robin Tal, Prentiss McNeil, and Alfonso Guillén. 2004. "Farmers, Herders, and Fishers: The Ecology of Revenge." *Evolution and Human Behavior* 25 (5): 336–53.

Filson, Darren, and Suzanne Werner. 2004. "Bargaining and Fighting: The Impact of Regime Type on War Onset, Duration, and Outcomes." *American Journal of Political Science* 48 (2): 296–313.

———. 2007. "Sensitivity to Costs of Fighting versus Sensitivity to Losing the Conflict: Implications for War Onset, Duration, and Outcomes." *Journal of Conflict Resolution* 51 (5): 691–714.

Fischer, David Hackett. 1989. *Albion's Seed: Four British Folkways in America*. New York: Oxford University Press.

Fletcher, Richard. 2004. *Bloodfeud: Murder and Revenge in Anglo-Saxon England*. New York: Oxford University Press.

Fox, James Alan, and Jack Levin. 1994. "Firing Back: The Growing Threat of Workplace Homicide." *The Annals of the American Academy of Political and Social Science* 536(1): 16–30.

——. 1998. "Multiple Homicide: Patterns of Serial and Mass Murder." *Crime and Justice* 23: 407–55.

Foyle, Douglas C. 1997. "Public Opinion and Foreign Policy: Elite Beliefs as a Mediating Variable." *International Studies Quarterly* 41 (1): 141–70.

——. 1999. *Counting the Public In: Presidents, Public Opinion, and Foreign Policy*. New York: Columbia University Press.

French, Peter A. 2001. *The Virtues of Vengeance*. Lawrence: University Press of Kansas.

Friedman, Lawrence. 1993. *Crime and Punishment in American History*. New York: Basic Books.

Fukuyama, Francis. 2004. "The Neoconservative Moment." *The National Interest* (76): 57–68.

Gallagher, Nancy W. 1993. "The Gender Gap in Popular Attitudes toward the Use of Force." In *Women and the Use of Military Force*, edited by Ruth H. Howes and Michael R. Stevenson, 23–38. Boulder, CO: Lynne Rienner.

Gallimore, Timothy. 2004. "Unresolved Trauma: Fuel for the Cycle of Violence and Terrorism." In *Psychology of Terrorism: Coping with the Continuing Threat*, edited by Chris E. Stout. Westport, CT: Praeger Publishers/Greenwood Publishing Group.

Gamson, William A., and Andre Modigliani. 1994. "The Changing Culture of Affirmative Action." In *Equal Employment Opportunity: Labor Market Discrimination and Public Policy*, edited by Paul Burstein, 373–94. Hawthorne, NY: Aldine de Gruyter.

Gartner, Scott Sigmund. 2008. "The Multiple Effects of Casualties on Public Support for War: An Experimental Approach." *American Political Science Review* 102 (1): 95.

Gartner, Scott Sigmund, and Gary M. Segura. 1998. "War, Casualties, and Public Opinion." *The Journal of Conflict Resolution* 42 (3): 278–300.

——. 2000. "Race, Casualties, and Opinion in the Vietnam War." *The Journal of Politics* 62 (1): 115–46.

Gartzke, Erik. 2007. "The Capitalist Peace." *American Journal of Political Science* 51 (1): 166–91.

Gaubatz, Kurt Taylor. 1999. *Elections and War: The Electoral Incentive in the Democratic Politics of War and Peace*. Stanford, CA: Stanford University Press.

Geddes, Barbara. 2003. *Paradigms and Sand Castles: Theory Building and Research Design in Comparative Politics*. Ann Arbor: University of Michigan Press.

Gelpi, Christopher, Peter D. Feaver, and Jason Reifler. 2006. "Success Matters: Casualty Sensitivity and the War in Iraq." *International Security* 30 (3): 7–46.

2009. *Paying the Human Costs of War: American Public Opinion and Casualties in Military Conflicts.* Princeton, NJ: Princeton University Press.

Gershkoff, Amy, and Shana Kushner. 2005. "Shaping Public Opinion: The 9/11–Iraq Connection in the Bush Administration's Rhetoric." *Perspectives on Politics* 3 (3): 525–37.

Ghosn, Faten, Glenn Palmer, and Stuart A. Bremer. 2004. "The MID3 Data Set, 1993–2001: Procedures, Coding Rules, and Description." *Conflict Management and Peace Science* 21 (2): 133–54.

Gibler, Douglas M., Steven V. Miller, and Erin K. Little. 2014. "A Replication and Analysis of the Militarized Interstate Dispute (MID) Dataset, 1816–2001." http://dmgibler.people.ua.edu/uploads/1/3/8/5/13858910/mid replication.dmgsvmekl.12014.pdf.

Gleditsch, Nils Petter. 1995. "Geography, Democracy, and Peace." *International Interactions* 20 (4): 297–323.

Gleditsch, Kristian Skrede, Idean Salehyan, and Kenneth Schultz. 2008. "Fighting at Home, Fighting Abroad How Civil Wars Lead to International Disputes." *Journal of Conflict Resolution* 52 (4): 479–506.

Goemans, H. E. 2000. "Fighting for Survival: The Fate of Leaders and the Duration of War." *Journal of Conflict Resolution* 44 (5): 555–79.

Goertz, Gary, and Paul F. Diehl. 1992. "The Empirical Importance of Enduring Rivalries." *International Interactions* 18 (2): 151–63.

Golby, James, Kyle Dropp, and Peter Feaver. 2013. "Listening to the Generals: How Military Advice Affects Public Support for the Use of Force." Center for a New American Security. www.cnas.org/publications/reports/listening-to-the-generals-how-military-advice-affects-public-support-for-the-use-of-force.

Gollwitzer, Mario, Linda J. Skitka, Daniel Wisneski, Arne Sjöström, Peter Liberman, Syed Javed Nazir, and Brad J. Bushman. 2014. "Vicarious Revenge and the Death of Osama Bin Laden." *Personality and Social Psychology Bulletin* 40 (5): 604–16.

Goren, Paul. 2001. "Core Principles and Policy Reasoning in Mass Publics: A Test of Two Theories." *British Journal of Political Science* 31(1): 159–77.

Gowa, Joanne. 2011. *Ballots and Bullets: The Elusive Democratic Peace.* Princeton, NJ: Princeton University Press.

Graham, Jesse, Jonathan Haidt, and Brian A. Nosek. 2009. "Liberals and Conservatives Rely on Different Sets of Moral Foundations." *Journal of Personality and Social Psychology* 96 (5): 1029.

Grasmick, Harold G., and Anne L. McGill. 1994. "Religion, Attribution Style, and Punitiveness toward Juvenile Offenders." *Criminology* 32 (1): 23–46.

Grasmick, Harold G., Robert J. Bursik Jr., and B. S. Blackwell. 1993. "Religious Beliefs and Public Support for the Death Penalty for Juveniles and Adults." *Journal of Crime and Justice* 16 (2): 59–86.

Grasmick, Harold G., Robert J. Bursik, and M'Lou Kimpel. 1991. "Protestant Fundamentalism and Attitudes toward the Corporal Punishment of Children." *Violence and Victims* 6 (4): 283–93.

Grégoire, Yany, Daniel Laufer, and Thomas M. Tripp. 2010. "A Comprehensive Model of Customer Direct and Indirect Revenge: Understanding the Effects of Perceived Greed and Customer Power." *Journal of the Academy of Marketing Science* 38 (6): 738–58.

Grégoire, Yany, Thomas M. Tripp, and Renaud Legoux. 2009. "When Customer Love Turns into Lasting Hate: The Effects of Relationship Strength and Time on Customer Revenge and Avoidance." *Journal of Marketing* 73 (6): 18–32.

Grieco, Joseph M., Christopher Gelpi, Jason Reifler, and Peter D. Feaver. 2011. "Let's Get a Second Opinion: International Institutions and American Public Support for War." *International Studies Quarterly* 55 (2): 563–83.

Gries, Peter Hays. 2005. "Nationalism, Indignation, and China's Japan Policy." *SAIS Review* 25 (2): 105–14.

Gross, Samuel R. 1997. "Update: American Public Opinion on the Death Penalty – It's Getting Personal." *Cornell Law Review* 83: 1448.

Gullace, Nicoletta. 2005. "Friends, Aliens, and Enemies: Fictive Communities and the Lusitania Riots of 1915." *Journal of Social History* 39 (2): 345–67.

Hafner-Burton, Emilie M., Stephan Haggard, David A. Lake, and David G. Victor. 2017. "The Behavioral Revolution and International Relations." *International Organization* 71 (S1): S1–S31.

Hafner-Burton, Emilie M., Brad L. LeVeck, David G. Victor, and James H. Fowler. 2014. "Decision Maker Preferences for International Legal Cooperation." *International Organization* 68 (4): 845–76.

Haidt, Jonathan, and Craig Joseph. 2004. "Intuitive Ethics: How Innately Prepared Intuitions Generate Culturally Variable Virtues." *Daedalus* 133 (4): 55–66.

Haidt, Jonathan, Silvia Helena Koller, and Maria G. Dias. 1993. "Affect, Culture, and Morality, or Is It Wrong to Eat Your Dog?" *Journal of Personality and Social Psychology* 65 (4): 613.

Hallpike, Christopher Robert. 1977. *Bloodshed and Vengeance in the Papuan Mountains: The Generation of Conflict in Tauade Society.* Oxford: Clarendon Press.

Hamber, Brandon, and Richard A. Wilson. 2002. "Symbolic Closure through Memory, Reparation and Revenge in Post-Conflict Societies." *Journal of Human Rights* 1 (1): 35–53.

Harkavy, Robert E. 2000. "Defeat, National Humiliation, and the Revenge Motif in International Politics." *International Politics* 37 (3): 345–68.

Hartwell, Marcia Byrom. 2005. "Perceptions of Justice, Identity, and Political Processes of Forgiveness and Revenge in Early Post-Conflict Transitions." DPhil/PhD thesis, University of Oxford.

Hayes, Danny, and Matt Guardino. 2013. *Influence from Abroad: Foreign Voices, the Media, and U.S. Public Opinion.* New York: Cambridge University Press.

Hayes, Timothy C., and Matthew R. Lee. 2005. "The Southern Culture of Honor and Violent Attitudes." *Sociological Spectrum* 25 (5): 593–617.

He, Yinan. 2007. "History, Chinese Nationalism and the Emerging Sino-Japanese Conflict." *Journal of Contemporary China* 16 (50): 1–24.

Hennessy, Dwight A., and David L. Wiesenthal. 2001. "Further Validation of the Driving Vengeance Questionnaire." *Violence and Victims* 16 (5): 565–73.

2002. "The Relationship between Driver Aggression, Violence, and Vengeance." *Violence and Victims* 17 (6): 707–18.

2005. "Driving Vengeance and Willful Violations: Clustering of Problem Driving Attitudes." *Journal of Applied Social Psychology* 35 (1): 61–79.

Henrich, Joseph, Steven J. Heine, and Ara Norenzayan. 2010. "The Weirdest People in the World?" *Behavioral and Brain Sciences* 33 (2–3): 61–83.

Henrich, Joseph, Richard McElreath, Abigail Barr, Jean Ensminger, Clark Barrett, Alexander Bolyanatz, Juan Camilo Cardenas, et al. 2006. "Costly Punishment across Human Societies." *Science* 312 (5781): 1767–70.

Hinckley, Ronald H. 1992. *People, Polls and Policy Makers: American Public Opinion and National Security*. New York: Lexington Books.

Hinton, Alexander Laban. 1998. "A Head for an Eye: Revenge in the Cambodian Genocide." *American Ethnologist* 25 (3): 352–77.

Holsti, Ole R. 1992. "Public Opinion and Foreign Policy: Challenges to the Almond-Lippmann Consensus." *International Studies Quarterly* 36 (4): 439–66.

1996. *Public Opinion and American Foreign Policy*. Ann Arbor: University of Michigan Press.

Horney, Karen. 1948. "The Value of Vindictiveness." *American Journal of Psychoanalysis* 8 (1): 3–12.

Horowitz, Donald L. 2001. *The Deadly Ethnic Riot*. Berkeley: University of California Press.

Horowitz, Michael C., and Matthew S. Levendusky. 2011. "Drafting Support for War: Conscription and Mass Support for Warfare." *Journal of Politics* 73 (2): 524–34.

Horowitz, Michael C., and Allan C. Stam. 2014. "How Prior Military Experience Influences the Future Militarized Behavior of Leaders." *International Organization* 68(3): 527–59.

Hudson, Valerie M., Mary Caprioli, Bonnie Ballif-Spanvill, Rose McDermott, and Chad F. Emmett. 2009. "The Heart of the Matter: The Security of Women and the Security of States." *International Security* 33 (3): 7–45.

Hurwitz, Jon, and Mark Peffley. 1987. "How Are Foreign Policy Attitudes Structured? A Hierarchical Model." *The American Political Science Review* 81 (4): 1099–120.

Huth, Paul. 2009. *Standing Your Ground: Territorial Disputes and International Conflict*. Ann Arbor: University of Michigan Press.

Inglehart, Ronald. 1990. *Culture Shift in Advanced Industrial Society*. Princeton, NJ: Princeton University Press.

1997. *Modernization and Postmodernization: Cultural, Economic, and Political Change in 43 Societies*. Princeton, NJ: Princeton University Press.

Isernia, Pierangelo, Zoltan Juhasz, and Hans Rattinger. 2002. "Foreign Policy and the Rational Public in Comparative Perspective." *Journal of Conflict Resolution* 46 (2): 201–24.

Iyengar, Shanto. 1991. *Is Anyone Responsible?: How Television Frames Political Issues*. Chicago: University of Chicago Press.

Iyengar, Shanto, and Adam Simon. 1993. "News Coverage of the Gulf Crisis and Public Opinion: A Study of Agenda-Setting, Priming, and Framing." *Communication Research* 20 (3): 365–83.

Jacobs, David, and Jason T. Carmichael. 2002. "The Political Sociology of the Death Penalty: A Pooled Time-Series Analysis." *American Sociological Review* 67 (1): 109–31.

Jacobs, Lawrence R., and Robert Y. Shapiro. 1999. "Lyndon Johnson, Vietnam, and Public Opinion: Rethinking Realist Theory of Leadership." *Presidential Studies Quarterly* 29 (3): 592–616.

——— 2000. *Politicians Don't Pander: Political Manipulation and the Loss of Democratic Responsiveness.* Chicago: University of Chicago Press.

Jacoby, Susan. 1983. *Wild Justice: The Evolution of Revenge.* New York: Harper & Row.

Jacoby, William G. 2006. "Value Choices and American Public Opinion." *American Journal of Political Science* 50 (3): 706–23.

——— 2013. "Individual Value Structures and Personal Political Orientations: Determining the Direction of Influence." Paper presented at the annual meeting of the Midwest Political Science Association, Chicago, IL.

Jentleson, Bruce W. 1992. "The Pretty Prudent Public: Post Post-Vietnam American Opinion on the Use of Military Force." *International Studies Quarterly* 36 (1): 49–73.

Jentleson, Bruce W., and Rebecca L. Britton. 1998. "Still Pretty Prudent: Post–Cold War American Public Opinion on the Use of Military Force." *Journal of Conflict Resolution* 42 (4): 395–417.

Johnson, Thomas H., and M. Chris Mason. 2008. "No Sign until the Burst of Fire: Understanding the Pakistan–Afghanistan Frontier." *International Security* 32 (4): 41–77.

Jones, David A. 2009. "Getting Even with One's Supervisor and One's Organization: Relationships among Types of Injustice, Desires for Revenge, and Counterproductive Work Behaviors." *Journal of Organizational Behavior* 30 (4): 525–42.

Kam, Cindy D., and Donald R. Kinder. 2007. "Terror and Ethnocentrism: Foundations of American Support for the War on Terrorism." *Journal of Politics* 69 (2): 320–38.

Kant, Immanuel. 1991. *Kant's Political Writings.* Edited by Hans Reiss. Cambridge: Cambridge University Press.

Karol, David, and Edward Miguel. 2007. "The Electoral Cost of War: Iraq Casualties and the 2004 US Presidential Election." *Journal of Politics* 69 (3): 633–48.

Kasser, Tim. 2011. "Cultural Values and the Well-Being of Future Generations: A Cross-National Study." *Journal of Cross-Cultural Psychology* 42 (2): 206–15.

Kennan, George Frost. 1951. *American Diplomacy.* Chicago: University of Chicago Press.

Kent, Stephanie L. 2010. "Predicting Abolition: A Cross-National Survival Analysis of the Social and Political Determinants of Death Penalty Statutes." *International Criminal Justice Review* 20 (1): 56–72.

Kernell, Samuel. 2007. *Going Public: New Strategies of Presidential Leadership.* Thousand Oaks, CA: CQ Press.

Kernsmith, Poco. 2005. "Exerting Power or Striking Back: A Gendered Comparison of Motivations for Domestic Violence Perpetration." *Violence and Victims* 20 (2): 173–85.

Kertzer, Joshua D. 2017. "Microfoundations in International Relations." *Conflict Management and Peace Science* 34(1): 81–97.

Kertzer, Joshua D., and Kathleen M. McGraw. 2012. "Folk Realism: Testing the Microfoundations of Realism in Ordinary Citizens." *International Studies Quarterly* 56 (2): 245–58.

Kinder, Donald R., and Lynn M. Sanders. 1996. *Divided by Color: Racial Politics and Democratic Ideals*. Chicago: University of Chicago Press.

King, Gary. 2001. "Proper Nouns and Methodological Propriety: Pooling Dyads in International Relations Data." *International Organization* 55 (2): 497–507.

Kinne, Brandon J., and Nikolay Marinov. 2013. "Electoral Authoritarianism and Credible Signaling in International Crises." *Journal of Conflict Resolution* 57 (3): 359–86.

Kissinger, Henry. 1994. *Diplomacy*. New York: Simon and Schuster.

Kleck, Gary. 1987. "America's Foreign Wars and the Legitimation of Domestic Violence." *Sociological Inquiry* 57 (3): 237–50.

Kohlberg, Lawrence. 1981. *The Philosophy of Moral Development Moral Stages and the Idea of Justice*. San Francisco, CA: Harper & Row.

Kohlberg, Lawrence, and Donald Elfenbein. 1975. "The Development of Moral Judgments Concerning Capital Punishment." *American Journal of Orthopsychiatry* 45 (4): 614.

Knoll, James L. 2010. "The 'Pseudocommando' Mass Murderer: Part I, The Psychology of Revenge and Obliteration." *Journal of the American Academy of Psychiatry and the Law Online* 38 (1): 87–94.

Krosnick, Jon A., and Donald R. Kinder. 1990. "Altering the Foundations of Support for the President through Priming." *The American Political Science Review* 84 (2): 497–512.

Kubrin, Charis E., and Ronald Weitzer. 2003. "Retaliatory Homicide: Concentrated Disadvantage and Neighborhood Culture." *Social Problems* 50 (2): 157–80.

Kuklinski, James H. 2001. "Introduction: Political Values." In *Citizens and Politics: Perspectives from Political Psychology*, edited by James H. Kuklinski, 355–65. Cambridge: Cambridge University Press.

Kull, Steven, and Clay Ramsay. 2001. "The Myth of the Reactive Public: American Public Attitudes on Military Fatalities in the Post–Cold War Period." In *Public Opinion and the International Use of Force*, edited by Philip P. Everts and Pierangelo Isernia. London: Routledge.

Lagerkvist, Johan. 2005. "The Rise of Online Public Opinion in the People's Republic of China." *China: An International Journal* 3 (1): 119–30.

Lai, Brian, and Dan Slater. 2006. "Institutions of the Offensive: Domestic Sources of Dispute Initiation in Authoritarian Regimes, 1950–1992." *American Journal of Political Science* 50 (1): 113–26.

Leblang, David, and Steve Chan. 2003. "Explaining Wars Fought by Established Democracies: Do Institutional Constraints Matter?" *Political Research Quarterly* 56 (4): 385–400.

Lebow, Richard Ned. 2010. *Why Nations Fight: Past and Future Motives for War*. New York: Cambridge University Press.

Lemke, Douglas, and William Reed. 2001. "The Relevance of Politically Relevant Dyads." *Journal of Conflict Resolution* 45 (1): 126–44.

Levy, Jack S., and William R. Thompson. 2009. *Causes of War.* Chichester: John Wiley & Sons.

Liberman, Peter. 2006. "An Eye for an Eye: Public Support for War against Evildoers." *International Organization* 60 (3): 687–722.

———. 2013. "Retributive Support for International Punishment and Torture." *Journal of Conflict Resolution* 57 (2): 285–306.

———. 2014. "War and Torture as 'Just Deserts.'" *Public Opinion Quarterly* 78 (1): 47–70.

Liberman, Peter, and Linda J. Skitka. 2017. "Revenge in US Public Support for War against Iraq." *Public Opinion Quarterly* 81 (3): 636–60.

Lippmann, Walter. 1922. *Public Opinion.* New York: Harcourt, Brace.

Lofquist, William S. 2001. "Putting Them There, Keeping Them There, and Killing Them: An Analysis of State-Level Variations in Death Penalty Intensity." *Iowa Law Review* 87: 1505.

Lotz, Roy, and Robert M. Regoli. 1980. "Public Support for the Death Penalty." *Criminal Justice Review* 5 (1): 55–66.

Lotz, Sebastian, Anna Baumert, Thomas Schlösser, Franz Gresser, and Detlef Fetchenhauer. 2011. "Individual Differences in Third-Party Interventions: How Justice Sensitivity Shapes Altruistic Punishment." *Negotiation and Conflict Management Research* 4 (4): 297–313.

Löwenheim, Oded, and Gadi Heimann. 2008. "Revenge in International Politics." *Security Studies* 17 (4): 685–724.

Lowry, Dennis T., Tarn Ching Josephine Nio, and Dennis W. Leitner. 2003. "Setting the Public Fear Agenda: A Longitudinal Analysis of Network TV Crime Reporting, Public Perceptions of Crime, and FBI Crime Statistics." *Journal of Communication* 53 (1): 61–73.

Lumsdaine, David Halloran. 1993. *Moral Vision in International Politics: The Foreign Aid Regime, 1949–1989.* Princeton, NJ: Princeton University Press.

Maggiotto, Michael A., and Eugene R. Wittkopf. 1981. "American Public Attitudes toward Foreign Policy." *International Studies Quarterly* 25 (4): 601–31.

Mansfield, Edward D., and Jack Snyder. 2005. *Electing to Fight: Why Emerging Democracies Go to War.* Cambridge, MA: MIT Press.

Maoz, Zeev, and Ben D. Mor. 1996. "Enduring Rivalries: The Early Years." *International Political Science Review* 17 (2): 141–60.

Maoz, Zeev, and Bruce Russett. 1993. "Normative and Structural Causes of Democratic Peace, 1946–1986." *American Political Science Review* 87 (3): 624–38.

Mauer, Marc. 2001. "The Causes and Consequences of Prison Growth in the United States." *Punishment & Society* 3 (1): 9–20.

———. 2003. *Comparative International Rates of Incarceration: An Examination of Causes and Trends.* Washington, DC: The Sentencing Project.

Maynard, Katherine, Jarod Kearney, and James Guimond. 2010. *Revenge versus Legality: Wild Justice from Balzac to Clint Eastwood and Abu Ghraib.* Abingdon: Birkbeck Law Press.

McCullough, Michael. 2008. *Beyond Revenge: The Evolution of the Forgiveness Instinct*. San Francisco, CA: Jossey-Bass.

McCullough, Michael E., C. Garth Bellah, Shelley Dean Kilpatrick, and Judith L. Johnson. 2001. "Vengefulness: Relationships with Forgiveness, Rumination, Well-Being, and the Big Five." *Personality and Social Psychology Bulletin* 27 (5): 601–10.

McCullough, Michael E., Robert Kurzban, and Benjamin A. Tabak. 2013. "Cognitive Systems for Revenge and Forgiveness." *Behavioral and Brain Sciences* 1 (1): 1–15.

McFarland, Sam G. 2005. "On the Eve of War: Authoritarianism, Social Dominance, and American Students' Attitudes toward Attacking Iraq." *Personality and Social Psychology Bulletin* 31 (3): 360–67.

McKee, Ian R., and N. T. Feather. 2008. "Revenge, Retribution, and Values: Social Attitudes and Punitive Sentencing." *Social Justice Research* 21 (2): 138–63.

Mearsheimer, John J. 2003. *The Tragedy of Great Power Politics*. New York: W. W. Norton & Company.

Meernik, James, and Michael Ault. 2001. "Public Opinion and Support for U.S. Presidents' Foreign Policies." *American Politics Research* 29 (4): 352–73.

Mendelberg, Tali. 2001. *The Race Card: Campaign Strategy, Implicit Messages, and the Norm of Equality*. Princeton, NJ: Princeton University Press.

Mendeloff, David. 2009. "Trauma and Vengeance: Assessing the Psychological and Emotional Effects of Post-Conflict Justice." *Human Rights Quarterly* 31 (3): 592–623.

Miller, William I. 1998. "Clint Eastwood and Equity: Popular Culture's Theory of Revenge." In *Law in the Domains of Culture*, edited by Austin Sarat and Thomas R. Kearns. Ann Arbor: University of Michigan Press.

Moghadam, Assaf. 2003. "Palestinian Suicide Terrorism in the Second Intifada: Motivations and Organizational Aspects." *Studies in Conflict & Terrorism* 26 (2): 65–92.

Mongeau, Paul A., Jerold L. Hale, and Marmy Alles. 1994. "An Experimental Investigation of Accounts and Attributions Following Sexual Infidelity." *Communications Monographs* 61 (4): 326–44.

Montell, William Lynwood. 1986. *Killings: Folk Justice in the Upper South*. Lexington: University of Kentucky Press.

Moreno-Jiménez, Bernardo, Alfredo Rodríguez-Muñoz, Juan Carlos Pastor, Ana Isabel Sanz- Vergel, and Eva Garrosa. 2009. "The Moderating Effects of Psychological Detachment and Thoughts of Revenge in Workplace Bullying." *Personality and Individual Differences* 46 (3): 359–64.

Morgan, T. Clifton, and Christopher J. Anderson. 1999. "Domestic Support and Diversionary External Conflict in Great Britain, 1950–1992." *The Journal of Politics* 61 (3): 799–814.

Morgan, T. Clifton, and Sally Howard Campbell. 1991. "Domestic Structure, Decisional Constraints, and War: So Why Kant Democracies Fight?" *The Journal of Conflict Resolution* 35 (2): 187–211.

Morgenthau, Hans Joachim, and Kenneth W. Thompson. 1985. *Politics among Nations: The Struggle for Power and Peace*. New York: Knopf.

Mueller, John E. 1973. *War, Presidents, and Public Opinion.* New York: Wiley.

Mueller, John. 1996. "Fifteen Propositions about American Foreign Policy and Public Opinion in an Era Free of Compelling Threats." Paper presented at the annual convention of the International Studies Association, San Diego, CA.

Murphy, Jeffrie G. 2000. "Two Cheers for Vindictiveness." *Punishment & Society* 2 (2): 131–43.

Nasr Bechwati, Nada, and Maureen Morrin. 2003. "Outraged Consumers: Getting Even at the Expense of Getting a Good Deal." *Journal of Consumer Psychology* 13 (4): 440–53.

——— 2007. "Understanding Voter Vengeance." *Journal of Consumer Psychology* 17 (4): 277–91.

Nelissen, Rob M. A., and Marcel Zeelenberg. 2009. "Moral Emotions as Determinants of Third-Party Punishment: Anger, Guilt, and the Functions of Altruistic Sanctions." *Judgment and Decision Making* 4 (7): 543–53.

Nelson, Thomas E., and Donald R. Kinder. 1996. "Issue Frames and Group-Centrism in American Public Opinion." *The Journal of Politics* 58 (4): 1055–78.

Nelson, Thomas E., Zoe M. Oxley, and Rosalee A. Clawson. 1997. "Toward a Psychology of Framing Effects." *Political Behavior* 19 (3): 221–46.

Neumayer, Eric. 2008. "Death Penalty: The Political Foundations of the Global Trend towards Abolition." *Human Rights Review* 9 (2): 241–68.

Newburn, Tim, and Trevor Jones. 2005. "Symbolic Politics and Penal Populism: The Long Shadow of Willie Horton." *Crime, Media, Culture* 1 (1): 72–87.

Niedenthal, Paula M. 2007. "Embodying Emotion." *Science* 316 (5827): 1002–5.

Nincic, Miroslav, and Donna J. Nincic. 2002. "Race, Gender, and War." *Journal of Peace Research* 39 (5): 547–68.

Nisbett, Richard. 2010. *The Geography of Thought: How Asians and Westerners Think Differently . . . and Why.* New York: Free Press.

Nisbett, Richard E., and Dov Cohen. 1996. *Culture of Honor: The Psychology of Violence in the South.* Boulder, CO: Westview Press.

Nunn, Nathan, and Leonard Wantchekon. 2011. "The Slave Trade and the Origins of Mistrust in Africa." *The American Economic Review* 101 (7): 3221–52.

Orth, Ulrich, Leo Montada, and Andreas Maercker. 2006. "Feelings of Revenge, Retaliation Motive, and Posttraumatic Stress Reactions in Crime Victims." *Journal of Interpersonal Violence* 21 (2): 229–43.

Ostrom, Charles W., and Dennis M. Simon. 1985. "Promise and Performance: A Dynamic Model of Presidential Popularity." *American Political Science Review* 79(2): 334–58.

Otterbein, Keith F., and Charlotte Swanson Otterbein. 1965. "An Eye for an Eye, a Tooth for a Tooth: A Cross-Cultural Study of Feuding." *American Anthropologist* 67 (6): 1470–82.

Page, Benjamin I., Robert Y. Shapiro, and Glenn R. Dempsey. 1987. "What Moves Public Opinion?" *The American Political Science Review* 81 (1): 23–43.

Pantoja, Adrian. 2006. "Against the Tide? Core American Values and Attitudes Toward US Immigration Policy in the Mid-1990s." *Journal of Ethnic and Migration Studies* 32 (3): 515–31.

Pape, Robert. 2005. *Dying to Win: The Strategic Logic of Suicide Terrorism.* New York: Random House.

Peceny, Mark, and Christopher K. Butler. 2004. "The Conflict Behavior of Authoritarian Regimes." *International Politics* 41 (4): 565–81.

Peffley, Mark, and Jon Hurwitz. 1992. "International Events and Foreign Policy Beliefs: Public Response to Changing Soviet-U.S. Relations." *American Journal of Political Science* 36 (2): 431–61.

Pérez, Louis A. Jr. 1989. "The Meaning of the Maine: Causation and the Historiography of the Spanish-American War." *Pacific Historical Review* 58 (3): 293–322.

Peristany, Jean G. 1966. *Honor and Shame: The Values of Mediterranean Society.* London: Weidenfeld and Nicolson.

Petersen, Roger D. 2011. *Western Intervention in the Balkans: The Strategic Use of Emotion in Conflict.* New York: Cambridge University Press.

Petersen, Roger, and Sarah Zukerman. 2009. "Revenge or Reconciliation: Theory and Method of Emotions in the Context of Colombia's Peace Process." *Law in Peace Negotiations*, FICHL Publication Series, no. 5: 151–74.

Pettiway, Leon E. 1987. "Arson for Revenge: The Role of Environmental Situation, Age, Sex, and Race." *Journal of Quantitative Criminology* 3 (2): 169–84.

Pickering, Jeffrey, and Emizet F. Kisangani. 2010. "Diversionary Despots? Comparing Autocracies' Propensities to Use and to Benefit from Military Force." *American Journal of Political Science* 54 (2): 477–93.

Pinker, Steven. 2011. *The Better Angels of Our Nature: Why Violence Has Declined.* New York: Penguin Books.

Pitt-Rivers, Julian. 1968. "Honor." In *International Encyclopedia of the Social Sciences*, edited by D. Sills. New York: Macmillan.

Pollock, Philip H., Stuart A. Lilie, and M. Elliot Vittes. 1993. "Hard Issues, Core Values and Vertical Constraint: The Case of Nuclear Power." *British Journal of Political Science* 23 (1): 29–50.

Posen, Barry R. 1993. "Nationalism, the Mass Army, and Military Power." *International Security* 18 (2): 80–124.

Posner, Richard A. 1980. "Retribution and Related Concepts of Punishment." *The Journal of Legal Studies* 9 (1): 71–92.

———. 1981. *The Economics of Justice.* Cambridge, MA: Harvard University Press.

Powell, Robert. 2002. "Bargaining Theory and International Conflict." *Annual Review of Political Science* 5 (1): 1–30.

———. 2017. "Research Bets and Behavioral IR." *International Organization* 71 (S1): S265–S277.

Powlick, Philip J. 1995. "The Sources of Public Opinion for American Foreign Policy Officials." *International Studies Quarterly* 39 (4): 427–51.

Powlick, Philip J., and Andrew Z. Katz. 1998. "Defining the American Public Opinion/Foreign Policy Nexus." *Mershon International Studies Review* 42 (1): 29–61.

Ramirez, J. Martin. 2007. "Justification of Aggression in Several Asian and European Countries with Different Religious and Cultural Background." *International Journal of Behavioral Development* 31(1 Ser.): 9–15.

Rathbun, Brian C., Joshua D. Kertzer, and Mark Paradis. 2017. "Homo Diplo-maticus: Mixed-Method Evidence of Variation in Strategic Rationality." *International Organization* 71 (S1): S33–S60.

Ray, James Lee. 2003. "Explaining Interstate Conflict and War: What Should Be Controlled For?" *Conflict Management and Peace Science* 20 (2): 1–31.

Reed, John Shelton. 1972. *The Enduring South: Subcultural Persistence in Mass Society.* Lexington, MA: Lexington Books.

——— 1982. *One South.* Baton Rouge: Louisiana State University Press.

Reifler, Jason, Harold D. Clarke, Thomas J. Scotto, David Sanders, Marianne C. Stewart, and Paul Whiteley. 2014. "Prudence, Principle and Minimal Heur-istics: British Public Opinion toward the Use of Military Force in Afghanistan and Libya." *The British Journal of Politics & International Relations* 16 (1): 28–55.

Reilly, James. 2013. *Strong Society, Smart State: The Rise of Public Opinion in China's Japan Policy.* New York: Columbia University Press.

Reiter, Dan. 2003. "Exploring the Bargaining Model of War." *Perspectives on Politics* 1 (1): 27–43.

Reiter, Dan, and Allan C. Stam III. 2002. *Democracies at War.* Princeton, NJ: Princeton University Press.

Reiter, Dan, and Erik R. Tillman. 2002. "Public, Legislative, and Executive Constraints on the Democratic Initiation of Conflict." *Journal of Politics* 64 (3): 810–26.

Renshon, Jonathan. 2015. "Losing Face and Sinking Costs: Experimental Evi-dence on the Judgment of Political and Military Leaders." *International Organization* 69 (3): 659–95.

Rho, Sungmin, and Michael Tomz. 2017. "Why Don't Trade Preferences Reflect Economic Self- Interest?" *International Organization* 71 (S1): S85–S108.

Rieder, Jonathan. 1984. "The Social Organization of Vengeance." In *Toward a General Theory of Social Control,* edited by Donald Black. Vol. 1. New York: Academic Press.

Risse-Kappen, Thomas. 1991. "Public Opinion, Domestic Structure, and Foreign Policy in Liberal Democracies." *World Politics* 43 (4): 479–512.

Rivers, Douglas, and Nancy L. Rose. 1985. "Passing the President's Program: Public Opinion and Presidential Influence in Congress." *American Journal of Political Science* 29 (2): 183–96.

Rokeach, Milton. 1973. *The Nature of Human Values.* New York: Free Press.

Roof, Wade Clark, and William McKinney. 1987. *American Mainline Religion: Its Changing Shape and Future.* New Brunswick, NJ: Rutgers University Press.

Rosenblatt, Alan J. 1998. "Aggressive Foreign Policy Marketing: Public Response to Reagan's 1983 Address on Lebanon and Grenada." *Political Behavior* 20 (3): 225–40.

Rottinghaus, Brandon. 2008. "Presidential Leadership on Foreign Policy, Opinion Polling, and the Possible Limits of 'Crafted Talk.'" *Political Communication* 25 (2): 138–57.

Ruddell, Rick, and Martin G. Urbina. 2004. "Minority Threat and Punishment: A Cross-National Analysis." *Justice Quarterly* 21 (4): 903–31.

Saideman, Stephen M., and R. William Ayres. 2012. *For Kin or Country: Xenophobia, Nationalism, and War*. New York: Columbia University Press.

Sasley, Brent E. 2011. "Theorizing States' Emotions." *International Studies Review* 13 (3): 452–76.

Saunders, Elizabeth N. 2011. *Leaders at War: How Presidents Shape Military Interventions*. Ithaca: Cornell University Press.

2017. "No Substitute for Experience: Presidents, Advisers, and Information in Group Decision Making." *International Organization* 71 (S1): S219–S247.

Schadt, Angela M., and Matt DeLisi. 2007. "Is Vigilantism on Your Mind? An Exploratory Study of Nuance and Contradiction in Student Death Penalty Opinion." *Criminal Justice Studies* 20 (3): 255–68.

Scheve, Kenneth F., and Matthew J. Slaughter. 2001. "What Determines Individual Trade-Policy Preferences?" *Journal of International Economics* 54 (2): 267–92.

Schumann, Karina, and Michael Ross. 2010. "The Benefits, Costs, and Paradox of Revenge." *Social and Personality Psychology Compass* 4 (12): 1193–205.

Schwartz, Shalom H. 1992. "Universals in the Content and Structure of Values: Theoretical Advances and Empirical Tests in 20 Countries." In *Advances in Experimental Social Psychology*, edited by Mark P. Zanna, 1–66. San Diego, CA: Academic Press.

1994. "Are There Universal Aspects in the Structure and Contents of Human Values?" *Journal of Social Issues* 50(4): 19–45.

1997. "Values and Culture." In *Motivation and Culture*, edited by D. Munro, J. F. Schumaker, and S. C. Carr, 69–84. New York: Routledge.

1999. "A Theory of Cultural Values and Some Implications for Work." *Applied Psychology* 48 (1): 23–47.

2014. "Values and Culture." In *Motivation and Culture*, edited by D. Munro, J. F. Schumaker, and S. C. Carr, 69–84. New York: Routledge.

Schwartz, Shalom H., and Wolfgang Bilsky. 1987. "Toward a Universal Psychological Structure of Human-Values." *Journal of Personality and Social Psychology* 53 (3): 550–62.

Scully, Diana, and Joseph Marolla. 1985. "'Riding the Bull at Gilley's': Convicted Rapists Describe the Rewards of Rape." *Social Problems* 32 (3): 251–63.

Senese, Paul D., and John A. Vasquez. 2008. *The Steps to War: An Empirical Study*. Princeton, NJ: Princeton University Press.

Shackelford. 2005. "An Evolutionary Psychological Perspective on Cultures of Honor." *Evolutionary Psychology* 3: 381–91.

Shah, Dhavan V., David Domke, and Daniel B. Wackman. 1996. "'To Thine Own Self Be True': Values, Framing, and Voter Decision-Making Strategies." *Communication Research* 23 (5): 509–60.

Shapiro, Robert Y., and Benjamin I. Page. 1988. "Foreign Policy and the Rational Public." *Journal of Conflict Resolution* 32 (2): 211–47.

Shen, Fuyuan, and Heidi Hatfield Edwards. 2005. "Economic Individualism, Humanitarianism, and Welfare Reform: A Value-Based Account of Framing Effects." *Journal of Communication* 55 (4): 795–809.

Sherry, Michael. 2005. "Dead or Alive: American Vengeance Goes Global." *Review of International Studies* 31 (Supplement S1): 245–63.

Shweder, Richard A., Manamohan Mahapatra, and Joan G. Miller. 1987. "Culture and Moral Development." In *The Emergence of Morality in Young Children*, edited by Jerome Kagan and Sharon Lamb. Chicago: University of Chicago Press.

Sigelman, Lee. 1980. "Gauging the Public Response to Presidential Leadership." *Presidential Studies Quarterly* 10 (3): 427–33.

Signorino, Curtis S., and Jeffrey M. Ritter. 1999. "Tau-b or Not Tau-b: Measuring the Similarity of Foreign Policy Positions." *International Studies Quarterly* 43(1): 115–44.

Simmons, Beth A. 2009. *Mobilizing for Human Rights: International Law in Domestic Politics*. New York: Cambridge University Press.

Simon, Dennis M., and Charles W. Ostrom. 1989. "The Impact of Televised Speeches and Foreign Travel on Presidential Approval." *The Public Opinion Quarterly* 53 (1): 58–82.

Singer, J. David. 1987. "Reconstructing the Correlates of War Dataset on Material Capabilities of States, 1816–1985." *International Interactions* 14: 115–32.

Siverson, Randolph M. 1995. "Democracies and War Participation: In Defense of the Institutional Constraints Argument." *European Journal of International Relations* 1 (4): 481–89.

Skarlicki, Daniel P., and Carol T. Kulik. 2004. "Third-Party Reactions to Employee (Mis) Treatment: A Justice Perspective." *Research in Organizational Behavior* 26: 183–229.

Skitka, Linda J., and David A. Houston. 2001. "When Due Process Is of No Consequence: Moral Mandates and Presumed Defendant Guilt or Innocence." *Social Justice Research* 14 (3): 305–26.

Skitka, Linda J., and Elizabeth Mullen. 2002. "The Dark Side of Moral Conviction." *Analyses of Social Issues and Public Policy* 2 (1): 35–41.

Skrondal, Anders, and Sophia Rabe-Hesketh. 2004. *Generalized Latent Variable Modeling: Multilevel, Longitudinal, and Structural Equation Models*. Boca Raton, FL: Chapman & Hall.

Slantchev, Branislav L. 2004. "How Initiators End Their Wars: The Duration of Warfare and the Terms of Peace." *American Journal of Political Science* 48 (4): 813–29.

Sniderman, Paul M., and Sean M. Theriault. 2004. "The Structure of Political Argument and the Logic of Issue Framing." In *Studies in Public Opinion: Attitudes, Nonattitudes, Measurement Error, and Change*, 133–65. Princeton, NJ: Princeton University Press.

Sniderman, Paul M., Richard A. Brody, and Phillip E. Tetlock. 1993. *Reasoning and Choice: Explorations in Political Psychology*. New York: Cambridge University Press.

Sobek, David, M. Rodwan Abouharb, and Christopher G. Ingram. 2006. "The Human Rights Peace: How the Respect for Human Rights at Home Leads to Peace Abroad." *Journal of Politics* 68 (3): 519–29.

Sobel, Richard. 2001. *The Impact of Public Opinion on U.S. Foreign Policy since Vietnam: Constraining the Colossus*. New York: Oxford University Press.

Solt, Frederick. 2009. "Standardizing the World Income Inequality Database." *Social Science Quarterly* 90 (2): 231–42.

2011. "Diversionary Nationalism: Economic Inequality and the Formation of National Pride." *The Journal of Politics* 73 (3): 821–30.

Sommers, Jennifer A., Terry L. Schell, and Stephen J. Vodanovich. 2002. "Developing a Measure of Individual Differences in Organizational Revenge." *Journal of Business and Psychology* 17 (2): 207–22.

Speckhard, Anne, and Khapta Ahkmedova. 2006. "The Making of a Martyr: Chechen Suicide Terrorism." *Studies in Conflict & Terrorism* 29 (5): 429–92.

Steele, Richard W. 1974. "The Pulse of the People: Franklin D. Roosevelt and the Gauging of American Public Opinion." *Journal of Contemporary History* 9 (4): 195–216.

Stewart, Frank Henderson. 1994. *Honor*. Chicago: University of Chicago Press.

Stinnett, Douglas M., and Paul F. Diehl. 2001. "The Path(s) to Rivalry: Behavioral and Structural Explanations of Rivalry Development." *Journal of Politics* 63 (3): 717–40.

Stuckless, Noreen, and Richard Goranson. 1992. "The Vengeance Scale: Development of a Measure of Attitudes toward Revenge." *Journal of Social Behavior & Personality* 7(1): 25–42.

1994. "A Selected Bibliography of Literature on Revenge." *Psychological Reports* 75 (2): 803–11.

Tabellini, Guido. 2008. "The Scope of Cooperation: Values and Incentives." *The Quarterly Journal of Economics* 123 (3): 905–50.

Tarar, Ahmer. 2006. "Diversionary Incentives and the Bargaining Approach to War." *International Studies Quarterly* 50 (1): 169–88.

Taylor, D. Garth, Kim Lane Scheppele, and Arthur L. Stinchcombe. 1979. "Salience of Crime and Support for Harsher Criminal Sanctions." *Social Problems* 26 (4): 413–24.

Throop, Susanna A. 2011. *Crusading as an Act of Vengeance, 1095–1216*. Burlington, VT: Ashgate Publishing.

Tomz, Michael R., and Jessica L. P. Weeks. 2013. "Public Opinion and the Democratic Peace." *American Political Science Review* 107 (4): 849–65.

Tonry, Michael. 1994. "Racial Disproportion in US Prisons." *British Journal of Criminology* 34 (S1): 97–115.

1999. "Why Are U.S. Incarceration Rates So High?" *Crime & Delinquency* 45 (4): 419–37.

Tripp, Thomas M., and Robert J. Bies. 2009. *Getting Even: The Truth about Workplace Revenge – And How to Stop It*. San Francisco, CA: Jossey-Bass.

2010. "'Righteous' Anger and Revenge in the Workplace: The Fantasies, the Feuds, the Forgiveness." In *International Handbook of Anger: Constituent and Concomitant Biological, Psychological, and Social Processes*, edited by Michael Potegal, Gerhard Stemmler, and Charles Spielberger, 413–31. New York: Springer.

Tversky, Amos, and Daniel Kahneman. 1981. "The Framing of Decisions and the Psychology of Choice." *Science* 211 (4481): 453–58.

Tyler, Tom R., and Robert J. Boeckmann. 1997. "Three Strikes and You Are Out, but Why? The Psychology of Public Support for Punishing Rule Breakers." *Law and Society Review*, 237–65.

Tyler, Tom R., and Renee Weber. 1982. "Support for the Death Penalty; Instrumental Response to Crime, or Symbolic Attitude?" *Law & Society Review* 17 (1): 21–45.

Uslaner, Eric M. 2008. "Where You Stand Depends upon Where Your Grandparents Sat: The Inheritability of Generalized Trust." *Public Opinion Quarterly* 72 (4): 725–40.

Valentino, Benjamin, Paul Huth, and Dylan Balch-Lindsay. 2004. "Draining the Sea: Mass Killing and Guerrilla Warfare." *International Organization* 58 (2): 375–407.

Valentino, Benjamin, Paul K. Huth, and Sarah E. Croco. 2010. "Bear Any Burden? How Democracies Minimize the Costs of War." *The Journal of Politics* 72 (2): 528–44.

Vandello, Joseph A., and Dov Cohen. 2004. "When Believing Is Seeing: Sustaining Norms of Violence in Cultures of Honor." In *The Psychological Foundations of Culture*, edited by Mark Schaller and Christian S. Crandell, 281. Mahwah, NJ: Lawrence Erlbaum Associates.

Van Evera, Stephen. 1994. "Hypotheses on Nationalism and War." *International Security* 18 (4): 5–39.

Voigtländer, Nico, and Hans-Joachim Voth. 2012. "Persecution Perpetuated: The Medieval Origins of Anti-Semitic Violence in Nazi Germany." *The Quarterly Journal of Economics* 127 (3): 1339–92.

Volcansek, Mary L. 2010. "Judicial Elections and American Exceptionalism: A Comparative Perspective." *DePaul Law Review* 60: 805.

Vossekuil, Bryan, Robert A. Fein, Marisa Reddy, Randy Borum, and William Modzeleski. 2002. "The Final Report and Findings of the Safe School Initiative: Implications for the Prevention of School Attacks in the United States." Washington, DC: United States Secret Service and United States Department of Education.

Walker, Samuel. 1998. *Popular Justice: A History of American Criminal Justice.* New York: Oxford University Press.

Warner, Jessica, Gerhard Gmel, Kathryn Graham, and Bonnie Erickson. 2007. "A Time-Series Analysis of War and Levels of Interpersonal Violence in an English Military Town, 1700–1781." *Social Science History* 31 (4): 575–602.

Washburn, Anthony N., and Linda J. Skitka. 2015. "Motivated and Displaced Revenge: Remembering 9/11 Suppresses Opposition to Military Intervention in Syria (for Some)." *Analyses of Social Issues and Public Policy* 15 (1): 89–104.

Way, Christopher, and Jessica L. P. Weeks. 2013. "Making It Personal: Regime Type and Nuclear Proliferation." *American Journal of Political Science* 58 (3): 705–19.

Weeks, Jessica L. 2008. "Autocratic Audience Costs: Regime Type and Signaling Resolve." *International Organization* 62 (1): 35–64.

———. 2012. "Strongmen and Straw Men: Authoritarian Regimes and the Initiation of International Conflict." *American Political Science Review* 106 (2): 326–47.

Western, Jon. 2005. *Selling Intervention and War: The Presidency, the Media, and the American Public.* Baltimore, MD: Johns Hopkins University Press.

Whitman, James Q. 2003. *Harsh Justice: Criminal Punishment and the Widening Divide between America and Europe.* New York: Oxford University Press.

Wiesenthal, David L., Dwight Hennessy, and Patrick M. Gibson. 2000. "The Driving Vengeance Questionnaire (DVQ): The Development of a Scale to Measure Deviant Drivers' Attitudes." *Violence and Victims* 15 (2): 115–36.

Wilcox, Clyde, and Robin Wolpert. 2000. "Gay Rights in the Public Sphere: Public Opinion on Gay and Lesbian Equality." In *The Politics of Gay Rights,* edited by Craig A. Rimmerman, Kenneth D. Wald, and Clyde Wilcox, 409–32. Chicago: University of Chicago Press.

Wildavsky, Aaron. 1987. "Choosing Preferences by Constructing Institutions: A Cultural Theory of Preference Formation." *American Political Science Review* 81 (1): 3–21.

Wilson, Richard. 2001. *The Politics of Truth and Reconciliation in South Africa: Legitimizing the Post-Apartheid State.* New York: Cambridge University Press.

Wittkopf, Eugene R. 1990. *Faces of Internationalism: Public Opinion and American Foreign Policy.* Durham, NC: Duke University Press.

Wood, Reed M., and Mark Gibney. 2010. "The Political Terror Scale (PTS): A Re-Introduction and a Comparison to CIRI." *Human Rights Quarterly* 32 (2): 367–400.

Woodwell, Douglas. 2004. "Unwelcome Neighbors: Shared Ethnicity and International Conflict during the Cold War." *International Studies Quarterly* 48 (1): 197–223.

Wu, Yuning, Ivan Y. Sun, and Zongxian Wu. 2011. "Support for the Death Penalty: Chinese and American College Students Compared." *Punishment & Society* 13(3): 354–76.

Wyatt-Brown, Bertram. 1986. *Honor and Violence in the Old South.* New York: Oxford University Press.

Yarhi-Milo, Keren. 2014. *Knowing the Adversary: Leaders, Intelligence, and Assessment of Intentions in International Relations.* Princeton, NJ: Princeton University Press.

Yoshimura, Stephen. 2007a. "Goals and Emotional Outcomes of Revenge Activities in Interpersonal Relationships." *Journal of Social and Personal Relationships* 24 (1): 87–98.

——— 2007b. "The Communication of Revenge: On the Viciousness, Virtues and Vitality of Vengeful Behavior in Interpersonal Relationships." In *The Dark Side of Interpersonal Communication,* edited by William R. Cupach and Brian H. Spitzberg. Mahwah, NJ: Lawrence Erlbaum Associates.

Young, Warren, and Mark Brown. 1993. "Cross-National Comparisons of Imprisonment." *Crime and Justice* 17 (January): 1–49.

Zaller, John. 1991. "Information, Values, and Opinion." *The American Political Science Review* 85 (4): 1215–37.

——— 1992. *The Nature and Origins of Mass Opinion.* New York: Cambridge University Press.

——— 1994. "Elite Leadership of Mass Opinion: New Evidence from the Gulf War." In *Taken by Storm: The Media, Public Opinion, and U.S. Foreign Policy in the Gulf War,* edited by W. Lance Bennett and David L. Paletz. Chicago: University of Chicago Press.

Zaller, John, and Dennis Chiu. 1996. "Government's Little Helper: US Press Coverage of Foreign Policy Crises, 1945–1991." *Political Communication* 13 (4): 385–405.

Zaller, John, and Stanley Feldman. 1992. "A Simple Theory of the Survey Response: Answering Questions versus Revealing Preferences." *American Journal of Political Science* 36 (3): 579–616.

Zimring, Franklin E., and Gordon Hawkins. 1997. *Crime Is Not the Problem: Lethal Violence in America: Lethal Violence in America.* New York: Oxford University Press.

Zorn, Christopher. 2001. "Estimating Between- and Within-Cluster Covariate Effects, with an Application to Models of International Disputes." *International Interactions* 27 (4): 433–45.

Zourrig, Haithem, Jean-Charles Chebat, and Roy Toffoli. 2009. "Consumer Revenge Behavior: A Cross-Cultural Perspective." *Journal of Business Research* 62 (10): 995–1001.

Index